THE OVER-60S DIRECTORY

THE OVER-60S DIRECTORY

Everything you need for a comfortable, enjoyable and rewarding old age

BELINDA HADDEN

Thorsons
An Imprint of HarperCollins*Publishers*

Thorsons
An Imprint of HarperCollins*Publishers*
77–85 Fulham Palace Road,
Hammersmith, London W6 8JB
1160 Battery Street,
San Francisco, California 94111–1213

Published by Thorsons 1995
10 9 8 7 6 5 4 3 2 1

© Belinda Hadden 1995

Belinda Hadden asserts the moral right to
be identified as the author of this work

Crown copyright is reproduced with the
permission of the Controller of HMSO.

A catalogue record for this book
is available from the British Library

ISBN 0 7225 3181 8

Printed in Great Britain by
HarperCollinsManufacturing Glasgow

All rights reserved. No part of this publication may be
reproduced, stored in a retrieval system, or transmitted,
in any form or by any means, electronic, mechanical,
photocopying, recording or otherwise, without the prior
permission of the publishers.

Please note that every effort has been made to ensure that the information in this book is correct and up to date at the time of going to press; the publishers cannot be held responsible for any changes to information given in this book since the date of publication.

Contents

	INTRODUCTION	9
1.	WHAT IS OLD?: Britain's Ageing Population	13
2.	HEALTH MATTERS: All You Need to Know to Promote Health and Fitness, and Organisations that Offer Advice on Prevention and Treatment	19
3.	WHO CARES?: Organisations to Turn to for Assistance, Counselling, Friendship and Practical Advice; Care and Nursing Services at Home	46
4.	WHERE TO LIVE: Adapting your Home; Finding a Suitable Alternative	64
5.	HOLIDAYS: Financing Them, Enjoying Them – All the Options	87
6.	FINANCIAL MATTERS: Benefits, Investments and How to Find Good Financial Advice	98
7.	LEGAL AND TAX MATTERS: Help with Understanding Powers of Attorney, Wills, Getting Out of Debt, Taxation	156
8.	SPECIAL EQUIPMENT FOR DAILY LIFE: Small Gadgets and More Sophisticated Equipment to Make Life Easier	171
9.	KEEPING SAFE: Home Protection, Basic Safety Guidelines and Where to Turn for Help	182
10.	MOBILITY AND GETTING AROUND: Transport Schemes and Special Vehicles to Help Older People Stay Mobile	189
11.	HOBBIES AND INTERESTS: Exploring Further Education, Volunteering and Other New Pursuits	197
12.	DEATH AND BEREAVEMENT: Arranging and Paying for the Funeral in Advance, What Friends and Relatives Need to Know after a Death, Coping with Grief and Loss and Administering the Estate	213
	INDEX	237

Introduction

TWO YEARS AGO I found myself looking after an elderly relative. I had no prior knowledge or experience of what to do in this new role and, somewhat daunted by the responsibility, I decided I must find out all I could. I started researching where to look for advice, information, literature and assistance.

The more I researched, the more I found: an incredible number of charitable, governmental and commercial organisations exist to provide help in so many ways. Their details can be found in surgeries, libraries, Citizens Advice Bureaux, Town Halls, DSS offices, telephone books – all over the place. Yet I was dismayed that, while there was fantastic help on offer, I had to look really hard to find out about it.

It made sense to gather all the information together and put it in one place. Which I did. It became a book – *The Ageing Parent Handbook: the directory of everything you need to know as relatives and friends grow older* (January, 1994). The book was remarkably well received and I received letters and telephone calls of congratulations from people all over the country who had found its references and information invaluable.

It soon became apparent, however, that I had underestimated the audience. I wrote the book for people like me who have older parents, relatives or friends to look after. But it seemed that the book was bought as much by the 'carees' as the 'carers' – the older friends and relatives were buying it *for themselves* and reading it from cover to cover. My publishers agreed, therefore, that it should be written for both audiences, which is why this new edition is called *The Over-60s Directory: Everything you need for a comfortable, enjoyable and rewarding old age*.

With 11.6 million people in the UK over 60 (and rising), this covers an enormous variety of people; from the fit, affluent retired to the frail aged who live below the poverty line. The differences are vast but it is important that they all keep their independence and dignity and are in touch with all the organisations which can help them.

I have checked and updated every entry and added many new ones. All details are correct at the time of going to press, although organisations may move and the availability of their publications may change.

Finally, my thanks to all the people who supplied further information for this year's issue, and particular thanks to everyone at Age Concern for their valuable assistance. Please accept my apologies for any errors or omissions that you may discover – and do tell me about them or request a free *Grey Agency Newsletter* by dropping me a line at the address below. I plan to send the newsletter, full of news and updated information, to as many readers as request it whenever there are enough new details to warrant it.

Belinda Hadden
September 1995

The Grey Agency
FREEPOST (SW8500)
PO Box 3054
London SW6 2HG

QUESTIONNAIRE

Everyone, particularly if they live alone, should ask themselves the questions below so that an accident or crisis does not force them to make hasty or ill-judged decisions. It may seem pessimistic or over-cautious, but it could save time, money and distress later.

If you are over 60, and particularly if you live alone:

- Does anybody see you every day?
- Does a neighbour have your telephone number?
- Do you have a relative or friend to whom you can or will turn for advice and support?
- Do they know:
  – where to contact you at all times?
  – what would happen in an emergency?
  – where your nearest hospital is in the event of an accident?
  – how to contact your doctor, bank manager, solicitor, vicar, rabbi, etc.?
- Have you ever considered the relative merits of sheltered accommodation, residential care or nursing homes? Do you understand the differences between these options?
- Do you know what is available locally and what the charges are?
- Are there any further state benefits for which you may be eligible?
- Is there a simple or sophisticated 'gadget' which might make your life easier?
- Is your home as safe as it could be from accidents or break-ins?
- Are you aware of the extensive range of concessions available for older people?
- Have you made a Will?
  Does somebody (perhaps your next-of-kin) know where it is kept?
  Who are your executors? And have you made your wishes clear?
- Do you know what a Power of Attorney is?
- Have you thought of the practical things that need to be done when someone dies?

I met someone recently who told me she had found some of the more delicate questions impossible to discuss with her family, who did not want even to consider a time when she might need to go into a nursing home or have a great deal of help with everyday life. In the end she had decided to write down her 'final requests' and give them to her daughter to keep in a sealed envelope until needed. Though the process had been difficult, she said it had been a great relief and source of comfort for her to know that her family were now instructed on what her wishes were.

chapter one

WHAT IS OLD?

Britain's Ageing Population

The length of our days is three score years and ten
Psalms 90.10

WHAT *DOES* OLD MEAN? The dictionary tells us that 'old' means 'advanced in years' or 'having lived for a relatively long time'. Legally, 'old age' is any age after 50, as defined by the Friendly Society Act of 1896.

'Old age' can include people in their late forties; if the end of working and raising a family defines the entry to old age! This is how the Centre for Policy on Ageing has defined the 13 million people in the 'Third Age' (55+) – one quarter of Britain's adult population.

Whatever it means, it is true to say that 'You're as young as you feel' – more now than ever before, with people living longer, healthier and more active lives. Some of them need care, but the vast majority of older people are fit and well, with a cheerful approach to the freedom that retirement affords them.

In the past 100 years longevity has almost doubled and the proportion of older people has trebled. In the 1890s a woman could expect to live to be 46; today she will probably live to be 77. By the year 2031, according to the Government publication *Social Trends*, 'those aged 80 and over are projected to number 3.4 million: over 60 per cent more than in 1990.'

A recent EU opinion poll[1] asked people over 60 what they preferred to be called. They came down overwhelmingly against 'elderly' and the majority was split between 'older people' and 'senior citizens'.

THE AGEING POPULATION – CAUSE FOR CONCERN

One in five people in the UK is now over 60 (11.6 million). In the first 30 years of the next century the number of pensioners is projected to rise by nearly 50 per

---

[1] Source: Family Policy Studies Centre special edition factsheet, 'Older People in the European Community'

cent – so that by the year 2031 almost 26 per cent of the population will be over pensionable age.[2] Conversely, the number of children born has been falling since the mid-1960s.

The growing number of retired people will exert an unsustainable strain on State provision of pensions and healthcare, particularly with people retiring earlier either through redundancy or choice. While many older people will have made provision for their later years, many will not, and the burden of support will fall on an already overburdened State and those still in employment. It has even been said that, in the next two decades, the State will have to choose between keeping the young *or* the old on Social Security. There will not be enough for *both*.

As John Major said at the 1993 G7 summit: 'We have to find new ways of delivering healthcare so that we can continue to treat more and more patients within the spending limits we can afford.' The controversial Community Care Act 1990, which came into effect in April 1993, reflects the gradual move to shift the costs of an ageing population away from the statutory services and onto families, friends, neighbours and the voluntary sector.

The costs of long-term care for elderly people, people with physical or learning disabilities and people with a mental illness have increased despite the policy of transferring people from long-stay hospitals to the community. The costs to the Department of Social Security (DSS) of residential care for those unable to live independently have also escalated at a frightening rate.

The implications for society are enormous. State pensions currently cost the nation £34.5 billion a year – 44 per cent of the total Social Security budget. Elderly people are the main consumers of health and social services in the UK. They are to be found in every type of care environment: general hospitals, residential care and nursing homes, mental health units, the community, day centres and day hospitals. The State's bill for residential care is expected to soar from its present £7.5 billion to £30 billion by the year 2031.

A bleak future is forecast. The young will look after the old for a few years, but pension funds will run dry and industries will close down for lack of young blood. We need to seek solutions *now* before the problems become severe. Much must be done to keep people healthy and active in their third age, to develop an effective community care service for dependent people and to plan ahead for the problems of the demographic time-bomb which will affect us all.

[2] Source: Age Concern, 'Older People in the United Kingdom'

Age Concern England
Astral House
1268 London Road
London SW16 4ER
Tel: 0181–679 8000

Age Concern Scotland
113 Rose Street
Edinburgh EH2 3DT
Tel: 0131–220 3345

Age Concern Wales
Fourth Floor
1 Cathedral Road
Cardiff CF1 9SD
Tel: 01222 371566

Age Concern Northern Ireland
6 Lower Crescent
Belfast BT7 1NR
Tel: 01232 245729

Age Concern is a registered charity whose governing body includes representatives of over 80 national organisations and six Departments of State. There are around 1,100 independent local Age Concern groups in England. Age Concern England (ACE) works closely with Age Concerns Scotland, Wales, and Northern Ireland and provides services to elderly people, stimulates innovation and research and works in partnership with other relevant statutory voluntary bodies.

Age Concern groups provide a wide range of services, often including day care, visiting services, lunch clubs, over-60s clubs and, in some areas, specialist services for physically and mentally frail older people. Its Information Department also maintains an open telephone helpline for older people themselves and their families. The Information and Training Departments of ACE provide a direct service of advice and support to professionals and volunteers working with elderly people throughout the country. ACE also gives grants to new projects and organisations and acts as an agent for government programmes such as Employment Training and Opportunities for Volunteers. ACE campaigns on many issues affecting older people and aims to inform public opinion through national reports, conferences, publicity, campaigning and the promotion of research.

ACE publications include numerous leaflets on health, financial and legal matters and safety. These are listed in the relevant chapters of this book – for further information covered in this chapter, its leaflet 'Older people in the United Kingdom. Some basic facts' contains statistics and details about our ageing population.

Help the Aged
St James Walk
London EC1R 0BE
Tel: 0171–253 0253

Help the Aged works to improve the quality of life of elderly people in the United Kingdom and internationally, particularly those who are frail, isolated or poor. By identifying needs, raising public awareness and through effective fundraising, Help the Aged promotes and develops aid programmes of a high standard which are practical and innovative.

Centre for Policy on Ageing
25–31 Ironmonger Row
London EC1V 3QP
Tel: 0171–253 1787

The Centre for Policy on Ageing (CPA) was formed in 1947. It promotes informed debate about issues affecting older age groups, stimulates awareness of the needs of older people and encourages the spread of good practice that will enable everyone to live the last third of life as fully as possible. Although CPA's work is primarily directed towards informing and influencing service providers, the fundamental touchstone of its approach is to discover and advocate what older people themselves want and need.

CPA's publications are aimed at all people who work with older people. These publications include analyses of research, policy and practice, and examine all aspects of life from the viewpoint of the older citizen. For example:
Growing Old Together (£10.50)
CPA World Directory of Old Age (£33)
Aspects of Ageism (£1)

Office of Population, Censuses and Surveys
St Catherine's House
10 Kingsway
London C2B 6LH
Tel: 0171–242 0262

The Office of Population Censuses and Surveys (OPCS) provides a breakdown and continuous analysis of statistics on population and demographics, with a summary of the projections. Results from the 1991 survey are now available. Many publications are available, including the 1991 Census statistics for Great Britain covering this topic: *Persons Aged 60 and Over, 1991*

The Family Policy Studies Centre
231 Baker Street
London NW1 6XE
Tel: 0171–486 8211

Family matters are changing and becoming a major issue, with declining marriage rates, increasing cohabitation, divorce, one-parent families and more dual-worker families. We are seeing an increasing need for families to care for an ageing population that has to be balanced with the demands of paid work. The Family Policy Studies Centre plays an important role in research, social policy and information about family matters. Numerous publications are available, including:
An Ageing Population (£3)
Disability and Dependency in Old Age (£7.95)
Innovations in Community Care (£5)

The Host Consultancy
Labour Market Intelligence Unit
Horsham
West Sussex RH12 1YS
Tel: 01403 211440

The Host Consultancy is an independent contract research and consultancy group which researches and produces publications concerning the effect of the increasing age of the labour force combined with the rising number of elderly in the population and its impact on care and employment policy. Example: *Eldercare, the case for employment policy* (£20)

Population Concern
178–202 Great Portland Street
London W1N 5TB
Tel: 0171–637 9582
Population Concern is an independent charity which aims to raise awareness of the size and complexity of world population and the resulting effect on social and economic development. It seeks to establish a balance between world population, natural resources and environment, and to raise funds to provide the knowledge and means of planned parenthood through projects in the UK and overseas.

Other organisations which monitor old age, its effects and policy thereon are:

Foundation for Age Research/Research into Ageing
Baird House
15–17 St Cross Street
London EC1N 8UN
Tel: 0171–404 6878

The Policy Studies Institute
100 Park Village East
London NW1 3SR
Tel: 0171–387 2171

Retirement Counselling and Courses

Pre-Retirement Association of Great Britain and Northern Ireland
Nodus Centre
University Campus
Guildford
Surrey GU2 5RX
Tel: 01483 39323
An independent, national charitable organisation with nearly 30 years' experience in the field of mid-life and retirement planning offering courses, research and information.

Godwins Ltd
Briarcliff House
Kingsmead
Farnborough
Hants GU14 7TE
Tel: 01252 521701

An independent company offering seminars or 'pre-retirement discussions' throughout the year, covering subjects such as health, finance, time-management and leisure, security, wills and taxation.

The Retirement Counselling Service
Turret House
The Avenue
Bucks HP7 0AB
Tel: 01494 433553
An independent company offering pre-retirement counselling seminars covering preparation, pensions, benefits, security, exercise, finance, health and activities.

Further Reading
An Ageing Population (Family Policy Studies Centre, 1991), £2.50
Active Retirement, positive steps to a secure future (The Which? Guide, Consumers Association, 1993), £12.99
The Good Retirement Guide, 1994, Rosemary Brown (Kogan Page), £14.99
The Carnegie Inquiry into the Third Age; Life, Work and Livelihood (Bailey Management Services, 127 Sandgate Road, Folkestone, Kent CT20 2BL), £19.50
Coping with Change – Focus on Retirement (available from The Health Education Authority; details *page 21*), £7.95

chapter two

HEALTH MATTERS

All You Need to Know to Promote Health and Fitness, and Organisations that Offer Advice on Prevention and Treatment

IT IS NEVER TOO LATE to change your lifestyle and habits in order to lead a healthier life. Whatever changes are made towards a more balanced diet and regular, gentle exercise will produce benefits which far outweigh any sacrifices.

Fortunately, there is a wealth of literature and advice on hand to advise you on the best way to stay healthy and get the best out of life. *Mens sana in corpora sana* – 'a healthy mind in a healthy body' – still holds good and there is no substitute for keeping fit and mentally alert, eating a healthy, balanced diet and having regular eye and dental check-ups.

Changes happen to everyone as they grow older – hair loses colour, names slip the mind, staircases seem steeper – but there is much you can do to improve the quality of your life and maintain good health into old age. Do not dismiss physical or mental problems as 'just old age'. Many conditions can be treated very easily and successfully; there are a large number of professional people who may be able to help, and there is much that can be done by older people to help themselves.

In recent years there have been many improvements in the quality and range of care available from the NHS, most of which are of particular importance to older people. For example, doctors must now offer an annual health check to all patients aged over 75. And there are a wide range of special clinics, occupational therapists, physiotherapists and specialists to help – all surgeries must now provide a leaflet explaining the range of services available.

The Department of Health publishes an extremely useful free guide called *Health and Well-being, a Guide for Older People*. It is available from:

HMSO Manchester
Print and Logistics Warehouse
Oldham Broadway
Business Park
Broadgate
Chedderton
Lancs OL9 0JA

Local pharmacists can also advise on health problems, including when a problem merits seeing a doctor. Men over 65 and women over 60 years of age are currently entitled to free prescriptions, and may be able to get help with the cost of dental care, sight tests and glasses. Your local authority Social Services Department will advise you as to which services are available. Their address and telephone number can be obtained from the library, Community Health Council, Citizens Advice Bureau or the telephone directory.

Age Concern's national 'Ageing Well' programme involves Age Concern, the Department of Health, the Health Education Authority, Merck Sharp and Dohme Ltd, and PPP in a partnership to support and encourage health and fitness and prevent ill-health and disability. Details are available from Age Concern (*see page 15*).

NHS PRESCRIPTIONS

Men over 65 and women over 60 are entitled to free prescriptions; those on Income Support or Family Credit are also eligible. In addition, sufferers of various medical conditions and people on War or MOD Disablement Pensions are also eligible; people may also have a low-income entitlement. Leaflet P11 (April 1993) from the Department of Health (or doctor's surgeries) explains who is eligible and how to claim an exemption certificate. Other Department of Health leaflets are:

AB11: Help with NHS Costs
D11: NHS Dental Treatment
G11: NHS Sight Tests and Vouchers for Glasses
H11: NHS Hospital Travel Costs
WF11: NHS Wigs and Fabric Supports
P11: NHS Prescriptions – How to get them free

These are also available from doctors. AB11 is available from some post offices. All can be obtained by writing to:

The Department of Health
The Health Publications Unit
No 2 Site
Heywood Stores
Manchester Road
Heywood
Lancs OL10 2PZ

The Health Education Authority

The HEA publishes numerous books and leaflets about all aspects of healthy living. In addition to numerous other publications about every aspect of health – heart disease, cancer, family health, alcohol, health and hygiene – of particular interest for older people are these leaflets:
'Cutting Down your Drinking'
'Diet and Cancer'
'Diet, Nutrition and Healthy Eating'
'Enjoy Healthy Eating'
'The Health Guide'
For a booklet detailing all the publications, get in touch with your local Health Education Unit. To obtain literature contact:

Health Education Authority Customer Services
Marston Book Services Ltd
PO Box 87
Osney Mead Ind Est
Oxford OX2 0DT
Tel: 01865 204745

Health Education Authority for Wales
Brunel House (Eighth Floor)
2 Fitzalan Road
Cardiff DF2 1EB
Tel: 01222 752222

Health Education Board for Scotland
Woodburn House
Canaan Lane
Edinburgh EH10 4SG
Tel: 0131–447 8044

Health Promotion Agency for Northern Ireland
18 Ormeau Avenue
Belfast BT2 8HS
Tel: 01232 311611
Other organisations which produce valuable information and publications:

The British Geriatrics Society
1 St Andrews Place
London NW1 4LB
Tel: 0171–935 4004
The British Geriatrics Society sets out to promote high standards of health for elderly people at home, in hospitals, in nursing and residential homes. It promotes research in age-related disease and strives to improve methods of care of elderly people. It also provides a forum for the exchange and dissemination of scientific information. The society promotes the teaching of geriatric medicine and the training of medical and paramedical staff in geriatric medicine and care of elderly people.

It publishes numerous invaluable leaflets which are available (free if you send an A4 sae), including:
'How to Eat Well When You Are Ill'
'How to Get the Sleep You Need'
'How to Help Yourself to a Well-Nourished Retirement'
'How to Keep Warm and Prevent Hypothermia'
'How to Look After your Food...and Yourself'
'How to Protect Yourself from Influenza'

Help the Aged
St James Walk
London EC1R 0BE
Tel: 0171–253 0253
Help the Aged publishes a number of useful advice leaflets which are available by writing to their information department, including:
'Better Hearing'
'Better Sight'
'Fight the Flu'
'Fitter Feet'
'Healthy Bones'
'Healthy Eating'
'Incontinence'
'Keeping Mobile'
'Managing your Medicines'
'Shingles'

Research into Ageing
Baird House
15–17 St Cross Street
London EC1N 8UN
Tel: 0171–404 6878
This charity directly funds research into diseases and conditions that affect the quality of life of older people. Useful free leaflets (please send sae) include:
Leaflet 1: *'Dementia'*
2: *'Osteoporosis'*
3: *'Urinary Incontinence'*
4: *'Exercise'*
5: *'Visual Problems in Old Age'*

SMOKING

It is a myth that smoking doesn't matter if you have smoked all your life without apparent ill effects. It is never too late to feel the benefits of stopping, in fact giving up smoking is the single most effective action anyone can take to improve his or her health.

All forms of smoking are bad: cigarettes, cigars and pipes all increase the risk of heart disease, lung disease (especially bronchitis and lung cancer) and osteoporosis (thinning of the bones). Smoking also reduces the chances of survival after a heart attack.

Every year, many people successfully give up smoking. There is plenty of help available: doctors are only too happy to help, and nicotine patches may be available on prescription to help you quit. In addition, useful leaflets can be obtained from:

Action on Smoking and Health (ASH)
109 Gloucester Place
London W1H 4EJ
Tel: 0171–935 3519
ASH provides information about smoking and its risks, and campaigns to promote policies that discourage smoking. A report 'As Time Goes By' was due out sometime in 1995 examining smoking and older women. Many other factsheets, posters and publications are available – send sae for publications list.

QUIT
Victory House
170 Tottenham Court Road
London W1P 0HA
Tel: 0171–388 5775
QUIT is there to assist those who wish to give up. Their QUITLINE

(0171–487 3000) offers free, one-to-one advice and referral to local stop-smoking groups. Also phone this number for a free QUITPACK.

DIET

It is the food we eat that gives us the energy and nourishment to keep us alive in mind, body and spirit. If our diet is not varied or if we do not eat enough, we are more liable to become ill. On the other hand, eating too much can also cause health problems.

As metabolic rate slows down it is harder to keep the weight off, and therefore it is important not to snack on the wrong sorts of food: those with a lot of salt or sugar. Similarly, as one gets older, one's sense of taste may diminish and it is important not to compensate by adding lots of salt. The addition of herbs and spices is a good way to stimulate the appetite.

The most important thing is a well-balanced diet which includes plenty of fruit and vegetables, foods high in starches (carbohydrate) and fibre or roughage where possible (wholemeal bread or potatoes with their skins on), and fish, especially oily fish like mackerel, sardines, tuna or pink salmon. Where possible, lean cuts of meat and poultry should be used. The saturated fats found in butter and cream should be taken in moderation. It is important to remember that the body burns more energy in the winter and, therefore, people need to eat more to stay warm.

Help the Aged (*see page 22*) produces a free advice leaflet called 'Healthy Eating'.

The British Nutrition Foundation
High Holborn House
52–54 High Holborn
London WC1V 6RQ
Tel: 0171–404 6504

The British Nutrition Foundation (BNF) is an independent scientific organisation which sets out to provide reliable information and scientifically-based advice on nutrition and related health matters. The ultimate objective is to help individuals to understand how they may best match their diet with their lifestyle. Its principal functions fall under the headings of information, education and research. The Foundation produces a wide range of publications to suit different levels of ability. In addition, nutrition scientists at the Foundation are happy to answer enquiries by letter or telephone. The BNF is a non-profit-making organisation. Publications include (and are free unless otherwise indicated):
'Diet and Heart Disease'
'Dietary Influences in Cancer'
'Nutrition and the Elderly'
'Nutritional Aspects of Fish'
'Nutritional Labelling'
'The Role of Diet in Dental Health'
'Salt in the Diet'
'Unsaturated Fatty Acids'
'Vegetarian Diets'
BNF: *Nutrition Facts (A5 leaflets, 50p per set)*

The Health Education Authority (*see page 21*) publishes a free leaflet called 'Enjoy Healthy Eating'.

Complan
Crookes Healthcare Ltd
PO Box 57
Central Park
Lenton Lane
Nottingham NG7 2LJ
Tel: 0115 950 7431
Complan is a nourishing drink for use during illness and recovery.

WeightWatchers UK Ltd
Kidwells Park House
Kidwells Park Drive
Maidenhead
Berks S16 8YT
Tel: 01628 777077
If your aim is to lose weight it is important to do it sensibly and not sacrifice a balanced diet and essential vitamins, minerals and nutrients. Sound advice, further information and the address of local WeightWatchers branches are available from WeightWatchers UK Ltd.

The Vegetarian Society of the United Kingdom
Parkdale
Dunham Road
Altrincham
Cheshire WA14 4QG
Tel: 0161–928 0793

The Vegetarian Society's aim is to increase the number of vegetarians in the UK in order to save animals, benefit human health and protect the environment and world food resources. It is a registered charity dedicated to campaigning, information, education and research.

Its information sheet (free with sae) 'Healthy Nutrition in Later Life' gives sensible guidelines for a vegetarian diet and a list of nutritional requirements for all the vital vitamins, minerals and nutrients, energy, fibre and protein. Other factsheets available (free with sae) include:
'Basic Nutrition'
'Iron'
'Protein'
'Stumbling Blocks'

The Vegan Society
7 Battle Road
St Leonard's-on-Sea
East Sussex
TN37 7AA
Tel: 01424 427393
Advice and information on a healthy vegan diet.

ALCOHOL

In moderation, alcohol is unlikely to cause harm. In fact, a glass of wine a day has been said to reduce stress and lower blood-pressure. But too much can seriously damage health and, in the long term, can lead to stomach disorders, high blood-pressure and brain damage.

Alcohol is more likely to stay in the body for longer in older people. Similarly, they may find that they are affected by a very small amount of alcohol.

Alcoholics Anonymous
PO Box 1
Stonebow House
Stonebow
York YO1 2NJ
Tel: 01904 644026
National organisation with self-help groups throughout the UK.

Al-Anon (for Relatives)
61 Great Dover Street
London SE1 4YF
Tel: 0171–403 0888
Al-Anon (part of Alcoholics Anonymous) provides understanding and support for the relatives and friends of problem drinkers, whether the alcoholic is still drinking or not. Literature and advice are available.

Alcohol Concern
Waterbridge House
32–36 Loman Street
London SE1 0EE
Tel: 0171–928 7377
The national information and resource centre supplying information and local counselling and medical advice groups. Leaflets include:
'Alcohol and Older People' (30p)
'Problem with Drink?' (40p)
'A Survivor's Guide to Parties' (20p)

Alcohol Problem Advisory Service
4 Greenland Road
London NW1 0AS
Tel: 0171–482 1173
Local organisation offering one-to-one or family group counselling and medical advice (linked to Alcohol Concern).

Alcohol Counselling and Prevention Services
34 Electric Lane
London SW9
Tel: 0171–737 3579
Local counselling and advice centre.

The Health Education Authority (*address page 21*) publishes a booklet, 'That's The Limit: A Guide to Sensible Drinking' (30p) and 'Cutting Down your Drinking' (30p)

SEXUALITY

Older people can enjoy sex just as much as younger people; indeed, some changes to an older person's body may enhance his or her own (or his or her partner's) pleasure. But other changes can cause difficulties. After the menopause women may experience physical changes, for example vaginal dryness, for which there are a variety of creams and lubricants. Some older men suffer from impotence, through an illness or certain medication that they are taking. Older people should not be embarrassed to seek the help of their doctor about this or any other sexual matter.

SPOD
286 Camden Road
London N7 0BJ
Tel: 0171–607 8851
SPOD provides information relating to sexuality and the needs of people with a disability. It can provide a wide range of information, advisory leaflets and publications (some free, others between 25p and 50p). Phone for their publications list.

Keeping Mentally Active

Keeping mentally alert is just as important as keeping physically active. For the older person, starting further education, joining a club or course or spending time on a favourite hobby can be both stimulating and rewarding.

Your local College of Further Education, Institute of Adult Education or Community College will have a list of the various courses on offer, both in the evening and the daytime. *See Chapter 11* of this book for more information and relevant names and addresses.

Many voluntary bodies welcome older people who would like to use their skills to benefit others and become a valuable help in the community. (*See Chapter 3, pages 61–2* and *Chapter 11, pages 199–200* for further information.)

Keeping Warm in Winter

This is a vital part of keeping well. At home, hot meals and hot drinks will keep the body warm, as will a warm bedroom and a hot drink before bed.

The best way to keep warm when going out is to wear several layers of clothing for better insulation. Above all, make sure that your head, hands and feet are well covered, especially if there is to be a long wait in the cold for a bus or train.

- For more information phone the Winter Warmth Line free on 0800 289 404 (England and Wales), 0800 838 587 (Scotland), 0800 616 757 (Northern Ireland). Text-only Minicom for the deaf: 0800 269 626.
- Age Concern's Factsheet No 1, 'Help with Heating', gives details of loans, grants, government benefits and other services (free with sae; *see page 15* for Age Concern's address).
- The British Geriatrics Society's leaflet 'How to Keep Warm and Prevent Hypothermia' gives valuable advice and information about helping the elderly to stay warm and well.
- SeniorLine (Freephone 0800 289 404) is run by Help the Aged (*see page 22*) and provides free information and advice.

  Help the Aged produces a free advice leaflet called 'Keep out the Cold', which suggests things you can do to keep warm, gives practical advice on keeping bills down and keeping heat in, and lists a range of simple energy-efficient measures.
- *Also see Chapter 6 (pages 121–2)* on the Social Fund/special payments in cold weather.

The following energy agencies may be able to offer help and information on energy waste, insulation and conservation, safety, payment and pre-payment terms and budget accounts:

Energy Action Grants Agency
Eldon Court
Eldon Square
Newcastle upon Tyne NE1 7HA
Tel: 0800 181 667
The Energy Action Grants Agency may give grants for loft insulation and draft-proofing. Its leaflet 'We Give Grants to Help You Keep Warm!' will be sent free of charge.

Neighbourhood Energy Action
St Andrews House
90–92 Pilgrim Street
Newcastle upon Tyne NE1 6SG
Tel: 0191–261 5677
A national charity which promotes energy efficiency as a solution to the heating and energy problems of low-income households. This may take the form of advice, leaflets or referral to grant providers.

Further leaflets, including those on 'Energy in your Home', 'Insulating your Home' and 'Heating your Home' may be obtained from:

The Energy Efficiency Office
Department of The Environment
1 Palace Street
London SW1E 5HE

Office of Electricity Regulation (OFFER)
Hagley House
Hagley Road
Edgbaston
Birmingham B16 8QG
Tel: 0121–456 6208
OFFER can supply the names of the regional electricity companies, all of whom publish a code of practice leaflet for the elderly and people with disabilities on how to conserve energy, and detailing special switches and controls and the addresses of companies which can supply this equipment. Its Code of Practice to elderly customers and customers with disabilities includes password schemes to protect you from bogus callers, braille bills, sympathetic hearing (a scheme to raise public awareness of the communication needs of the hard of hearing) and other helpful strategies.

The Office of Gas Supply
Southside
105 Victoria Street
London
SW1E 6QT
Tel: 0171–828 0898

EYES

It is normal for people's eyesight to change as they get older. For example, they may find that they have to hold books at arm's length to read them.

It makes sense for older people to have regular sight tests to check the health of their eyes and see whether they need glasses, or whether their glasses need changing. These tests are done by an optometrist or ophthalmic optician. Older people may be entitled to a free NHS sight test and an NHS Spectacle Voucher if they are on a low income. They can apply for this on form AG1, obtainable from their optician, doctor or local Social Security office.

Two common eye conditions that affect older people, cataracts and glaucoma, are both treatable. Cataracts can be treated through a straightforward operation. Glaucoma can be treated with eye drops, tablets or surgery. People with glaucoma and their close relatives aged 40+ are entitled to free sight tests.

To help your eyes, make sure that there is good lighting in your home, particularly for activities like reading and sewing. By placing lights near to where they are needed, you can avoid having to use a stronger bulb. A bright light over the stairs and in other places where someone might trip is very important, especially if they have to get up in the night.

Further information is available from:

The Eye Care Information Service (EIS)
PO Box 3597
London SE1 6DY
Tel: 0171–357 7730
Voluntarily funded by both the optical industry and the profession, the EIS is dedicated to promoting the importance of good optical health, an interest in eye wear and improved awareness of modern optical technology. A range of information leaflets, factsheets, posters and audio-visual aids are published – a new leaflet, provisionally entitled 'Eyecare after 60' along with 'Radiation Hazards to the Eye', 'The Eye Examination, Your Questions Answered', 'Clear Vision, Safe Driving' and 'Retiring with Good Vision' are available if you send the EIS a stamped addressed envelope.

Royal National Institute for the Blind
224 Great Portland Street
London W1N 6AA
Tel: 0171–388 1266
The RNIB publishes a selection of leaflets on eye conditions, prevention and treatment. It publishes catalogues for special products to aid daily life (*see page 178*) and publishes a number of useful books and publications, including leaflets such as 'All About Cataracts', 'All About Diabetic Retinopathy' and 'All About Glaucoma' (price 25p each).

Partially Sighted Society
Redbridge House
7 Manor Road
Woodford Bridge
Essex IG8 8ER
Tel: 0181–559 2779
The Society provides counselling and training, information, advice and mail order aids. Telephone for further information.

The International Glaucoma Association
Kings College Hospital
Denmark Hill
London SE5 9RS
Tel: 0171–737 3265
The International Glaucoma Association is a charity which provides information about glaucoma, its detection, treatment and management. It campaigns to increase public awareness of this insidious condition and will answer questions by letter and telephone (during office hours). It funds research into glaucoma, its causes and treatment.

Further Reading
The British Geriatrics Society (*see page 21*) publishes a leaflet called 'Visual Problems in Old Age'.
Help the Aged (*see page 22*) produces a free advice leaflet called 'Better Sight'.
Better Sight without Glasses, Harry Benjamin (Thorsons, 1995)

HEARING

There are 7.5 million people in Great Britain with some degree of hearing loss. As they grow older, many people lose the ability to hear high-pitched sounds. If you or someone you know finds it hard to follow a conversation or hear the telephone or the television, contact a GP. There may be a simple cause such as wax in the ears, which can be easily removed (don't try to do it yourself and *never* poke anything in your ears).

Hearing aids are free through the NHS to everyone who needs them, as are batteries and repairs. It takes time to get used to them, but do be patient and, if you have problems or the hearing aid stops working properly, do take it back.

If you have difficulty hearing the telephone, doorbell or television, you can get special equipment. Ask your local Social Services Department or *see pages 50–1* of this book.

The Royal National Institute for Deaf People
105 Gower Street
London WC1E 6AM
Tel: 0171–387 8033
Text: 0171–388 2346
Qwerty: 300 band
Minicom: 0171–383 3154
The RNID is the UK's largest voluntary organisation representing the needs of deaf, deafened, hard of hearing and deaf-blind people. The RNID provides a range of quality services, including deaf awareness training, assistive devices (through manufacturer *Sound Advantage*), information, specialist telephone services (through Typetalk), communication support and residential care for deaf people with special needs. The RNID also raises awareness about the needs of deaf people and campaigns to remove discrimination and create full access to information. The RNID provides a range of quality services for deaf people and the professionals who work with them, including information, residential care and training. A publications list provides details of the many factsheets that are available (one copy free, please call for bulk order details), which include:
'*Buying a Hearing Aid*'
'*Telephone Adaptations*'
'*Typetalk Information Sheet*'
'*Tinnitus Perception, Retraining and Habituation*'
'*Lipreading – A Practical Guide*'
'*Understanding Dizziness and Imbalance*'
'*Noise Exposure and Hearing Loss*'

Hearing Concern – The British Association of the Hard of Hearing
7–11 Armstrong Road
London W3 7JL
Tel: 0181–743 1110 (voice and minicom)
The Association provides advice, information and support for anyone with acquired hearing loss. It provides information on hearing aids, lip-reading and equipment to help with the television, telephone, etc. It also operates the sympathetic hearing scheme, to raise public awareness of the communication needs of hard of hearing people, and produces a quarterly magazine, *Hearing Concern*. Most publications are free with sae, including:
'Facing Up to Hearing Loss'
'Lip-Reading'
'How Clearly Do You Speak?'
'You and your Hearing Aid'

Breakthrough Deaf-Hearing Integration
Charles Gillett Centre
998 Bristol Road
Selly Oak
Birmingham B29 6LE
Tel: 0121–472 6447
Text: 0121–471 1001
A voluntary organisation that integrates deaf and hearing people of all ages through self-help programmes of social activities, practical projects and training. These show that, through improved communication, deaf people can achieve even greater independence and share, with hearing people, a better quality of life.
Facilities at the Birmingham Centre include a Total Communication Course and an open learning centre, self-help contact groups for all ages, a youth group and an information and library service.

The British Deaf Association
38 Victoria Place
Carlisle CA1 1HU
Tel: 01228 48844
The Association gives information, advice and support for the profoundly deaf and campaigns on behalf of deaf people who use sign language. It produces a wide range of publications, magazines and videos and arranges holidays for older deaf people, as well as conferences and health promotion.
The Association has the largest membership organisation in the UK led by deaf people. Local branches throughout the country arrange group activities and education, and supply publications – list available on request.

British Tinnitus Association
Room 6
14–18 West Bar Green
Sheffield S1 2DA
Tel: 0114 279 6600
This charity gives information, leaflets and advice for tinnitus sufferers. There are local self-help groups, a quarterly journal and an annual conference. In addition, the Tinnitus Helpline is available on 0345 090 210, Monday to Friday 10 a.m. to 3 p.m.

National Association of Deafened People
103 Heath Road
Widnes
Cheshire WA8 7NU
Tel: 01494 482355
NADP is a charity which provides information and support for those who have a profound acquired hearing loss. There are local groups in some areas.

A quarterly newsletter and occasional publications are free to members. Books and materials available include: *Deaf People Can Compete on Equal Terms in the Workplace* (1992), £3.50 *Introduction to Cochlear Implants* (1993), £2.50
poster (produced 1994), free
publicity leaflet (1990), free
information pack and booklet (price on application)

The National Deaf–Blind League
18 Rainbow Court
Paston Ridings
Peterborough PE4 6UP
Tel: 01733 573511
Organisation offering information, advice, help, holidays and benefits advice.

Further Reading
Living with Tinnitus, Richard Hallam (Thorsons, 1993), £5.99
Help the Aged (*details page 22*) produces a free advice leaflet called 'Better Hearing'.

TEETH

With proper care a person should be able to keep his or her teeth for a lifetime. Brushing well every day with fluoride toothpaste and avoiding eating sugary foods certainly helps.

It is as important to take as much care of false teeth as of natural teeth. They should be cleaned carefully and the wearer should visit the dentist regularly. Whether your teeth are real or false, a dentist should examine your mouth from time to time; he or she may be able to make a house call if you are housebound.

People on a low income may get help with the cost of dental treatment. Leaflet D11 (available from dentists or your local Social Security office) explains how to get help.

BONES

Many older people suffer from osteoporosis, a condition in which the bones become thinner, weaker and more susceptible to breaking. This can be prevented or treated. The National Osteoporosis Society runs national education campaigns to work towards eradicating this preventable bone disease. The Society aims to increase awareness and to provide advice on prevention and treatment, information and support for sufferers through patient literature, a national helpline and a network of local groups. This is the only charity raising funds for research into the causes, treatment and prevention of osteoporosis and working nationally and locally to ensure that sufferers can obtain the treatment and support they need. Send sae for further information to:

The National Osteoporosis Society
PO Box 10
Radstock
Bath BA3 3YB
Tel: 01761 437903

Further Reading
Help the Aged (*see page 22*) produces a free advice leaflet called 'Healthy Bones'. The British Geriatric Society (*see page 21*) publishes a leaflet called 'Osteoporosis'.
Osteoporosis, Kathleen Mayes (Thorsons, 1991)

FEET

Looking after one's feet is vital whatever one's age, as minor problems can easily lead to major ones. Older people should make sure that shoes fit well and are comfortable, and should try not to wear slippers all day. Looking after your feet is undoubtedly the single most important contribution to continued mobility.

Chiropodists can provide very useful assistance, from help in cutting toenails to treatment for corns and bunions. If you or anyone you know has a problem finding shoes that will fit, contact a specialist footwear company (*see opposite*). A GP will be able to put you in touch with an NHS chiropodist.

The Society of Chiropodists
53 Welbeck Street
London W1M 7HE
Tel: 0171–486 3381
Can offer books, leaflets and details of local chiropodists. Lists State Registered Chiropodists in private practice and in stated geographical areas (please send sae if list is required). The following publications are free individually (telephone for prices of bulk orders):
'Ingrowing Toenails'
'Bunions and other Toe Deformities'
'Ageing Feet'
'Chilblains'
'Arthritic Feet'

British Footwear Manufacturers Association
5 Portland Place
London W1N 3AA
Tel: 0171–580 8690
People who have needs which lie outside the scope of footwear normally on offer in shops may find useful help and advice in the BFMA booklet 'Footwear for Special Needs' (£2), which lists hundreds of companies who can help to sort out their special needs.

Cosyfeet

Cosyfeet
5 The Tanyard
Leigh Road
Street
Somerset BA16 0HR
Tel: 01458 447275

Cosyfeet 'fit feet others won't fit'; it is a leading footwear company whose mail order catalogue is aimed mainly at the housebound elderly. It specialises in wider, deeper, roomier slippers, sandals and shoes. As people grow older the size and shape of their feet may change, so comfortable, well-fitting shoes are an essential aid to mobility. Cosyfeet dispatch 'same day', and offer a no-quibble money back guarantee.

The Disabled Living Foundation
380–384 Harrow Road
London W9 2HU
Tel: 0171–289 6111

The Disabled Living Foundation runs the Footwear Advisory Service which can help if you have problems finding shoes to fit or need advice on how to adapt your shoes to make them more comfortable.

Sole-Mates
46 Gordon Road
London E4 6BU
Tel: 0181–524 2423

Sole-Mates offers a partnering service so that people whose feet are not the same size (that is, one foot is a different size than the other) can be 'matched' with other people and share the cost of buying shoes. Please send sae for further information.

Further Reading
Help the Aged (*see page 22*) produces a free advice leaflet called 'Fitter Feet'.
The Foot Care Book, an A–Z of Fitter Feet by Judith Kemp (Age Concern, 1988), £2.95

GIDDINESS

This is common with older people and can often be treated. Doctors can provide useful help and advice. It is important for the affected person not to get up or turn suddenly and, if an older person does feel giddy, he or she should try to sit or lie down for a few minutes, or hold on to something secure until he or she feels steady again.

MEDICINES

To use medicines safely, do observe the following precautions:
- Make sure that you (or whoever is taking them) takes them exactly as prescribed or according to the instructions.
- Never take medication that has passed its expiry date.
- Never mix prescribed and bought medicines without first checking with the doctor or pharmacist who prescribed them.
- Dispose safely of any medicines no longer in use.

- Keep all medicines out of the reach of children.
- Consult a doctor about whether alcohol will react badly with any medicines being taken.

Help the Aged (*see page 22*) produces a free advice leaflet called 'Managing your Medicines'. Further information on safety with medicines is in Chapter 9.

INCONTINENCE

Urinary and faecal incontinence are distressing for sufferers – many are afraid of leaving the house lest they should have an accident. A great deal of help is available so that even severe cases can be managed with the help of special garments, pads, appliances and deodorants. Doctors or District Nurses should be able to prescribe these aids.

The Continence Foundation
2 Doughty Street
London WC1N 2PH
Tel: 0171–404 6875
The Continence Foundation is a charity which operates a confidential information helpline staffed by experienced nurse continence advisors who can answer queries about all aspects of incontinence and other bladder and bowel problems. The helpline operates Monday to Friday, 9 a.m. to 6 p.m. on 0191–213 0050. Letters will also be answered (please include sae). A range of information leaflets and a mail order book service are also available. Publications include:

Coping Successfully with Prostate Problems (£5.99)
Incontinence and Inappropriate Urinating (£8.55)
Managing Incontinence – A Guide to Living with Loss of Bladder Control (£8.95)
'The Continence Guide', 'Pelvic Floor Exercises', 'You and your Prostate' (free with sae)

Association for Continence Advice
The Basement
2 Doughty Street
London WC1N 2PH
Tel: 0171–404 6821
The Association can supply leaflets and information for local advice groups.

Further Reading
Help the Aged (*see page 22*) produces a free advice leaflet called 'Incontinence'.
The British Geriatrics Society (*see page 21*) publishes a leaflet called 'Urinary Incontinence'.
The Disabled Living Foundation (*see page 33*) offers an advisory service and a number of publications about incontinence, stress incontinence, adult bed-wetting and bowel problems (priced between £1.50 and £8.50 – send sae for publications lists).
Age Concern England has a leaflet about urinary and faecal incontinence. Please send sae (*address page 46*).

Counsel and Care for the Elderly (*address page 47*) has produced a leaflet, 'A Positive Approach to Incontinence for Older People', which is available free with sae.
Overcome Incontinence, Richard J. Millard (Thorsons, 1993), £5.99

The following associations provide information and local self-help groups for anyone living with a urostomy, colostomy or ileostomy:

The British Colostomy Association Group
15 Station Road
Reading
Berks RG1 1LG
Tel:01734 391537
Person-to-person help with any aspect of daily life, free information packs and referrals to local organisations who can assist.

Ileostomy Association of Great Britain and Northern Ireland
PO Box 23
Notts NG18 4TT
Tel: 01623 28099

The Urostomy Association
Buckland
Beaumont Park
Danbury
Essex
Tel: 01245 224294

EXERCISE

It is never too late to start! Exercise is good for you at any age. However, it is sensible to consult a doctor first if you have been ill or are unused to physical activity.

We all know that exercise keeps us fitter and physically healthier – new evidence now shows that it can keep the brain younger and more agile. Research at Manchester University has revealed that super-fit 70-year-olds can have brains as powerful as the average 50-year-old. It is believed that aerobic exercise actually keeps the brain active.

Exercise improves strength, suppleness and stamina. Activities like gardening, bowls, dancing and walking are all excellent forms of exercise. Swimming is particularly good if a person is overweight or has any backache, stiffness or disability, as the water supports the body.

Many local authorities offer older people reduced rates of entry and special classes at sports centres and, if they do not, it may be possible to arrange through the Sport and Recreation Department at your local town hall (*see* Hobbies and Interests, *pages 197–212*). Information on local keep-fit, exercise or swimming classes may be obtained at your local library or town hall. A number of organisations exist to help people start their own swimming groups, yoga classes or even windsurfing teams – further details of these are given in Chapter 11.

Further Reading
The British Geriatrics Society (*see page 21*) publishes a leaflet called 'Exercise'.
Sixty-Something, Dr Joan Gomez (Thorsons, 1993)

The Dark Horse Venture
Kelton
Woodlands Road
Liverpool L17 0AN
Tel: 0151–729 0092
The Dark Horse Venture encourages older people to take up new activities and discover hidden talents, encouraged by someone with professional training or proven experience in your chosen activity. One of the activity categories is 'Exploring and Exercising', which encourages people to undertake travel, explorations or physical recreation. *See Chapter 11* for further details.

Yoga for Health Foundation
Ickwell Bury
Biggleswade
Beds SG18 9EF
Tel: 01767 627271
Special courses for 'third age' guests are held during the year, led by lecturers and teachers who are themselves over 70. The courses are aimed at maximising abilities and gaining as much as possible from later years. The Yoga for Health Centre is open all year round and welcomes senior guests at any time, aiming to provide a balanced programme which benefits older people, including those with chronic disability. The Centre is modified for wheelchair use and provides a care staff throughout the day.

Relaxation for Living
168–170 Oatlands Drive
Weybridge
Surrey KT13 9ET
Tel: 01932 831000
Relaxation for Living is a national educational charity founded in 1972. It exists to promote the teaching of physical relaxation as a means of stress control, to combat the strain, anxiety and tension of modern life and to reduce fatigue. The charity offers a free information pack, a quarterly newsletter, audio tapes, leaflets, books, courses in relaxation and stress management, a correspondence course and courses to train teachers in relaxation and stress management.

The Medau Society
8b Robson House
East Street
Epsom
Surrey KT17 1HH
Tel: 01372 729056
The Medau movement classes improve posture, co-ordination, muscle tone and suppleness and give a feeling of well-being, relaxation and enjoyment. Active recreational classes and chair-based exercise classes are available when appropriate; free literature and information are available with sae. Telephone for the address of local Medau classes.

Extend Exercise Training Ltd
22 Maltings Drive
Wheathampstead
Herts AL4 8QJ
Tel: 01582 832760
Extend is a charity which provides recreational movement to music classes for over-60s and people of all ages with disabilities. They have 600 teachers in the UK – please telephone for an exercise booklet or to find out about the class nearest you.

The Women's League of Health and Beauty
52 London Street
Chertsey
Surrey KT16 8AJ
Tel: 01932 564567
Over 280 centres in the UK provide exercise classes for women of all ages.

Further Help and Advice on Prevention and Treatment

The British Heart Foundation
14 Fitzhardinge Street
London W1H 4DH
Tel: 0171–935 0185
Heart disease accounts for nearly half of all deaths in the UK. 'Don't smoke, watch your weight, take regular exercise and choose food wisely' is the advice from The British Heart Foundation, the largest heart charity. It raises money to fund research into all forms of heart and circulatory disease, education programmes for the public and health professionals, rehabilitation and support groups for heart patients and cardiac equipment for hospitals and ambulance services. It also promotes life-saving training techniques.

  A large number of publications are available from the BHF free of charge (donations are welcome) on subjects such as 'The Heart', exercise, diet, resuscitation, smoking, heart medicines, blood-pressure and reducing the risks of heart disease, and 'Food Should Be Fun'. A £5 donation is usually asked towards the cost of videos.

The Coronary Prevention Group
Plantation House
Suite 5/4
31–33 Fenchurch Street
London EC3M 3NN
Tel: 0171–626 4844

The Medical Department
The Wellcome Foundation
Crewe Hall
Crewe
Cheshire CW1 1UB
Tel: 01270 583151
The Medical Department provides patients with information leaflets on a variety of conditions such as shingles, genital herpes and HIV.

The Alzheimer's Disease Society (England)
Gordon House
10 Greencoat Place
London SW1P 1PH
Tel: 0171–306 0606
Alzheimer's Disease is a physical disease which causes a progressive decline in the ability to remember, to learn, to think and to reason. The Society is a charity that gives support

to families of sufferers throughout the UK, and publishes booklets and factsheets on a wide range of topics. Members receive a free monthly newsletter.

The Society offers assistance through membership and a national network of branches and support groups to provide practical help, information and guidance for carers and professionals. The Society also campaigns for adequate and high-quality services and promotes research and public awareness. The free recorded information numbers are:

Alzheimer's Disease: 0800 318 771
Other Dementias: 0800 318 772
The Society – How We Help: 0800 318 773
Who Can Help – Services: 0800 318 774
Legal and Financial Information: 0800 318 775
Free leaflets include:
'If you are looking after a confused relative...'
General leaflet – 'Who are we and how can we help?'
'Alzheimer's Disease: What Is It?'
'Other Causes of Dementia'
'Safe as Houses – Living Alone with Dementia'

Alzheimer's Scotland
8 Hill Street
Edinburgh EH2 3JZ
Tel: 0131–225 1453
Helpline: 0131–220 6155 (24 hours)
Alzheimer's Scotland exists to help people with dementia and their carers with a network of local groups and branches which provide a chance for carers to meet others in their situation. Projects throughout Scotland provide services such as home support and day centres in order to give carers a valuable break and to provide stimulation and social contact for the person with dementia. Many publications are available, priced 10p to £2 – send sae for a publications list. Examples include:
'What is Dementia?' (10p)
'Getting Help from your Doctor' (75p)
'Personal Care' (20p)
'Aluminium and Alzheimer's Disease' (20p)

Alzheimer's Disease Society (Wales)
Tonne Hospital
Neath
West Glamorgan SA11 3LX
Tel: 01639 641938

Alzheimer's Disease Society (Northern Ireland)
11 Wellington Park
Belfast BT9 6DJ
Tel: 01232 664400

Dementia Services Development Centre
University of Stirling
Stirling FK9 4LA
Tel: 01786 467740
This charity/research centre exists to extend and improve services to people with dementia and their carers. It provides information, development assistance, conferences and seminars, publications, research and training.

Further Reading
The British Geriatrics Society (*see page 21*) publishes a leaflet called 'Dementia'.
Caring for Confusion, Paulette Micklewood (Scutari Press, 1991). A book about the care of patients with Alzheimer's Disease.
The 36-hour Day by Nancy Mace and Peter Rabins (Hodder and Stoughton), £9.99.
Living with Alzheimer's Disease by Gordon Wilcock (Penguin), £5.99
Alzheimer's Disease, Isobelle Gidley and Richard Shears (Thorsons, 1988)
See also Mental Health, *below*.

The Arthritis and Rheumatism Council
PO Box 177
Chesterfield
Derbyshire S41 7TQ
Tel: 01246 558033
Only one person in 50 will escape arthritis or rheumatism to one degree or another; in Britain these afflictions affect up to eight million people severely. The Arthritis and Rheumatism Council funds research to find a cure and publishes over 40 free booklets and leaflets to help people understand and cope with their illness.

Arthritis Care
18 Stephenson Way
London NW1 2HD
Tel: 0171–916 1500
Helpline: 0800 289 170
Arthritis Care is the only national voluntary organisation working with and for people of all ages with arthritis and rheumatism. It aims to promote their health, well-being and independence through services, support, self-help, campaigning and information. It has over 600 branches and 67,000 members.

Arthritis Care provides an information counselling service by telephone and letter, and the freephone AC Barclays helpline (above) is available from Monday to Friday, 12 noon to 4 p.m. Other services include holidays, mobility equipment, and a basic information pack. Free publications (with sae) include:
'Keeping on the Move'
'Osteoporosis and Arthritis'
'Hip Replacement'

The Arthritic Association
Hill House
Little New Street
London EC4A 3TR
Tel: 0171–491 0233

Further Reading
Life without Arthritis – The Maori Way, Jan de Vries (Mainstream Publishing, 1991), £4.99
Arthritis, Stephen Terrass (Thorsons, 1994)
Diets to Help Arthritis, Helen MacFarlane (Thorsons, 1988)
New Self Help: Arthritis, Leon Chaitow (Thorsons, 1987)

The National Back Pain Association
16 Elmtree Road
Teddington
Middlesex TW11 8ST
Tel: 0181–977 5474

A small registered medical charity devoted entirely to helping back pain sufferers, the NBPA funds research into causes and treatment of back pain and educates people to use their bodies sensibly and reduce the risks of back pain. The Association runs nationwide branches to help sufferers; members are entitled to four issues of its magazine *Talkback* per year, access to local self-help groups, and its information line. The NBPA offers a range of publications for 10p plus sae:
'Self-care'
'Better Backs for Gardeners'
'Better Backs for Drivers'
'Handy Hints'
A Carer's Guide (£1.50)
Better Backs for Gardeners (video, £7.49)

Further Reading
Back Pain, Roger Newman Turner (Thorsons, 1993), £5.99
New Self Help: Backache and Disc Troubles, Arthur White (Thorsons, 1989)

The Chartered Society of Physiotherapy
14 Bedford Row
London WC1R 4ED
Tel: 0171–242 1941

The Society helps to promote good health and publishes a range of leaflets and pamphlets which are free with sae. For instance:
'Physiotherapy and Older People'
'Mobility is a Must'
'Look After your Back'
'Take the Strain Out of Gardening'

BACUP (The British Association of Cancer United Patients, Their Families and Friends)
3 Bath Place
Rivington Street
London EC2A 3JR
Tel: 0171–613 2121 (admin only)
Info: 0800 181 199

BACUP offers up-to-date information and emotional support to people with cancer, their families and friends. Free, confidential services include a nationwide telephone information service staffed by cancer nurses.

A London-based one-to-one counselling service is available to cancer sufferers and their, families, friends and colleagues. Appointments may be made on 0171–696 9000.

BACUP publishes over 40 booklets on different cancers and their treatments and on the practical and emotional issues faced by people with cancer. The books are helpful and clearly written; a publications list is available with sae.

Cancer Relief Macmillan Fund
15–19 Britten Street
London SW3 3TB
Tel: 0171–351 7811

The Fund works to improve the quality of life for people with cancer. It builds and maintains day care and in-patient centres, finances a medical education programme to improve the cancer care skills of NHS nurses and doctors, gives grants directly to patients in need and funds four associate charities which provide information and support.

The charity is perhaps best known for Macmillan nurses: trained specialists in caring for people with cancer. There are now more than 950 Macmillan nurses in the UK, offering advice and support at all stages of the illness and in any setting – home, hospital and care centres. Macmillan nurses work with the NHS at all times.

Free leaflets include:
'Help is There: National Contacts for People with Cancer'
'Breast Cancer, How to Help Yourself'

Cancer Help Centre
Grove House
Cornwallis Grove
Clifton
Bristol BS8 4PG
Tel: 0117 974 3216
Cancer Help runs a holistic healing programme to complement medical treatment, with a one-day or one-week residential course (costing around £500 for a week).

The Hodgkin's Disease Association
PO Box 275
Haddenham
Aylesbury
Bucks HP17 8RU
Tel: 01844 291479
The Association offers emotional and practical support and literature for sufferers of Hodgkin's Disease (cancer of the lymphatic system) and their friends and relatives.

Cancerlink
17 Britannia Street
London WC1X 9JN
Tel: 0171–833 2451
Cancerlink offers cancer patients, their friends and relatives support, literature and an information service.

Cancer Care Society
21 Zetland Road
Redland
Bristol BS6 7AH
Tel: 0117 942 7419
Cancer Care offers counselling, self-help and support groups throughout the UK.

Further Reading
Cancer: How to Reduce your Risks (The Health Education Authority, *see page 49*), 50p
Cancer Special Diet Cookbook, Richard Turner and Elizabeth Simonsen (Thorsons, 1991)

The British Diabetic Association
10 Queen Anne Street
London W1M 0BD
Tel: 0171–323 1531

The BDA offers information and education for people with diabetes, professionals and their families, supporting medical and social research, local branches and self-help groups.

Further Reading
Diets to Help Diabetes, Martin Budd (Thorsons, 1994), £2.99
The Diabetes Handbook: Insulin Dependent, John L. Day (Thorsons, 1986)

Action for Dysphasic Adults
1 Royal Street
London SE1 7LL
Tel: 0171–261 9572
Dysphasia is a communication handicap resulting from the loss or impairment of speech and language after a stroke or head injury. This organisation provides information and advice for sufferers and their carers. It supports development of and research into new methods of assessment and treatment, and aims to increase public awareness of the abilities and needs of sufferers.

National Eczema Society
163 Eversholt Street
London NW1 1BU
Tel: 0171–388 4097
Practical information, advice, information packs and quarterly journal.

The Haemophilia Society
123 Westminster Bridge Road
London SE1 7HR
Tel: 0171–928 2020
For leaflets, advice and help, please send sae.

Mental Health

Depression Alliance
PO Box 1022
London SE1 72B
Tel: 0171–721 7672
Write (with sae) for information.

MIND
National Association for Mental Health
Granta House
15–19 Broadway
London E15 4BQ
Tel: 0181–519 2122

Richmond Fellowship for Mental Welfare
8 Addison Road
Kensington
London W1N
Tel: 0171–603 6373
A charity helping mental health sufferers though therapy or a short- or long-term stay in a home.

Scottish Action on Dementia
8 Hill Street
Edinburgh EH2 3JZ
Tel: 0131–225 1453

Multiple Sclerosis Society
25 Effie Road
London SW6 1EE
Tel: 0171–736 6267
For advice and literature

The Parkinson's Disease Society of the United Kingdom
22 Upper Woburn Place
London WC1H 0RA
Tel: 0171–383 3513
The Parkinson's Disease Society exists to help all people with Parkinson's Disease, their families, friends and the professionals involved in their care. The areas of work include welfare, research, information, education, publicity and fundraising. There are

approximately 200 local branches offering self-help and mutual support. The Society can provide many books and leaflets about the disease, some of which are free with sae. Send for a publications list.

The Motor Neurone Disease Association
PO Box 246
Northampton NN2 2PR
Tel: 01604 250505
Helpline (9 a.m.–10.30 a.m.): 01345 626262
The Association supports people with MND and their families by providing advice and information, support groups, a network of regional care advisors, an equipment loan scheme and limited financial assistance. It funds research into the cause of MND, supports clinical trials and provides grants for applied research.

The Stroke Association
CHSA House
Whitecross Street
London EC1Y 8JJ
Tel: 0171–490 7999

The Stroke Association is the only national charity solely concerned with combating strokes. It funds research and helps stroke patients and their families by offering advice, publications and welfare grants. It has 20 regional information centres; its community services, dysphasic support and family support schemes provide (in many areas) home visits for stroke victims and their families to help with speech problems and provide emotional support. More than 400 stroke clubs are affiliated to the Association; details of local groups are available on request.

Volunteer Stroke Scheme
7 Albion Street
London W2 2AS
Tel: 0171–262 8385
VSS is a charity which provides help for people who suffer from speech and other problems as a result of a stroke. It provides family support and rehabilitation in the greater London area.

ALTERNATIVE MEDICINE

The Institute of Complementary Medicine
PO Box 194
London SE16 1QZ
Tel: 0171–237 5165
Organisation which can direct the public to local practitioners of osteopathy, hypnotherapy, homoeopathy, massage, counselling, etc.

The British Acupuncture Association and Register
34 Alderney Street
London SW1V 4EU
Tel: 0171–834 1012

The Register of Traditional Chinese Medicine
19 Trinity Road
London N2 8JJ
Tel: 0181–883 8431
For list of registered acupuncturists send £2.50 plus sae.

The British School of Osteopathy
1–4 Suffolk Street
London SW1Y 4GH
Tel: 0171–930 9254
The BSO is building a community care clinic for the treatment of people with disabilities, and provides a low-fee system for the treatment of elderly people.

The British Chiropractic Association
29 Whitley Street
Reading
Berks RG2 0EG
Tel: 01734 757557
The registering association for chiropractitioners, it can direct members of the public to their local practitioner.

The Shiatsu Society
5 Foxcote
Wokingham
Berks RG11 3PG
Tel: 01734 730836

Society of Homoeopaths
2 Artisan Road
Northampton NN1 4HU
Tel: 01604 21400
Send for free register of local practitioners.

The British Homoeopathic Association
27a Devonshire Street
London WC1N 3HR
Tel: 0171–935 2163
The Association exists to encourage the understanding and use of homoeopathy and provide answers to all enquiries. It maintains a large library and publishes a bi-monthly magazine. Send large sae for further information.

The National Institute of Medical Herbalists
56 Longbrook Street
Exeter EX4 6AH
Tel: 01392 426022
Send 29p sae for general information and list of practitioners.

The British College of Naturopathy and Osteopathy
Frazer House
6 Netherall Gardens
London NW3 5RR
Tel: 0171–435 3630
The BCNO is a teaching college which runs clinics (£15 for the first consultation and £10 for subsequent visits). The college provides a particular type of osteopathic education – that of holistic or naturopathic osteopathy, which is unique.

The Incorporated Society of Registered Naturopaths
328 Harrogate Road
Leeds LS17 6PR
Tel: 0113 268 5992
Send sae for free practitioners list and publications list.

The National Federation of Spiritual Healers
Old Manor Farm Studio
Church Street
Sunbury on Thames
Middlesex TW16 6RG
Tel: 01932 783164
Phone 0891 616 080 for healer referrals.

Further Reading
Better Health through Natural Healing, Ross Trattler (Thorsons, 1993), £7.99
The Complete System of Chinese Self-healing, Dr Stephen T. Chang (Thorsons, 1994), £6.99
The Science of Homoeopathy, George Vithoulkas (Thorsons, 1993), £14.99
The Book of Pain Relief, Leon Chaitow (Thorsons, 1993), £6.99
Keeping Well – A Guide to Health in Retirement, Anne Roberts (Faber and Faber, 1991), £4.99
Look Younger, Feel Better: A Top-to-toe Programme for Health and Vitality, Dr James Scala and Barbara Jacques (Piatkus Books, 1993), £9.99
The Magic of Movement: A Tonic for Older People, Laura Mitchell (Age Concern, 1988), £3.95
The New Case for Exercise (Health Education Authority, tel: 0171–383 3833), £2.95
You Can Feel Good Again, Richard Carlson (Thorsons, 1993), £4.99
Your Health in Retirement – An A to Z Guide, J.A. Muir (Age Concern, 1990), £4.50

chapter three

WHO CARES?

Organisations to Turn to for Assistance, Counselling, Friendship and Practical Advice; Care and Nursing Services at Home

OVER THE YEARS a massive network of caring organisations has emerged to assist and advise people from all walks of life with all manner of problems.

I have already listed charitable and other organisations concerned with health and diseases in the previous chapter, as most assist with prevention as well as care and cure of the condition.

There are so many caring organisations which provide advice, information, counselling, financial grants or accommodation that it may be hard to know which does what or, indeed, that they exist at all. Here they are listed with a description of the products, services and/or information they can provide.

Age Concern England
Astral House
1268 London Road
London SW16 4ER
Tel: 0181–679 8000

Age Concern Scotland
113 Rose Street
Edinburgh EH2 3DT
Tel: 0131–220 3345

Age Concern in Wales
Fourth Floor
1 Cathedral Road
Cardiff CF1 9SD
Tel: 01222 371566

Age Concern Northern Ireland
6 Lower Crescent
Belfast BT17 1NR
Tel: 01232 245729

Age Concern England (ACE) is the main charity concerned with research, aid, training and publications for older people. Together with its affiliated organisations Age Concern Scotland, Northern Ireland and Wales, ACE provides a wide range of community services, including day centres, lunch clubs, visits for the lonely as well as transport and many other schemes. It also takes an active part in policy formulation by advising the UK Government on legislation affecting older people and campaigning on their behalf. ACE publishes information sheets on the following subjects (send for publications list and prices before ordering; a *9-inch x 6-inch sae* will be required for a maximum of five): heating, holidays, wills, legal matters, accommodation, finance, and disability.

Age Concerns throughout Britain also exist to promote effective care of and to encourage choice and opportunity for older people. Relevant publications include:
'Finding Help at Home'
'Abuse of Elderly People, Guidelines for Action' (25p)

Help the Aged
St James Walk
London EC1R 0BE
Tel: 0171–253 0253

Help the Aged works to improve the quality of life of elderly people, particularly those who are frail, isolated or poor. The charity is primarily a fundraising organisation, making grants to community-based projects.

Help the Aged's SeniorLine is a free national information service staffed by advice workers who can respond to callers' questions about housing, health, welfare and disability benefits, mobility, support for carers, community alarms, sources of local practical help and other voluntary organisations. If they are unable to help they can usually tell you who can. Call free on 0800 289 404, Monday to Friday 10 a.m. to 4 p.m.

The charity also has a range of free advice leaflets on welfare and disability benefits, money matters, home safety and health. Write to the Information Department for a list.

Help the Aged also cares for nearly 600 residents in its nine extra-sheltered developments, 32 semi-sheltered dwellings, four registered residential homes and many donated properties.

Counsel and Care for the Elderly
Twyman House
16 Bonny Street
London NW1 9PG
Tel: 0171–485 1550

Counsel and Care is a charity which offers free, confidential advice, practical help and an information service for older people, their carers and families and health professionals. It can supply grants to support older people in residential or nursing homes, or in their own homes and, where possible, can access financial resources administered by other agencies for the benefit of older people and their carers. It updates information on services and benefits for older people by visiting residential and nursing establishments and building up and revising details of the resources available. If Counsel and Care cannot help callers it is usually able to direct them to whoever can.

A wide range of information sheets, reports and leaflets are available (25p if more than one is required). These include:
'About Counsel and Care'
'Older People in Britain: Fact and Fiction'
'Help at Home'
'The Social Fund for Older People'
'Disability Living Allowance'
'Dementia'
'Which Charity?'

Carers

Carers are people who look after a relative, friend or neighbour who cannot manage without help because of disability, illness or the effects of old age. It is estimated that 6.8 million people – one in seven people over 16 – has some kind of caring role. Most commonly these people are caring for their parents.[1]

Carers are involved in personal care tasks such as washing, administering medications and offering practical help. Many carers have had problems themselves as a result, ranging from financial difficulties if they have to give up their job, no personal help or support, or their own health suffering owing to stress and exhaustion.

Seeking Help

If you feel you need help because you or someone you know becomes unable to cope through illness or disability, you should talk to:
- your doctor for information about health services
- the Social Services Department for an assessment of care needs, housing needs and help in the home and other services
- voluntary organisations and charities.

If you are caring for a relative or friend who has an illness or disability that makes daily life difficult, you could claim money – the Invalid Care Allowance (which currently works out at less than £35 per week) – and receive other kinds of support. A leaflet, 'Caring for Someone?' produced by the DSS, details:
- the help available from Social Security and your local council, including information on benefits and allowances, and protecting state pension rights (*see page 67*)
- a list of useful telephone numbers and addresses
- information on practical help such as district nurses and home helps or someone to give you a break from caring.

The Citizens Advice Bureau can advise on problems relating to help and care at home and, if they cannot help you themselves, invariably know who can. *See page 51* for national headquarters or look in the phone book or in the Yellow Pages under 'Social Service and Welfare Organisations'.

Further Reading

The Department of Health (*see page 220*) publishes a leaflet called 'Community Care Changes' (April 1993), free.

Age Concern (*details page 46*) publishes a booklet, 'Getting and Paying for Care, advice for older people and their families'. It also publishes an invaluable factsheet called 'Finding Help at Home'.

The Policy Studies Institute (tel: 0800 262 260) publishes *Attendance Allowance and the Costs of Caring* by Janet Horton and Richard Berthoud (£9.95).

---

[1] Source: Carers National Association (*see page 49*)

RADAR (tel: 0171–250 3222) publishes *What Is Community Care?* (£1.50), which gives advice on the duties of local authorities.

The Community Care Handbook, the new system explained, Barbara Meredith (available from Age Concern Books), £11.99

The Health Education Authority publishes:

Who Cares? Information and Support for Carers of Confused People (30p)

Caring: How to Cope, Janet Horwood (£4.99). An invaluable guide to one of the most demanding jobs around, covering feelings, health, grants and allowances, help, money and bereavement.

Working with Carers (£3.95)

Call for Care (£1.95)

A booklet is also available detailing other titles and prices. For more information contact:

Health Education Authority
Customer Services Department
Marston Book Services
PO Box 87
Oxford OX2 0DT
Tel: 01865 204745

The Carers National Association (England)
20–25 Glasshouse Yard
London EC1A 4JS
Tel: 0171–490 8818
The CNA was formed to address the needs of carers and support them and enable them to speak and campaign. It provides advice and information and has a network of 200 local branches throughout UK. Publications and free leaflets on advice, how to cope, benefits, holidays and respite care and residential care are available.

CNA Scotland
Tel: 0141–333 9495

CNA Wales
Tel: 01222 880176

The Princess Royal Trust for Carers
16 Byward Street
London EC3R 5BA
Tel: 0171–480 7788
The Trust provides support, advice and help on all issues affecting carers at local level through its growing network of carer centres. These centres offer emotional support, practical help, access to existing care attendance schemes or voluntary sitting services, mutual support and advocacy when necessary. The Trust aims to raise funds in order to enter into funding partnerships to set up carer centres in each local authority area.

The Association of Crossroads Care Attendant Schemes – ACCAS (England)
10 Regent Place
Rugby
Warwickshire CV21 2PN
Tel: 01788 573653

ACCAS Wales
5 Cooper's Yard
Curran Road
Cardiff CF1 5DF
Tel: 01222 222282

ACCAS Northern Ireland
7 Regent Street
Newtownards
County Down ET23 4AB
Tel: 01247 814455

ACCAS Scotland
contact the Warwickshire address, above
This Association provides care attendants who come into the home to give the carers of people with disabilities a break. The objectives are to relieve the stresses experienced by the carer by offering respite and, in exceptional circumstances, to provide Care Attendants to people with disabilities living on their own.

There are 180 autonomous schemes and eight regional offices throughout England, Scotland and Wales. Care is provided free of charge and follows the routine of the carer as closely as possible.

The National Extension College
18 Brooklands Avenue
Cambridge CB2 2HN
Tel: 01223 316644

The National Extension College is an education charity. Its Caring and Health materials can provide guidance, support and skills for all carers, whether they are looking after someone at home, working in the community or within the Health Service. Titles include:
Caring at Home – Information and Advice Aiming to Combat Isolation and Helplessness (£6.95)
Coming into Hospital – An Information Booklet for Patients (£15)
Coping with the System – An Outline Guide to the Citizen's Everyday Rights (£15.95)

The Winged Fellowship (*see page 94*) offers a series of special weeks of holidays for Alzheimer's Disease sufferers and their carers each year.

The book *Equipment and Services for People with Disabilities* is prepared by the Department of Health and the Central Office of Information. It is full of information about what services may be obtained from doctors, health services, social services, charities and government bodies. The leaflet may be obtained from The Health Publications Unit (*see page 90*).

If you or someone you know needs practical services at home, the Social Services Department of the local council should be able to assist, depending on where you live. These services may include the following:

- home care help
- chiropody at home
- laundry or incontinence service
- hairdressing at home
- gardening, decorating, minor repairs
- transport to the shops or to clubs and day centres
- leisure activities for housebound people
- equipment loans
- mobile library services
- visiting schemes
- meals on wheels.

Meals on Wheels provides hot, midday meals for people who cannot prepare their own food, often assisted by the Women's Royal Voluntary Service and the British Red Cross Society with transport. There is a small charge for this service.

The Social Services Department is also responsible for social workers and home care help, and for assessing care needs for either care in the home or referral to a residential or nursing home. The appropriate department can be contacted either by looking under 'Social Services' in the local telephone directory or through the Citizens Advice Bureau (*see below*).

The National Association of Citizens Advice Bureaux (NACAB)
115–123 Pentonville Road
London N1 9LZ
Tel: 0171–833 2181
There are over 1,000 Citizens Advice Bureaux in the UK providing information and advice free of charge on every subject. These include financial and legal matters, and consumer and employment problems. To find your nearest CAB phone the NACAB office or look in your telephone directory.

CARE AND NURSING SERVICES AT HOME

Hundreds of independent organisations throughout the UK provide social or nursing care for older people or people with disabilities in their own homes. There are licensed employment and/or nursing agencies as well as charitable or voluntary organisations. The fees will vary according to the duties and hours involved, and you should check the agency's charges (including commission, VAT, joining fee) and its code of practice before making a commitment. It may be possible to receive some Social Security Benefit to help pay for care – *see* the Financial Benefits section (*pages 147–53*).

Government policy suggests that home care services are to become the preferred approach of community care and that a 'mixed economy of care' should be promoted. A responsible and effective independent body, The United Kingdom Home Care Association (UKHCA), has been formed to speak for the independent providers of home care and home nursing services and raise the profile of home care services generally with its 'UKHCA Code of Practice'. A recommended complaints procedure is now available. The Association's representatives work closely with colleagues in the public sector. For further information:

The United Kingdom Home Care Association
42 Banstead Road
Carshalton Beeches
Surrey SM5 3NW
Tel: 0181–288 1551
It also publishes a list of member organisations (priced £15) and local lists of members (free of charge).

Cleshar Community Care
108 Fortis Green Road
London N10 3HN
Tel: 0181–444 0954
Cleshar provides a home care nursing service (telephone for their charges).

Somerset Care Ltd
Acacia House
Swingbridge
Bathpool
Taunton
Somerset TA2 8BY
Tel: 01823 323584
Somerset Care is a private company which can supply home care and a range of domestic services for people needing help throughout Somerset and in neighbouring counties – telephone for scale of charges.

British Nursing Association
North Place
82 Great North Road
Hatfield
Herts AL9 5BL
Tel: 01707 263544
The British Nursing Association provides fully qualified nurses, carers or auxiliaries to private patients in their own homes. Telephone for scale of fees.

Care Alternatives
206 Worple Road
Wimbledon
London SW20 8PN
Tel: 0181–946 8202
Care Alternatives introduces reliable caring staff to the elderly or people with disabilities. Write or telephone for further details and rates.

Someone to Talk to

Saneline
199–205 Old Marylebone Road
London NW1 5QP
Tel: 0171–724 6570 (admin only)
SANELINE London: 0171–724 8000
SANELINE outside London: 01345 678000 (charged at local rate)
Saneline is a national helpline for all people coping with mental illness. Trained volunteers give support and practical information to sufferers of mental illness, their families and friends. Saneline is open from 2 p.m. to midnight, 365 days a year.

The British Association for Counselling
1 Regent Place
Rugby
Warwicks CV21 2PJ
Tel: 01788 578328
Please send an A4 sae for information such as a list of local counsellors or information about carers and training.

The British Red Cross Society
9 Grosvenor Crescent
London SW1X 7EJ
Tel: 0171–235 5454
The British Red Cross provides a range of services throughout the UK, including domiciliary respite care to allow carers to take a short break, and emergency personal care, a 'home from hospital' service and transport and escort services.

The Samaritans (National Headquarters)
10 The Grove
Slough S4 1QP
Tel: 01753 532713
The Samaritans is a voluntary organisation offering confidential emotional support 24 hours a day every day of the year, to those in distress, despair or feeling tempted to suicide irrespective of age, race, creed or status. Their service is free and confidential and anyone can phone, visit or write to any of the 200 branches throughout the UK and Republic of Ireland.

The over-65s are at high risk of suicide and The Samaritans want to reach retired people who either feel isolated and despairing or who now have the time and desire to volunteer to listen to others in crisis without judgement.

Free leaflets include:
'Older People Needing Support'
'Older Volunteers'

Relate/National Marriage Guidance
Herbert Gray College
Little Church Street
Rugby
Warwicks CV21 3AP
Tel: 01788 573241/560811
Local organisations throughout the UK offering relationship counselling. Write to locate your local branch or look in your telephone directory.

The National Association of Widows
54–57 Allison Street
Digbeth
Birmingham B5 5TH
Tel: 0121–643 8348
Information, advice and friendly support for widows, particularly helping them to overcome the problems of loneliness, isolation and financial difficulties.

See also the sections in this book on Help and Friendship (*pages 55–7*) and The War Widows Association (*page 59*).

ELDERLY ABUSE

It is estimated that up to 10 per cent of elderly people may suffer some form of abuse. This occurs either when the immediate carer is no longer able to care in a loving and sensitive way, or when other family members or visitors to the household may be abusing them.

Abuse may manifest itself in one or a combination of ways:

- physical abuse: hitting, slapping, restraining
- verbal or psychological abuse: blackmail, blaming or swearing
- deprivation: of food, heat, clothing, comfort or cleaning
- forcible isolation: not letting others see or talk to them
- sexual abuse
- misusing medication
- financial abuse: misuse or misappropriation of monies or property.

Much abuse of elderly people is the result of carers being stressed, exhausted or isolated. This may happen in one of the following situations:

- when the elderly person has a disability affecting his or her physical, mental or communications performance
- when the person has behavioural or personality disturbances which the carer finds inconsistent and/or hard to understand
- when the family is under stress due to low income or poor housing
- when family relationships are poor or there is a history of violent behaviour.

Elderly abuse is a crime. If you suspect that someone you know is being abused you should contact the Social Services or the police immediately. They will know what action to take and may be able to offer relief to both the carer and the cared for. A leaflet, 'Action on Elder Abuse' is available (with sae) from Age Concern England (*see page 46*).

Crime or Attack

Victim Support
National Office
Cranmer House
39 Brixton Road
London SW9 6DZ
Tel: 0171–735 9166
A small number of older people become victims of crime each year, whether through attack or a break-in. Local Victim Support schemes are listed in the telephone book or can be contacted through the local library, Citizens Advice Bureau or Age Concern group.

Victim Support Scotland
14 Frederick Street
Edinburgh EH2 2HB
Tel: 0131–225 7779
VSS is an independent, voluntary organisation offering free practical help, advice, information and emotional support to victims of crime.

Policy

Centre for Policy on Ageing
Ironmonger Row
London EC1V 3QP
Tel: 0171–253 1787
The CPA is an independent organisation that aims to influence public policy affecting the lives of the 13 million older people in the UK. It also seeks to develop and promote policies that will enable people to lead fulfilled lives and maintain independence for as long as possible. The CPA publishes a number of informative leaflets and guides aimed at those who work with older people. Send 6-inch by 8-inch sae for publications list.

The British Pensioner and Trade Union Action Association (BPTUAA)
Norman Dodds House
315 Bexley Road
Erith
Kent DA8 3EZ
Tel: 01322 335464
The BPTUAA is a voluntary organisation which actively campaigns on behalf of all pensioners, aiming to maintain living standards. It has regular meetings with the all-party Committee for Pensions in the House of Commons on health and welfare matters and tries to secure an increased universal state pension. It publishes a quarterly journal, price 25p.

Help and Friendship

Your local Age Concern will know of all the groups and associations which can offer help and friendship. The following will also give information on what is available in your area.

The Samaritans provide a 24-hour a day listening service to those in distress, despair or tempted to commit suicide (*see page 199*).

Association of Jewish Friendship Clubs for the Over-60s
Woburn House
Upper Woburn Place
London WC1H 0EP
Tel: 0171–387 8980
The Association forms friendship clubs for the over-60s to alleviate loneliness and to provide friendship and activities.

Age-Link
9 Narborough Close
Brackenbury Village
Ickenham
Middlesex UB1D 8TN
Tel: 0181–571 5324
Age-Link aims to befriend lonely or housebound elderly people by arranging outings on a Sunday afternoon once a month, often to the homes of other Age-Link members.

Methodist Homes for the Aged
Epworth House
Stuart Street
Derby DE1 2EQ
Tel: 01332 296200
A befriending initiative, 'Live at Home' helps improve the quality of life for older people who choose to remain in their own homes.

National Association of Women's Clubs
5 Vernon Rise
King's Cross Road
London WC1X 9EP
Tel: 0171–837 1434
For information about what clubs are available in your area.

Contact
15 Henrietta Street
Covent Garden
London WC2E 8QH
Tel: 0171–240 0630
Contact aims to provide companionship and regular outings within a Contact group of elderly people who live alone without family support and who are no longer able to get out without assistance.

Lewisham Pensioners Link
74 Deptford High Street
London SE8 4RT
Tel: 0181–691 0938
Lewisham Pensioners Link is a London-based group which arranges projects for pensioners, as well as offering friendship and home help, health advice and information, welfare rights assistance and physical help to keep out the cold. Contact them to find out more or to locate local branches.

Elders Voice
Carlton Centre
Granville Road
London NW6 2BX
Tel: 0171–624 3480
For pensioners in the Brent area.

RUKBA – The Royal United Kingdom Beneficent Association
6 Avonmore Road
London W14 8RL
Tel: 0171–602 6274

RUKBA is a national charity (charity registration number 210729) helping some 5,000 elderly people on very low incomes to stay in their own homes. The provision of a regular, small additional income and special grants alleviates severe financial hardship and helps maintain independence. The charity's network of 750 volunteers also offers local friendship and practical support.

Sixty Plus
1 Thorpe Close
London W10 5XL
Tel: 0181–969 9105

Sixty Plus offers welfare rights advice, help with dealing with benefit claims, pensions, council tax, income support, disability, housing benefit, general benefit checks, money problems and debt counselling for pensioners in the Kensington and Chelsea areas of London. In addition it runs a practical help service which includes shopping trips, events and activities and a befriending scheme.

In addition, Sixty Plus runs a 'Coldline' – a hypothermia prevention 24-hour emergency line which gives advice and referrals for heating repairs and draughtproofing. Information from:

Coldline
31 Dalston Lane
London E8 3DF
Tel: 0171–241 0440

The Distressed Gentlefolks Aid Association
1 Derry Street
London W8 5HY
Tel: 0171–229 9341

The DGAA makes regular allowances and emergency grants for those of professional and similar backgrounds who find themselves in need or distress. These grants sometimes are made in conjunction with other charities and are designed to help beneficiaries stay in their own homes. In addition, the Association runs 13 homes around England. Some of these provide residential care for the elderly; others provide more intensive nursing care. Entry conditions can be checked with head office.

SOLITAIRE – Friends Indeed
PO Box 2
Hockley
Essex SS5 4QR

SFI is an organisation to help combat loneliness. It is voluntary in every way and non-profit-making. Membership is open to single women only, age range 40 and over (enquiries by post only). The aim is to promote friendship nationwide and, wherever possible, at local level. Holiday companions and pen-friend schemes are some of the advantages covered by the £6 yearly donation but people are invited to try, free, by sending sae to the above address.

Women's Royal Voluntary Service
234–244 Stockwell Road
London SW9 9SP
Tel: 0171–416 0146
The UK's largest voluntary organisation, this is a charity whose services include social clubs for the elderly and people with disabilities, meals on wheels, books on wheels, social transport, carers' support groups, and a laundry service. Short-term help is available for shopping, collection of prescriptions, and escort to appointments with the doctor, dentist or optician. Local offices and telephone numbers are listed in the telephone book.

The National Association of Leagues of Hospital Friends
Second Floor
Fairfax House
Causton Road
Colchester
Essex CO1 1RJ
Tel: 01206 761227/761243
The aim of NALHF is to help patients and former patients in hospitals, healthcare establishments and in the community (in both the NHS and private sector) throughout the UK. The range of services includes everything from staffing shops, canteens, libraries and telephone-hotlines to befriending, reception and escort duties, arranging outings, flower arranging, hairdressing, writing letters, finding amenities – the list is endless. Each LHF is autonomous. The national office acts as a support and advice centre to its members and volunteers and provides mail order services, insurance, etc. A wide variety of goods and leaflets is available – catalogue on request.

WHICH CHARITY?

Counsel and Care (*see page 47*) produces a factsheet called 'Which Charity?' It helps people to identify what sort of grant they require (one-off or continuing) and advises them how best to apply.

The Association of Charity Officers
c/o RICS Benevolent Fund Ltd
Tavistock House North
Tavistock Square
London WC1H 9RJ
Tel: 0171–383 5557

The Association has some 250 members, all of whom are registered charities, giving non-contributory relief and helping people from all walks of life. Its objective is to promote efficiency and encourage co-operation between charities – it aims to put those in need of help in touch with those who can give most help, but it has no funds of its own to distribute.

Charity Search
25 Portview Road
Avonmouth
Bristol BS11 9LD
Tel: 0117 982 4060
A charity providing a free advice service that will respond to telephone or written enquiries about helping elderly people in genuine financial difficulties to find established charities that might help them. They publish a book called *Charity Made Clear* (Auriel James; £4.95, send a cheque with every order). The book is written for ordinary people and for those concerned with the welfare of others who are faced with an overwhelming and bewildering mass of charities.

Help for Ex-Servicemen and -women

The Forces Help Society and Lord Roberts Workshops
122 Brompton Road
London SW3 1JE
Tel: 0171–589 3243
The Society helps, according to need, men and women who have served at any time in HM forces, which includes a large proportion of those now elderly, as so many served in the Second World War or did National Service. It provides help to people in need, which includes advice on obtaining benefits and services to which individuals may be entitled. This help is channelled through a network of trained voluntary case-workers organised in co-operation with the Soldiers', Sailors' and Airmen's Families Association (*see page 58*). Local contact addresses and telephone numbers may be found at the library or post office and in the telephone directory.

The Society also maintains Cottage Homes for people with disabilities and elderly men and women and their partners. Some of these homes are purpose-built for those suffering from disabilities (not necessarily the result of active service).

The Lord Roberts Workshop provides training and employment for disabled ex-servicemen and -women in Dundee and Edinburgh. They produce a range of goods and furniture.

The RAF Association
Beachcroft Stanleys
20 Furnival Street
London EC4A 1BN
Tel: 0171–242 1011
The majority of the RAF Association's welfare work is undertaken in the local community by some 600 volunteers who offer assistance to approximately 45,000 individuals providing advice and help with benefit regulations or war pensions claims, and visiting sick people in hospital or at home. It relies totally on voluntary income to fund its welfare work.

The Soldiers', Sailors' and Airmen's Families Association
Room 24
19 Queen Elizabeth Street
London SE1 2IP
Tel: 0171–403 8783
This charitable organisation aids the families of people who were in the Services.

The British Limbless Ex-Servicemen's Association (BLESMA)
185–187 High Road
Chadwell Heath
Romford
Essex RM6 6NA
Tel: 0181–590 1124

BLESMA provides pre- and post-amputation counselling to individuals and visits to check on the welfare of members and their widows. It provides advice on pensions and allowances; it also represents members at Appeal Tribunals. It provides financial assistance in the form of grants, and offers limited funding for research and development in the field of prosthetics and orthotics. BLESMA also acts as a consumer watchdog in respect of artificial limbs, wheelchairs and appliances, and has a nationwide branch structure. Publications include:
'Better Health for the Amputee' (75p)
'Out on a Limb' (£3)
BLESMAG – in house journal (published three times a year, price £1 p.a.)

Royal British Legion
48 Pall Mall
London SW1Y 5JY
Tel: 0171–973 0633

The Royal British Legion is a charity and Britain's premier ex-Service organisation which promotes the welfare of service and ex-servicemen and -women and their dependents, relieving hardship where it exists. It employs over 2,270 ex-servicemen and -women and their dependents, 31 per cent of whom are registered disabled, making the Legion one of the largest private employers of people with disabilities in the UK. It represents 18 million people.

The War Widows Association of Great Britain
Bryn Hyfryd
1 Coach Lane
Matlock
Derbyshire DE4 2NA
Tel: 01629 636374

The Association is a national, voluntary organisation and registered charity. It was founded to improve conditions for all war widows and their families from 1949 to the present day. It works with other ex-Service and Service organisations including the Central Committee on War Pensions. It has about 50 regional organisers throughout Britain and keeps its members informed via its regular newsletter, *Courage*; it also holds meeting around the country.

HELP FOR PEOPLE WITH DISABILITIES

The Disabled Living Foundation
380–384 Harrow Road
London W9 2HU
Tel: 0171–289 6111

The DLF was established in 1970 to serve people with special physical needs by providing practical advice and information on all aspects of independent living. The DLF's professional advisors respond to some 30,000 enquiries each year, mainly on equipment for people with disabilities. A large number of specialist publications are available on many subjects including health, equipment, clothing and shoes: for a publications list send sae.

The British Red Cross Society
9 Grosvenor Crescent
London SW1X 7EJ
Tel: 0171–235 5454
The British Red Cross provides a range of services throughout the UK, including medical loans and mobility aids, an escort and transport service, therapeutic beauty care and domiciliary services. Its medical loan service includes equipment such as wheelchairs, backrests, bath seats, commodes and walking sticks. It also operates an international tracing and message service, first-aid duties and training and, in parts of the UK, a home from hospital scheme and day care services.

The Physically Handicapped and Able Bodied (PHAB) (England)
Level 7
New England House
New England Street
Brighton
East Sussex BN1 4GH
Tel: 01273 674643

PHAB Northern Ireland
25 Alexandra Gardens
Belfast BT15 3LJ
Tel: 01232 370240

PHAB Scotland
Princes House
5 Shandwick Place
Edinburgh EH2 4RG
Tel: 0131–229 3559

PHAB Wales
First Floor
179 Penarth Road
Cardiff CF1 7JW
Tel: 01222 223677
PHAB exists to further the integration of people with and without disabilities. This is done through over 500 clubs throughout the UK.

RADAR (Royal Association for Disability and Rehabilitation)
Unit 12, City Forum
250 City Road
London EC1V 8AF
Tel: 0171–250 3222
RADAR is a national organisation working with and for people with physical disabilities to remove architectural, economic and attitudinal barriers. RADAR is particularly involved in the areas of education, employment, mobility, health, social services, housing and access. The Association produces a number of publications and operates in conjunction with an affiliated network of over 500 local and national organisations.

RADAR offers a large number of publications. For prices and details, send for a publications list. Subjects covered include: access, education, employment, health services, holidays, housing, legal and parliamentary matters, mobility and travel, national key scheme, Social Security and finances, Social Services and community living, sport and leisure.

The Greater London Association of Disabled People
336 Brixton Road
London SW9 7AA
Tel: 0171–274 0107
GLAD promotes the rights of people with disabilities in London and helps with training, research and information. It publishes 'The London Disability Guide' (telephone for p & p charges) and a large number of other publications.

VOLUNTEERS

Many organisations desperately need volunteers to help with fundraising, home visits, even organising community work – the activities are numerous and varied. Voluntary work can be enormously rewarding and a good means of keeping active and meeting people.

Listed below are just few of the organisations that welcome volunteers. Others are listed in the 'Hobbies and Interests' section of this book. Older people could contact their favourite charity to offer their services or go to their Citizens Advice Bureau, library, church or hospital. Please *see also* the Volunteering section of the chapter on Hobbies and Interests (*pages 199–200*).

Community Service Volunteers
237 Pentonville Road
London N1 9NG
Tel: 0171–278 6601
CSV's Retired and Senior Volunteer Programme (RSVP – *see below*) harnesses the skills and experience of older people to enrich schools, hospitals and community projects and to help protect the environment. Older volunteers use their business experience to advise younger people starting out on their own. Younger full-time volunteers work face-to-face with older people to help them live independently in their own homes.

Retired and Senior Volunteer Programme (RSVP)
237 Pentonville Road
London N1 9NG
Tel: 0171–278 6601
RSVP encourages over 3,000 retired and senior people a year to volunteer in their own communities. Anyone 50+ who wants to be involved in the community may participate in volunteering and choose what they want to do. It recognises the skills of older people and provides group commitment and support. Each group plans its own activities, which might include working with elderly people locally, using business experience to advise young people starting out on their own, or going into primary or secondary schools to help individual pupils or small groups of pupils and support teachers. Free leaflets include: 'Your Hidden Talent'; the RSVP video is priced £14.

Women's Royal Voluntary Service (England)
234–244 Stockwell Road
London SW9 9SP
Tel: 0171–416 0146

WRVS Scotland
19 Grosvenor Crescent
Edinburgh EH12 5EL
Tel: 0131–337 2261

WRVS Wales
26 Cathedral Road
Cardiff CF1 9LJ
Tel: 01222 228386
Help for elderly people is just part of the range of help supplied by the WRVS: this includes welfare services, care relief holidays, supplies of clothing and bedding, home services and luncheon clubs.

National Association of Volunteer Bureaux
St Peter's College
College Road
Saltley
Birmingham B8 3TE
Tel: 0121–327 0265
The National Association of Volunteer Bureaux puts people in touch with their local voluntary agency, which can inform them what volunteer work is available in their area.

Society of Voluntary Associates
350 Kennington Road
London SE11 4LH
Tel: 0171–793 0404
The SVA recruits and trains volunteers to work with offenders, with projects all over Great Britain.

The National Council for Voluntary Organisations
Regents Wharf
8 All Saints Street
London N1 9RL
Tel: 0171–713 6161
The National Council for Voluntary Organisations supplies information sheets on paid and unpaid work opportunities for people of all ages.

Caring for a Pet

The Animal Welfare Trust
Tylers Way
Watford Bypass
Watford
Herts WD2 8HQ
Tel: 0181–950 8215
The Animal Welfare Trust is a national charity dedicated to taking in and caring for unwanted animals. It finds suitable new homes for dogs, cats and other animals which would otherwise be abandoned, left to stray or put to sleep. No healthy animal is put to sleep however long its stay.

Its 'Pet Concern' programme provides assistance towards boarding fees for the pets of senior citizens and those with disabilities during hospital treatment or convalescence, bringing peace of mind in an emergency. The scheme is co-ordinated with the Social Services.

The Trust recognises the benefits of pets for the older person. It is hoped that many older people will feel able to take on pets in the knowledge that the Trust will provide help and advice whenever necessary. Free publications include:
'Animal Aid for the Elderly'
'Emergency Pet Care'
'Guide to Making a Will'

National Canine Defence League
17 Wakley Street
London EC1V 7LT
Tel: 0171–837 0006
The NCDL promotes animal ownership for older people and undertakes to find homes for animals whose owners are incapacitated.

The Cinnamon Trust
Poldarves Farm
Trescowe Common
Penzance
Cornwall TR20 9RX
Tel: 01736 850291

This national charity helps elderly and terminally ill people with pets. Through its network of 800 volunteers it provides short-term fostering of pets if their owner has to go into hospital or cannot care for them, and it will make arrangements for long-term care if the owner dies. In addition, they will help with the day-to-day care of pets when this poses a problem, i.e. walking a pet or making visits to the vet if the owner is unable to cope. The Trust has a register of nursing homes, residential homes and sheltered housing throughout the UK that will accept residents with pets.

Homesitters
Buckland Wharf
Buckland, Bucks HP22 5LQ
Tel: 01296 630730

This organisation suggests that people make all the necessary arrangements now so that if they have to go into hospital unexpectedly a properly briefed homesitter can, at short notice, move into your home to ensure security and care for your possessions and pets.

People's Dispensary for Sick Animals
Whitechapel Way
Priorslee
Telford
Salop TF2 9PQ
Tel: 01952 290999

The People's Dispensary for Sick Animals will help people who cannot afford vets' fees – the level of assistance is means-tested by the amount of Income Support, Family Credit or Housing Benefit one is receiving.

Canine Concern Scotland Trust
East Lodge
Caldarvan
Gartocharn
Strathclyde
Tel: 01389 83325

Volunteers from this agency will assist dog owners who fall ill.

Further Reading

Age and Vulnerability: A Guide to Better Care, Olive Stevenson (Edward Arnold, 1989), £8.25
Care for the Carer, Christine Orton (Thorsons, 1989), £4.99
Caring at Home, Nancy Kohner (King's Fund Informal Caring Programme, 1988), £3
Caring for Parents in Later Life, Avril Rodway (Consumers Association, 1992), £9.95
Coping with Ageing Parents, Chris Gilleard and Glenda Watt (W & R Chambers, 1983), £3.95
Counselling Carers – Supporting Relatives of Confused Elderly People at Home, Andrew Papadopoulos (Winslow Press, 1990), £6.95
Handbook for Care Assistants: A Practical Guide for Carers (Scottish Action on Dementia, 1991), £3 (approx)
Loneliness: How to Overcome It, Val Marriott and Terry Timblick (Age Concern England, 1988), £3.95

chapter four

WHERE TO LIVE

Adapting your Home, Finding a Suitable Alternative

WHILE RESEARCHING THIS BOOK I came across the widest possible spectrum of older people, from the 96-year-old lady who lives happily and successfully on her own to the merchant banker in his early sixties with Alzheimer's Disease who requires full nursing care.

While no two situations are ever exactly the same, certain criteria do exist to help you assess where it would be best for you or someone you are caring for to live. This involves answering certain questions:

- How capable is the older person (or persons) concerned?
- Can they look after themselves: cooking, hygiene, security, taking medication when necessary?
- Can they look after their house and garden?
- Can they get out and about: to the doctor, on visits, holidays, for leisure activities?
- How suitable is their current accommodation in terms of:
  size and manageability?
  accessibility (stairs, ramps) and potential for adaptation?
  location (proximity to neighbours, family, shops)?
- Do they have any special needs now (or will they have in the foreseeable future) concerning:
  company (i.e. loneliness)?
  finances?
  provision of food?
  health?
  looking after the house, repairs and maintenance?
- Has the future ever been discussed in terms of where they will live if they become less able to cope on their own?

It is remarkable how seldom this last question has ever been broached within families so that, when the time comes, there has been no preparation or consideration of finances, location or type of accommodation, and certainly no visits made to compare the alternatives before a decision *has* to be made.

Usually the decision has to be made quickly, more often than not prompted by an accident or illness which leaves the older person unable to look after themselves as competently as before, sometimes after a stay in hospital. Lack of advance preparation could mean a hasty decision or a series of moves until the right place is available, which might make the whole process far more traumatic than it need be.

The Alternatives

Two broad accommodation options exist for older people:
1. Adapting their existing home so that it is more suitable for advancing years (see 'Staying Put', below).
2. Moving to alternative accommodation: sheltered housing or a residential or nursing home (*see pages 68–86*).

Staying Put

There is no doubt that older people should be encouraged to continue to live in their own homes for as long as possible. There is no substitute for the surroundings, friends, neighbours and neighbourhood with which they are familiar.

Local Authority grants may be available to assist with adaptation work, but individuals will be means-tested according to the type of grant required and the circumstances of the applicant. It is important to obtain agreement from the Authority before proceeding with any alterations. Applicants should contact the Renovation Grants section of their local council, who will be able to suggest what sort of grant to apply for.

The Social Fund, which is run by the Benefits Agency, provides grants and loans for people on Income Support. Older people may be able to get help with repairs by applying for a Local Authority Grant. Any income (dependent on age and marital status) or savings (over £5,000) may be taken into account, but even if you are above this threshold you may be eligible for a grant to cover a part of the work. You should not proceed with the work until approval is received. Leaflets SB16 'A Guide to the Social Fund' and SFL2 'How the Social Fund Can Help You' are available free from Benefits Agency offices.

Age Concern (*see page 85*) produces a leaflet (No 13) called 'Older Home Owners – financial help with repairs', which explains the options in more detail.

Disabled facilities grants are available for tenants and owner-occupiers with disabilities to adapt their homes so that they can manage more independently – applicants should contact the Renovations Grants section of their local council. Anyone having difficulties getting help may be assisted by The Royal Association for Disability and Rehabilitation (RADAR, *see page 60*).

A number of organisations exist to assist with the process of adapting homes and helping with the cost, both in terms of physical changes and the use of additional local services in order that older homeowners may stay in their homes. These agencies run the adaptation schemes and can give advice about building repairs, adaptations and costs, as well as about any loans or grants that may be available. Some of the agencies arrange and supervise the building work.

Care and Repair Ltd was chosen to be the national co-ordinating body for all home improvement agencies. Home improvement agencies help people who are older, have disabilities and/or are living on low income to repair or adapt homes which are unfit or unsuitable. Staff visit people in their own homes and help them through the process of deciding what repairs or adaptations are needed, arranging the financing and organising the building work. The work ranges from small items such as handrails or new locks through to major jobs such as building a specially adapted bathroom or renewing the roof. Over £31 million worth of building work was organised for nearly 14,500 clients by agencies in England during 1992–3.

Central enquiries:

Care and Repair Ltd (England)
Castle House
Kirtley Drive
Nottingham NG7 1LD
Tel: 0115 979 9091

Care and Repair Scotland
Fifth Floor
Mercantile Chambers
53 Boswell Street
Glasgow G2 6TS
Tel: 0141–248 7177

Care and Repair Cymru Ltd
Norbury House
Norbury Road
Cardiff CF5 3AS
Tel: 01222 576286

Other organisations that can help to identify repairs or adaptations that need to be carried out or considered, and that can recommend contractors and assist with loans are:

Northern Ireland Housing Executive
The Housing Centre
2 Adelaide Street
Belfast BT2 8PB
Tel: 01232 240588 or 01232 317000

Homelife DGAA
1 Derry Street
London W8 5HY
Tel: 0171–396 6700
Homelife is a charity which gives people financial help either to stay in their homes, including assistance with bills, equipment and repairs, or to help get into a nursing home.

RUKBA – The Royal United Kingdom Beneficent Association
6 Avonmore Road
London W14 8RL
Tel: 0171–602 6274
RUKBA is a national charity (charity registration number 210729) helping some 5,000 elderly people on very low incomes to stay in their own homes. The provision of a regular, small additional income and special grants alleviates severe financial hardship and helps maintain independence. The charity's network of 750 volunteers also offers local friendship and practical support.

The Centre for Accessible Environments
60 Gainsford Street
London SE1 2NY
Tel: 0171–357 8182
The Centre is the only UK charity whose role is to help ensure that buildings are convenient and safe for all

users, including the elderly and people with disabilities. The Centre can advise on how to make a house or flat more comfortable and convenient and can put people in touch with experienced architects in their locality.

Care in the Community
The Government's new community care approach, 'Care in the Community' came into effect on 1 April 1993, and is all about assessing older people's need for help and helping them either to remain in their own homes for as long as they are willing and able or to move to residential or nursing accommodation. Different people need different kinds of help, and a range of services can enable them to stay in their own homes – for example meals on wheels or home help (*see* Who Cares? *pages 46–63*) and help with repairs, improvements or adaptations to the home (see Who Pays? *page 75*).

Who Can Help?
If you need help or assistance of any kind you should telephone your local Social Services Department, or Social Work Department in Scotland, for further information or assessment of the help you might need (phone number in the telephone book under the name of your local council). Local authority grants towards the cost of repair and maintenance may be available, but they are means-tested and are dependent on the local authority's own resources.

For advice on Care in the Community, and how it affects Attendance Allowance, Disability Living Allowance and Housing Benefit you can contact Freeline Social Security on 0800 666 555 or contact your local Benefits Agency office.

All sorts of equipment is available to make life easier around the home. Stairlifts, bath seats, handrails – further details are given in Chapter 8.

Local Citizens Advice Bureaux and the Department of Social Security also provide a wealth of information as to additional services available. If required, a social worker will visit you at home to discuss and advise about any services that might be needed. These may include:

- home help
- laundry service
- waste disposal services
- meals on wheels
- district nurses
- day centres.

SeniorLine, Help The Aged's freephone advice line, will be able to give advice on community care, housing options and welfare and disability benefits. Phone 0800 289 404.

Shelter – National Campaign for Homeless People
88 Old Street
London EC1V 9HU
Tel: 0171–253 0202
Shelter provides free, confidential advice through a network of Housing Aid Centres to people experiencing housing problems.

Care and Nursing Services at Home

A large range of independent, voluntary and statutory services are available and are detailed in the chapter entitled 'Who Cares?' (*see pages 46–63*).

Your local Age Concern group will be able to advise on special services in the area run by them or by other groups. Age Concern (*details page 46*) publishes a booklet 'Getting and Paying for Care, advice for older people and their families'. It also publishes an invaluable factsheet called 'Finding Help at Home'. In addition, it publishes *Your Rights* (£1.95), which gives information about Social Security benefits and other sources of financial help, including retirement pension, disability benefits and income-related benefits.

Capital Release

Several companies assist retired homeowners with capital release, enabling them to raise a tax-free lump sum or regular income against their property. This allows them to continue to live in their homes with guaranteed occupancy; the money can be spent to increase their standard of living, pay for home improvements, buy a holiday or be invested in any way. Alternatively, a home income plan (mortgage annuity scheme) may be considered. This gives the owner a monthly income for life while he or she retains ownership of the home.

As with any financial undertaking, arrangements with any such company should be supervised by a solicitor (*see pages 144–7 for further details about these plans*).

MOVING TO ALTERNATIVE ACCOMMODATION

The choice here is dependent upon the level of support required. There are three distinct accommodation options, each of which is supplied by both the private and public sectors, as well as some which are aided or funded by charitable or voluntary organisations. These are:
1. sheltered housing
2. residential care homes
3. nursing homes.

Sheltered Housing

Sheltered housing involves a collection of apartments or bungalows within a defined and protected area offering a degree of privacy and some communal facilities. These are provided by councils, housing associations and private developers and may be available to rent or to buy. Housing associations are non-profit-making bodies which receive funding from government or other sources and provide homes for people in housing need. Waiting lists may be long, as demand is high.

Residences are self-contained and are generally unfurnished – residents are encouraged to bring their own furnishings. There is usually a warden on duty to oversee residents and there may be a communal laundry, common room, or dining room: services differ from scheme to scheme. Sheltered housing is usually conveniently located for shops and other local facilities.

Be sure to check not only the rent or purchase price, but also the service charges that cover facilities and services such as provision of a warden, laundry facilities, alarm systems, home and garden maintenance, etc. Also, ensure that the property complies with the National House Building Council's Sheltered Housing Code of Practice, which ensures that residents' rights are fully protected. Some developers offer schemes by which a person is offered housing at a discount in return for the ownership of the property when that person dies. *You should always take independent legal and financial advice before making any commitment.*

It is also important to check the maintenance and service charges before committing. Any complaints or queries about service charges, maintenance, etc., if normal complaints procedures are not successful, should be addressed to the **Sheltered Housing Advisory and Conciliation Service** on 0171–383 2006.

Your local Social Services Department or Age Concern group (address and telephone numbers on *page 46*) should know if there are any sheltered housing schemes in your area for sale or rent.

Age Concern England also produces a free factsheet: 'Sheltered Housing for Sale' (*address page 46*). A book, *Housing Options for Older People* (£4.95 including p & p) is available from the Mail Order Department, Age Concern England.

Help the Aged produces a free information sheet: 'Sheltered Housing' (*address page 47*). Counsel and Care also produces a factsheet: 'Special Accommodation for Older People' (25p) (*address page 85*).

The Elderly Accommodation Counsel
46a Chiswick High Road
London W4 1SZ
Tel: 0181–995 8320
The Counsel maintains a national central database of all types of private and voluntary accommodation suitable to meet the needs of those over the age of retirement. This includes sheltered housing for sale or rent, and homes and hospices. The charity conducts an ongoing programme into the medical acceptance criteria for entry into such types of accommodation together with details and statistics on costs. Information can also be given on sources of top-up funding for those unable to meet all the fees in a home. Free publications include 'For You and Yours' (general information booklet), 'Choosing the Right Home – advice and guidance', and 'Looking for Retirement Housing' (please send sae).

The Counsel also publishes regional registers of retirement housing available for rent, covering homes offered by local authorities, housing associations, Abbeyfield Societies and Almshouse charities, detailing nearly 500,000 sheltered homes. Write or telephone for prices and p & p charges.

Housing Organisations Mobility and Exchange Services (HOMES)
26 Chapter Street
London SW1P 4ND
Tel: 0171–233 7077
HOMES is a government organisation which helps people who live in local authority or housing association accommodation to move home, perhaps to be

nearer relatives or employment. Its HOMESWAP scheme provides councils with a list of people who want to swap homes into their area.

The National Association of Estate Agents
Arbon House
21 Jury Street
Warwick CV34 4EH
Tel: 01926 496800
The NAEA can offer free referral to anyone wishing to buy or sell property in another town or district through its National Homelink Service. This service is free to the public.

Local authorities, voluntary organisations, private schemes, charitable and housing trusts and housing associations offer a large number of properties for sale or rent. A few of these organisations are listed below:

The Abbeyfield Society
53 Victoria Street
St Albans
AL1 3UW
Tel: 01727 857536
The Abbeyfield Society provides 'very sheltered' *rental* housing for older people within their chosen community. Abbeyfield Houses strive to be non-institutional and care is given in family-type houses, built or adapted in accordance with statutory requirements. Residents have their own room which they can furnish with their own belongings. Abbeyfield 'supportive' houses have resident housekeepers, and 'extra care' houses provide 24-hour personal care for frail older people. Abbeyfield has a range of literature – further details on request.

Anchor Housing Association
Fountain Court
Oxford Spires Business Park
Kidlington
OX5 1NZ
Tel: 01865 854000
Anchor is the leading charity providing housing and care for older people in England. This housing and care is provided through sheltered housing for rent and special housing-with-care for very frail older people. A number of publications are available – please send for a publications list.

McCarthy and Stone
Homelife House
26–32 Oxford Road
Bournemouth BH8 8EZ
Tel: 01202 292480
McCarthy and Stone sells comfortable, secure retirement flats and homes with security alarms, communal laundry facilities, house managers and maintenance teams. Further details and rates on request.

The North British Housing Association
4 The Pavilions
Portway
Preston
Lancs PR2 2YB
Tel: 01772 897200
One of the country's leading housing associations, North British provides a range of good quality, affordable housing for older people, including carefully designed warden-assisted flats and bungalows, sheltered accommodation and 'housing with care' schemes for frail elderly people. It is a non-profit-making organisation, active in most parts of the country.

Castle Rock Housing Association Ltd
2 Wishaw Terrace
Meadowbank
Edinburgh EH7 6AF
Tel: 0131–652 0152
This is a not-for-profit organisation which rents sheltered homes.

Community Home Care 'Orchard Lea'
Arkley Nursing Home
Barnet Road
Barnet
Herts EN5 3LJ
Tel: 01279 600282
Community Home Care owns and operates retirement homes, hospitals and nursing homes throughout the UK. Its Orchard Lea development is a new concept of 'close care' which allows older people to buy a home; all insurance, maintenance, light, heat and even some cooking are covered by the monthly service charge. A 24-hour emergency call is in operation and other assistance may be called upon as needed.

The Country Houses Association
41 Kingsway
London WC2B 6UB
Tel: 0171–836 1624
This company has converted nine historic mansions into apartments which are available for sale.

The Humanist Housing Association
1 Holmes Road
London NW5 3AA
Tel: 0171–485 8776

The HHA is a charitable housing association which is committed to providing homes for rent for people who are most in need. It is based in London and the home counties and manages 1,000 units which are primarily sheltered housing for the elderly.

Retirement Lease Housing Association
19 Eggars Court
St George's Road East
Aldershot
Hants GU12 4LN
Tel: 01252 318181
This company sells sheltered housing in sites in Hampshire and Sussex.

The English Courtyard Association
8 Holland Street
London W8 4LT
Tel: 0171–937 3890
This association sells two- and three-bedroomed country cottages with garden (and gardener) offering privacy, security and freedom.

Orbit Housing Association
44/45 Queens Road
Coventry CV1 3EH
Tel: 01203 632231
Properties for sale and rent.

Sheltered Housing Services Ltd
8–9 Abbey Parade
London W5 1EE
Tel: 0181–997 9313
SHS operates an up-to-date national register of privately-owned sheltered housing for sale throughout the UK.

The National Federation of Housing Associations
175 Gray's Inn Road
London WC1X 8UP
Tel: 0171–278 6571
This is the representative body for housing associations, trusts and societies in England. It covers organisations which provide housing and do not trade for profit. Over 1,600 members agree to abide by a code of conduct.

The Scottish Federation of Housing Associations
38 York Place
Edinburgh EH1 3HU
Tel: 0131–556 5777

The Welsh Federation of Housing Associations
Norbury House
Norbury Road
Fairwater
Cardiff CF5 3AS
Tel: 01222 555022

The Northern Ireland Federation of Housing Associations
88 Clifton Street
Belfast BT13 1AB
Tel: 01232 230446

Help the Aged
St James Walk
London EC1R 0BE
Tel: 0171–253 0253
Help the Aged has nine extra-sheltered developments and 32 semi-sheltered dwellings.

Raglan Housing Association
Wright House
12–14 Castle Street
Poole
Dorset BH15 1BQ
Tel: 01202 678731
A not-for-profit organisation offering general purpose sheltered housing with some accommodation for people with disabilities.

The Beth Johnson Housing Association Ltd
Three Counties House
Festival Way
Stoke on Trent ST1 5PX
Tel: 01782 219200
A not-for-profit organisation offering sheltered housing.

Kirk Care Housing Association
3 Forres Street
Edinburgh EH3 6BJ
Tel: 0131–225 7246

Methodist Homes for the Aged
Epworth House
Stuart Street
Derby DE1 2EQ
Tel: 01332 296200
Methodist Homes provides a range of accommodation and care services based on Christian principles which are open to all older people in need, whatever their beliefs. It cares for older people in 37 residential homes throughout England and Wales and its housing association manages 20 sheltered housing schemes which are available for rent.

Nationwide Housing Trust
Moulton Park
Northampton NN3 1NL
Tel: 01604 794189
Sells sheltered housing.

North Housing
Ridley House
Regent Centre
Newcastle upon Tyne NE3 3JE
Tel: 0191–285 0311
Not-for-profit organisation offering sheltered housing, mainly to rent (some with joint ownership).

Northern Counties Homes
Princes Buildings
Oxford Court
Oxford Street
Manchester M2 3WQ
Tel: 0161–228 3388
Not-for-profit organisation offering sheltered housing, for sale or to rent.

Northern Ireland Co-ownership Housing Association Ltd
Murray House
Murray Street
Belfast BT1 6DN
Tel: 01232 327276
Not-for-profit organisation offering sheltered housing for sale or to rent.

Presbyterian Housing Association Northern Ireland Ltd
Lamont House
Purdy's Lane
Newtorn Breda BT8 4AX
Tel: 01232 491851
Not-for-profit organisation offering sheltered housing for rent.

The William Sutton Housing Trust
Sutton Court
Tring
Herts HP23 5BB
Tel: 01442 891100
Not-for-profit organisation offering sheltered housing, to rent.

Hanover Housing Association
Hanover House
18 The Avenue
Egham
Surrey TW20 9AB
Tel: 01784 438361
A national charity and sheltered housing specialist for 30 years, Hanover manages over 9,000 rented and 4,500 owner-occupied properties across England, 98 per cent purpose-built for older people. Most estates have fully-trained resident managers and all are connected to emergency control centres. Hanover aims to meet the housing and support needs of older people with care, efficiency and economy. Details, including ethnic language leaflets and rates, on request.

Church of Ireland Housing Association (Northern Ireland) Ltd
27 Lisburn Road
Belfast BT9 7AA
Tel: 01232 242130
Not-for-profit organisation offering sheltered housing to rent or buy.

Derwent Housing Association Ltd
Phoenix Street
Derby DE1 2ER
Tel: 01332 46477
A not-for-profit organisation offering sheltered housing, for sale and to rent.

English Churches Housing Group
Sutherland House
70–78 West Hendon Broadway
London NW9 7BT
Tel: 0181–203 9233
A charitable trust offering sheltered housing to rent.

Fold Housing Association
3 Redburn Square
Holywood
Co Down BT18 9HZ
Tel: 01232 428314
Not-for-profit organisation offering sheltered housing for rent, leasehold sheltered housing, housing with care for frail older people or for dementia sufferers. It also runs day and respite care for dementia sufferers and their carers, and a 'staying put' home improvement agency service.

The Guinness Trust
17 Mendy Street
High Wycombe
Bucks HP11 2NZ
Tel: 01494 535823
A charity which offers flats and houses for rent.

Friends of the Elderly and Gentlefolks Help
42 Ebury Street
London SW1W 0LZ
Tel: 0171–730 8263
A charity offering residential houses and flats to rent. The Society is pleased to accept donations to help it bridge the gap between what the costs of running these homes and what is received back through fees.

James Butcher Housing Association
39 High Street
Theale
Reading RG7 5AH
Tel: 01734 323434
A charity offering sheltered homes for sale or for rent.

Jephson Homes Housing Association Ltd
Jephson House
Blackdown
Leamington Spa
Warwicks CV32 6RE
Tel: 01926 339311
A not-for-profit organisation offering sheltered housing, for rent.

Merseyside Improved Homes
46 Wavertree Road
Liverpool L7 1PH
Tel: 0151–709 9375
A charity offering sheltered housing to rent.

Retirement Lease Housing Association
19 Eggar's Court
St George's Road
Aldershot
Hants GU12 4LN
Tel: 01252 318181
A not-for-profit organisation offering sheltered housing to rent.

Royal Air Forces Association
Portland Road
Malvern
Worcs WR14 2TA
Tel: 01684 892505
A charity offering sheltered housing to rent.

The Royal British Legion Housing Association Ltd
PO Box 32
St John's Road
Penn
High Wycombe
Bucks HP10 8JF
Tel: 01494 813771
A charity offering sheltered housing to rent.

Hadleigh Retirement Homes
Highfield House
27 South Street
Tarring
Worthing BN14 7LG
Tel: 01903 204106
A company offering sheltered housing, for sale and for rent.

Select Retirement
Manor View Offices
Ringwood Road
Burley
Hants BH24 4BR
Tel: 01425 403777
A company offering sheltered housing, for rent and for sale in Hampshire.

Further Reading
A Buyer's Guide to Retirement Housing, Age Concern England (Central Books), £4.95

Residential Homes and Nursing Homes

Residential or care homes are for people who, although still fairly independent, do require some assistance (perhaps with washing, dressing or cooking). Residents are generally encouraged to bring some of their own belongings when they move in. When considering a home it is important to check that it is near shops and other facilities so that the resident's sense of independence may be maintained.

By law any private or voluntary residential care home with four or more residents has to be registered with the Local Authority Social Services Department.

Nursing homes are residential or care homes which provide 24-hour nursing cover. They must be run by a qualified doctor or nurse and are more suitable for people who need constant attention from trained nurses. By law any home providing nursing care to more than one person has to be registered with the District Health Authority.

Who Pays?

Care in the Community

The Government's new community care arrangements have meant changes to the Income Support available for people going into residential care or nursing homes. If you need financial help to enter a residential care or nursing home you must first contact your local authority's Social Services Department (Social Work Department in Scotland). They will discuss the most suitable type of care and, if appropriate, find you a place in a home or help you choose one. The Department will pay the home's fees and will work out how much you can afford to contribute, based on your income, benefits and capital. You will also be allowed a personal expenses allowance.

In summary, if you have:

- more than £8,000 in savings you pay the full fee. You may be able to claim Attendance Allowance or Disability Living Allowance.

- £8,000 or less in savings, your income will be taken into account, including any Income Support you may be entitled to. The local authority pays the rest – up to what is needed to meet your 'assessed care needs'.

You have the right to choose the home to which you go. If you have chosen a more expensive home than the local authority will usually pay for, someone else may make up the difference – a relative or charity, for instance. In the case of problems or disagreement with the assessment you should use the complaints procedure – details from your Local Authority Social Services Department.

If you have a home of your own to sell, and £8,000 or less in savings, the local authority could arrange a place for you and help with the fees. They would then claim back the money you owe them when your property is sold.

The value of your home is not counted if your stay in a home is temporary, or if your spouse or partner or relative is aged 60 or over, or under 60 and with a disability, and is living there.

Further information can be obtained from Freeline Social Security on 0800 666 555. Leaflet IS50, 'Help If You Live in a Residential Care Home or Nursing Home', is available from local Benefits Agency offices.

Age Concern (*see page 46*) produces a factsheet (No 10) called 'Local Authority charging procedures for residential and nursing home care'.

Choosing a Residential or Nursing Home

About three quarters of the 14,000 residential care homes in the UK are run by private or voluntary organisations, the rest by local authorities. If you are able to pay for it yourself, you may apply for a place in the home of your choice. Fees in the run-for-profit homes vary enormously. Before committing to a particular home it is vital to check and compare not only the facilities and services on offer, but also the projected fee increases over the next few years.

Choosing a residential home is a decision which should be made jointly and carefully. Here are a few of the factors to consider when deciding:

- *Are visitors made welcome?* Good homes operate an open-door policy whereby visitors are made welcome, within the limitations of meal- and bedtimes.
- *Is the level of care offered suitable and/or adequate?* If continual care is required because of illness, disability or frailness then a nursing home registered with the Local Health Authority is needed. More active elderly persons are recommended to a Residential Care Home registered with the Social Services Department (or Social Work Department in Scotland).

Some homes have dual registration, which ensures residents a home even if they do become frail and in need of continuous care.
- *Personal relationships:* On your exploratory visits try to observe the relationship between residents and staff – is it friendly and happy?
- *Physical needs:* Are there aids to mobility and independence to help residents as they become less mobile and steady?
- *Independence and privacy:* Can residents choose at what time they rise and retire? Do they have freedom or are their movements regimented? Do residents have single or shared room and, if shared, do they have a choice about with whom they share? It is important that they maintain their independence.
- *Location:* Is the home near where relatives live? Is it near public transport and other amenities and shops to help make visits there easier and so that you may get out and about when friends and relatives visit?
- *Happiness:* No amount of physical care can substitute for happiness and homeliness. Talk to residents and see whether they seem completely comfortable and happy.

Age Concern England (*address page 46*) produces a free factsheet, 'Finding Residential and Nursing Home Accommodation'. Help the Aged (*address page 80*) publishes an information sheet 'Residential and Nursing Homes', which details how to choose and how to pay for one. Counsel and Care (*address pages 85–6*) produces 'Finding Suitable Residential and Nursing Accommodation' (London only) (10p).

Further Reading
At Home in a Home, Pat Young (Age Concern, 1988), £3.95
Directory of Residential Care Facilities in Scotland, Margaret Scott (ed.), (Scottish Council for Voluntary Organisations, 1989), £7.50
Laing's Review of Private Health Care 1992/93 and Directory of Independent Hospitals, Residential and Nursing Homes and Related Services (Laing and Buisson, 1993), £35
The Daily Telegraph Guide to Living and Retiring Abroad, Mike Furnell (Kogan Page Ltd, 6th edn, 1992), £8.99

How to Find a Private Nursing Home or a Private or Voluntary Residential Care Home
Your local Age Concern group, Citizens Advice Bureau, Social Services Department or Community Health Council may offer general advice and lists of residential care or nursing homes in your area.

The Registration Officer for Private Nursing Homes will be able to give a list of private homes in your area. Contact the District Health Authority (address in the telephone book).

Some charities assist people to find homes; these are listed later in this chapter (*see pages 79–85*).

The Relatives Association
Twyman House
5 Tavistock Place
London WC1H 9SS
Tel: 0171–916 6055/0181–201 9153

The Relatives Association was founded in 1992 for the relatives and friends of elderly people in all types of residential care, nursing homes and long-stay hospitals. It aims to provide a framework nationally (and eventually, locally) through which relatives can work together to maintain and improve the quality of residential care for older people and to assist in creating common understanding between staff, relatives and residents. A newsletter is circulated quarterly and deals with varied topics such as procedure, feelings of guilt and government policy. A publication, *Relative Views*, is available on request (voluntary donations welcome).

The United Kingdom Home Care Association
42 Banstead Road
Carshalton Beeches
Surrey SM5 3NW
Tel: 0181–288 1551

The United Kingdom Home Care Association (UKHCA) has been formed to speak for the independent providers of home care and home nursing services and raise the profile of home care services generally with its 'UKHCA Code of Practice'. A recommended complaints procedure is now available. The Association's representatives work closely with colleagues in the public sector. It also publishes a list of member organisations (priced £15) or local lists of members (free of charge).

The Registered Nursing Home Association
Calthorpe House
Hagley Road
Edgbaston
Birmingham B16 8QY
Tel: 0121–454 2511

The Registered Nursing Home Association is the trade association for nursing home owners. With a membership of 1,600 homes representing 30 per cent of the private nursing home sector, it looks after 60,000 patients. All homes have to submit to an independent inspection visit. It publishes a directory of nursing homes which reach certain high standards. They can also give details of homes in particular areas.

The British Federation of Care Home Proprietors
852 Melton Road
Thurmaston
Leicester LE4 8BN
Tel: 0116 264 0095

The BFCHP promotes professional standards in the delivery of quality care. It operates a registry of care homes and helps and advises on selecting residential and nursing care by providing a list of homes in the area. Leaflets include 'How to Choose a Care Home' (free with sae).

National Care Homes Association
5 Bloomsbury Place
London WC1A 2QA
Tel: 0171–436 1871

The National Care Homes Association is a confederation of private care homes meeting certain standards. They can offer advice on choosing a private residential care home.

Other sources of information to help you to choose a residential care or nursing home are:

- Personal recommendation

If someone knows a particular home this can be the best way to make a choice.

- Yellow Pages

Look under Residential and Retirement Homes or Nursing Homes. Make sure you visit several and use the checklist at the beginning of this chapter (*page 64*) before making a choice.

- Social workers

Based at the Social Services Department (or Social Work Department in Scotland) or, if you are currently in hospital, the hospital itself may be able to provide a list of homes and general advice.

- Counsel and Care for the Elderly

This charity visits private residential and nursing homes in the London area and can provide a list of homes as well as a general advisory service (*address pages 85–6*).

Placement Agencies

A number of specialist agencies can give professional advice on care options, costs, appraisal of need and a choice of what is available.

SMD Agency
37 Taylors Crescent
Cranleigh
Surrey GU6 7EN
Tel: 01483 274085

A member of the Association of Independent Care Advisors (*see below*), the SMD Agency provides a free advisory service to clients and relatives and offers a comprehensive selection of residential and nursing homes in Surrey and the surrounding areas to suit all needs and financial requirements. It personally and regularly inspects the hundreds of homes on their books.

Network Homesearch
51a Brighton Road
Horsham
West Sussex RH13 6EZ
Tel: 01403 271281

A member of the Association of Independent Care Advisors (*see below*), Network Homesearch is a placement service offering independent advice on sheltered, residential and nursing homes. Staff have personal interviews and a local up-to-date knowledge of properties in Suffolk, South Hampshire, South Buckinghamshire, Hertfordshire, West Sussex, East Surrey, Leicestershire, Lancashire and Majorca. Additional services include advocacy and regular visiting.

Other agencies which assist in this way are **Carequest**, tel: 01223 872884, and **Grace**, tel: 01483 304354. Always be sure to check the scale of fees before committing to use private services such as these.

Association of Independent Care Advisors
Faldonside
Kinglsey
Bordon
Hants GU35 9ND
Tel: 01420 472273
The Association of Independent Care Advisors is the governing association of organisations which help older people and their families to find suitable care homes, sheltered housing and domiciliary care services.

Independent Health Care Association
22 Little Russell Street
London WC1A 2HT
Tel: 0171–430 0537
The Independent Health Care Association is a registered charity representing the majority of the UK's independent healthcare providers: independent hospitals, psychiatric hospitals and nursing and residential homes. It acts as a focal point for promoting innovative thinking on a wide range of health policy issues and promotes the independent sector by influencing Parliament, Whitehall and the media on the issues which affect health and social care.

Help the Aged
St James Walk
London EC1R 0BE
Tel: 0171–253 0253
Help the Aged has four registered residential homes.

John Groom's Association for the Disabled
10 Gloucester Drive
Finsbury Park
London N4 2LP
Tel: 0181–802 7272
The Association is a charity which runs projects to help people with disabilities – including residential homes, respite care and holiday accommodation.

The Leonard Cheshire Foundation
26–9 Maunsel Street
London SW1P 2QN
Tel: 0171–828 1822
This is a charity which runs residential homes for the people with disabilities, and provides part-time care attendants to go into the homes of those with disabilities.

Methodist Homes for the Aged
Epworth House
Stuart Street
Derby DE1 2EQ
Tel: 01332 296200
A charity which cares for older people in need (not necessarily Methodists) in 37 residential homes, one home for those who are mentally frail, and a nursing home. The homes respect the individuality and dignity of those in their care, enabling them to live life to the full.

Somerset Care Ltd
Acacia House
Swingbridge
Bathpool
Taunton
Somerset TA2 8BY
Tel: 01823 323584

Somerset Care is a charitable trust which owns and operates 26 care and nursing homes in Somerset and neighbouring counties. Details and rates on request.

Friends of the Elderly and Gentlefolks Help
42 Ebury Street
London SW1W 0LZ
Tel: 0171–730 8263

A charity offering residential accommodation.

Two Care
13 Harwood Road
London SW6
Tel: 0171–371 0118

Two Care is a charitable housing association with 10 residential and psychiatric rehabilitation homes for people recovering from mental illness.

Ashbourne Homes plc
3 Atlantic Quay
York Street
Glasgow G2 8JH
Tel: 0141–331 2222

A company operating private homes in Scotland, England and Wales.

Royal British Legion
48 Pall Mall
London SW1Y 5JY
Tel: 0171–973 0633

The Royal British Legion is a charity and Britain's premier ex-Service organisation which promotes the welfare of service and ex-service men and women and their dependents, relieving hardship where it exists. It provides seven residential homes and three convalescent homes.

The British Limbless Ex-Servicemen's Association (BLESMA)
185–187 High Road
Chadwell Heath
Romford
Essex RM6 6NA
Tel: 0181–590 1124

BLESMA provides permanent residential and respite accommodation through its two nursing and residential care homes at Blackpool and at Crieff in Perthshire.

The Brendoncare Foundation
Brendon
Park Road
Winchester
Hampshire SO23 7BE
Tel: 01962 852133

The Brendoncare Foundation is a not-for-profit organisation and registered charity providing what they call 'Total Care' for older people in residential, nursing and terminal care homes. The homes offer 'security, dignity and a warm, caring atmosphere'.

Sue Ryder Foundation
Cavendish
Sudbury
Suffolk CO10 8AY
Tel: 01787 280252

The Foundation is a registered charity which has over 20 nursing homes in the UK.

St George's Nursing Home
61 St George's Square
London SW1V 3QR
Tel: 0171–821 9001/2
The St George's Nursing home in London's Victoria offers 24-hour RGN nursing care in this quiet, residential area with easy access to public transport and local shopping.

Disabled Housing Trust
Norfolk Lodge
Oakenfield
Burgess Hill
West Sussex RH15 8SJ
Tel: 01444 239123
The DHT is a charitable trust providing residential care for the physically handicapped.

Greenacre Group plc
Kenwood House
15 Reading Road
Pangbourne
Berks RG8 7LR
Tel: 01734 844414
Provider of nursing and residential care accommodation in Oxfordshire, Berkshire, Wiltshire, Somerset, Gloucestershire and Scotland.

The Arkle Lodge Nursing Home
Sprents Lane
Overton
Hants RG25 3HX
Tel: 01256 771353
A private nursing home.

Tameside Care Group Ltd
Enterprise House
Grange Road South
Hyde
Cheshire SK14 5NY
Tel: 0161–368 9099

Private company operating residential and nursing homes.

The Forces Help Society and Lord Roberts Workshops
122 Brompton Road
London SW3 1JE
Tel: 0171–589 3243
The Society helps, according to need, men and women who have served at any time in HM forces, which includes a large proportion of those now elderly who served in the Second World War or did National Service. It provides help to people in need, which includes advice on obtaining benefits and services to which individuals may be entitled.

The Society also maintains Cottage Homes for those with disabilities and elderly men and women and their partners. Some of these homes are purpose-built for those suffering from disabilities (not necessarily the result of active service).

Takare plc
Takare House
Whitechapel Way
Priorslee
Telford
Salop TF2 9SP
Tel: 01952 292392
A private company operating nursing homes in the UK.

Westminster Healthcare plc
48 Leicester Square
London WC2H 7FB
Tel: 0171–839 9302
A private company operating 65 nursing homes in the UK.

Crestacare Ltd
Wesley House
Huddersfield Road
Bircstall
Nr Batley
West Yorks WF17 0EJ
Tel: 01924 422221
Operates nursing homes in the UK and Ireland.

Court Cavendish Group Ltd
Maple House
2–6 High Street
Potters Bar
Herts EN6 5QR
Tel: 01707 664400
Nursing and residential care group, with 34 homes in the UK.

Country House Retirement Homes Ltd
Tannery House
Tannery Lane
Send
Woking
Surrey GU23 7EF
Tel: 01483 211571
Company offering 30 homes, mainly in southeast England.

Community Hospitals Group plc
Priory Terrace
24 Bromham Road
Bedford MK40 2QD
Tel: 01234 273473
Company operating 14 nursing homes in England.

Caledonian Nursing Homes Ltd
St Joseph's Nursing Home
Lochwinnoch
Renfrewshire
Tel: 01505 843390
Company operating eight nursing homes in Scotland.

Sandown Private Nursing Homes
646 Shore Road
Whiteabbey
Co Antrim BT37 0PR
Tel: 01232 853134
Company operating 29 nursing homes in Northern Ireland.

Lodge Care plc
Pond Road
Shoreham by Sea
West Sussex BN43 5WU
Tel: 01273 464724
Company operating 14 nursing homes on the south coast, in the Midlands and the North.

Northern Caring Homes Ltd
Administration Centre
Winlaton Care Village
Winlaton
Tyne and Wear NE21 6JY
Tel: 0191–499 0366
Company operating 11 nursing and residential homes.

Quality Care Homes Ltd
18–20 St Cuthbert's Way
Darlington
Co Durham DL1 1GB
Tel: 01325 364586
Company operating 24 nursing homes in Cleveland, Durham, Darlington, Newcastle and Sunderland.

The Almshouse Association
Billingbear Lodge
Wokingham
Berks RG11 5RU
Tel: 01344 52922
The 2,000 UK almshouse charities provide housing for needy elderly people, usually those who have previously resided in the area. Vacancies are advertised in the local press and names

and addresses of correspondents to almshouse charities may be obtained from the local authority (Housing or Social Services Departments) or the Citizens Advice Bureau. The Almshouse Association is a national charity advising almshouse charities on matters of finance, current legal requirements, standards of accommodation and all aspects of almshouse administration.

Homes for Minorities and Special Needs

A number of minorities and special needs homes are detailed below. There may also be some Asian, Afro-Caribbean or Cypriot housing schemes for frail elderly people in your area – the Social Services Department will be able to help you find out what is available.

Jewish Care
221 Golders Green Road
London NW11 9DW
Tel: 0181–458 3282
Jewish Care runs residential and nursing homes and sheltered housing schemes for Jewish people.

The Cinnamon Trust
Poldarves Farm
Trescowe Common
Penzance
Cornwall TR20 9RX
Tel: 01736 850291
The Trust has a register of nursing homes, residential homes and sheltered housing throughout the UK that will accept residents with pets.

ANS Contract Healthcare
1 Battersea Square
London SW11 3PZ
Tel: 0171–924 3026
Associated Nursing Services plc works with Health Authorities to provide the best long-term care for the elderly and mentally ill. It is one of the largest operators, with 28 nursing homes and 1,200 beds throughout the country. Further details and rates on request.

The Royal National Institute for the Blind
224 Great Portland Street
London W1N 6AA
Tel: 0171–388 1266
The RNIB provides high-quality residential care in pleasant surroundings in homes in Harrogate, North Yorks, Westgate-on-Sea, Kent, Burnham-on-Sea, Somerset and Hove (*see also* Health Matters, *pages 19–45*).

The Hospice Information Service
St Christopher's Hospice
51–59 Lawrie Park Road
Sydenham
London SE26 6DZ
Tel: 0181–778 9252
The Hospice Information Service is a worldwide network and resource which can give information and advice on hospice and palliative care. Palliative care is the total care of patients with a terminal illness for whom the goal must be the best quality of life for them and their families. Although hospice care is principally for patients with advanced cancer, many hospices will consider applications from patients with other illnesses. There are facilities for in- and out-patients and home care teams. *The Directory of*

Hospice Services in the UK and Ireland is available free on receipt of an 11-inch x 9-inch sae with three second class stamps.

Further Information

Help The Aged
St James Walk
London EC1R 0BE
Tel: 0171–253 0253
Help the Aged operates SeniorLine, a freephone advice line for older people, their relatives, carers and friends. Advice workers can give information and advice on a wide range of issues including community services, housing, welfare and disability benefits. Telephone SeniorLine on 0800 289 404, 10 a.m. to 4 p.m. Monday to Friday. The charity also produces a range of advice leaflets covering money matters, home safety and health.

Age Concern England
Astral House
1268 London Road
London SW16 4ER
Tel: 0181–679 8000

Age Concern Scotland
113 Rose Street
Edinburgh EH2 3DT
Tel: 0131–220 3345

Age Concern Wales
Fourth Floor
1 Cathedral Road
Cardiff CF1 9SD
Tel: 01222 371566

Age Concern Northern Ireland
6 Lower Crescent
Belfast BT7 1NR
Tel: 01232 245729
Most areas have an Age Concern group which provides services, leaflets and advice. Relevant factsheets include:
'Rented Accommodation for Older People'
'Rented Accommodation for Older People in Greater London'
'Sheltered Housing for Sale'
'Finding Residential and Nursing Home Accommodation'
'Local Authorities Charging Procedures for residential and nursing home care'
'Preserved Rights to Income Support for residential and nursing homes'
'Raising Income or Capital from your Home'
Age Concern also publishes a book, Housing Options for Older People (£4.95).

Counsel and Care for the Elderly
Twyman House
16 Bonny Street
London NW1 9PG
Tel: 0171–485 1566 (Monday, Tuesday, Thursday and Friday, 10.30 a.m. to 4 p.m.)

Counsel and Care visits establishments and has a list of available resources. Relevant publications (free unless otherwise indicated) include:
'Older People at Risk of Abuse in a Residential Setting'
'Special Accommodation for Older People'
'Community Care Choices for Older People'
'Community Care – a Guide to Making a Complaint'
'Help at Home'
'Which Charity?'

'What to Look for in a Private or Voluntary Registered Home'
'The Social Fund for Older People'
'Finding Suitable Residential and Nursing Accommodation' (London only), 10p

chapter five

HOLIDAYS

Financing Them, Enjoying Them – All the Options

THESE DAYS THE CHOICE of holidays is fantastic. Practically every country in the world is accessible: there are hotels, villas and apartments to stay in; sporting, adventure, camping, hobby and health holidays; rail, coach, fly-drive, group travel or 'solo' holidays; stays in one place or multi-centre holidays – the list is endless.

Travel agents are there to advise people of every interest, ability or disability about what is available and what would suit their needs and budget. Some tour operators have holidays specifically for older age groups and, in recent years, the long-stay holiday has become popular with older people who can live relatively well and inexpensively through the winter months in resort hotels or other accommodation in a warmer climate, even receiving their pensions while they are away.

Social Service Departments have the power to give financial help towards holidays. Having said this, some Authorities do not make grants at all, while others may offer holidays at places of their own choice instead of giving help. In addition, the amounts are never large and are likely to involve means-testing to determine the amount they will give.

TRAVELLING ABROAD

If an operator is chosen who is a member of the Association of British Travel Agents (ABTA, 55–57 Newman Street, London W1P 3PG, tel: 0171–637 2444), the booking conditions will meet the ABTA Code of Conduct. Should the company fail financially the holiday or money will still be guaranteed. Any grievances should be taken up with the tour operator first. If this is not satisfactory, ABTA runs an arbitration scheme to deal with complaints, whose special telephone number is 0171–307 1907.

Travel agents will be able to advise on whether any visas or special inoculations are needed. It is wise always to check in advance – people have been known to be refused entry into the country they wanted to visit. Masta's Travellers

Health Line is an automated system which will send you printed advice tailored to your trip. As well as health precautions, this includes the latest health news and Foreign Office travel advice; tel: 0891 224 100 (39p a minute cheap rate, 49p at other times).

Technically passports are not strictly necessary for travel to EU countries, but many transport carriers do ask for one and it is useful for identification purposes when cashing traveller's cheques or checking into a hotel.

Long-stay Holidays

These holidays have become very popular, offering reduced-price accommodation in milder climes over the winter months. In fact, some tour operators claim it can be cheaper to take a holiday than to stay at home.

Airtours Golden Years Holidays is one company that can help if you need information about long-stay holidays (brochure and information from travel agents, or call 01706 260000). Last year, Airtours Wintersun apartments cost from as little as £3.79 per day.

All persons going for less than three months can cash all their retirement pension orders when they return. Pension orders cannot be cashed later than three months after the date printed on them. If going abroad for three months or more, the local Social Security office should be warned well in advance to make arrangements for the payment of the pension, which can be paid into a bank in the UK for the duration.

If a person is receiving other Social Security benefits such as Housing Benefit and Income Support he or she should contact the local Social Security office before leaving the country.

Further Reading
Life in the Sun: A Guide to Long-stay Holidays and Living Abroad in Retirement, Nancy Tuft (Age Concern England, 1989), £6.95

Travel Insurance

It is advisable to take out insurance against the possible risks that may be encountered while on holiday. Household policies may cover loss or theft, but travellers should be sure to have coverage for medical and personal emergencies, which will cover cancellation and/or curtailment of the trip. Check that the cover required has been obtained, as most insurers impose terms or restrict cover for persons over 70.

Age Concern (*see opposite*) offers Holiday and Travel Insurance which does not automatically increase because of age, and there are discounts for people travelling for more than 31 days – ideal for long-stay holidays. They also offer home, motor, injury cash plan and pet insurance and can be contacted at:

Age Concern Insurance Services
Garrod House
Chaldon Road
Caterham
Surrey CR3 5YZ
Tel: 01883 341122

The **Holiday Care Service** offers a holiday insurance policy specifically designed for people with disabilities and their families. Phone TravelCare on 0800 181 532 for further information.

Travellers should be sure to check their household policy to find out what cover they have, as some policies can become invalid if the home is unoccupied for more than two weeks. **Housewatch** is one of the agencies which will literally 'babysit' houses while their owners are away (*see page 90*).

A free leaflet about holiday and car insurance is available with sae from:

The Association of British Insurers
51 Gresham Street
London EC2V 7HQ
Tel: 0171–600 3333
Other companies offering travel insurance for older people are:

Europ Assistance Ltd
Sussex House
Perrymount Road
Haywards Heath
West Sussex RH16 1DN
Tel: 01444 440 202

Extrasure Holdings
Lloyd's Avenue House
6 Lloyds Avenue
London EC3N 3AX
Tel: 0171–480 6871

Medical Treatment Overseas

Medical treatment overseas may not be free nor of the same standard as in the UK. For emergency medical treatment in an EU country a person needs to have completed form E111 (available at post offices). It should then be stamped, signed and returned so that it may be taken along on the holiday. With the form is a useful leaflet, 'Health Advice for Travellers Inside the European Community'.

In non-EU countries emergency treatment may be provided on the same terms as for residents of the country being visited. A wealth of useful advice is listed in leaflet T5, *Health Advice for Travellers* (available from doctors' surgeries and Social Security offices, or from the Health Publications Unit – address below). It contains essential information on:

- how to avoid the need for healthcare when abroad
- immunisation advice
- how to plan for healthy travelling
- how to obtain emergency medical treatment in countries throughout the world
- how to obtain and use Form E111, which will provide free or reduced-cost emergency medical treatment in most European countries.

Health Publications Unit
No 2 Site
Heywood Stores
Manchester Road
Heywood
Lancs OL10 2PZ
Freephone: 0800 555 777

Home Security While Away

The security of one's home can be a nagging worry in the back of one's mind throughout a holiday. Housewatch can provide live-in security, including answering the telephone, caring for pets, watering plants, mowing the lawn and general housework. They can drive people to and from the airport and have some groceries awaiting their return.

Housewatch Ltd
Little London
Berden
Bishop's Stortford
Herts CM23 1BE
Tel: 01279 777412

Homesitters Ltd
Buckland Wharf
Buckland
Aylesbury
Bucks HP22 5LQ
Tel: 01296 630730

Homesitters can, at short notice, move into your home and ensure security and care for possessions and pets.

Animal Aunts
Wydwooch
45 Fairview Road
Headley Down
Hants GU35 8HQ
Tel: 01428 712611
This company will look after pets in their owner's home.

Holiday and Specialist Organisations

Saga Holidays
The Saga Building
Middelburg Square
Folkestone
Kent CT20 1AZ
Tel: 0800 300 456
This is the largest provider of holidays for people over 50 and offers a huge range of holidays in the UK and overseas, including short breaks, cruises, university and college centres, coach holidays, touring centres, singles holidays, arts and special-interest holidays, holiday villages and holidays in practically every country in the world.

Travel Companions (060)
110 High Mount
Station Road
London NW4 3ST
Tel: 0181–202 8478
This organisation provides a nationwide service for people aged 25–75 who like to share their holidays. Clients are offered a choice of companions with similar interests and they meet their travel companion before they decide to make their holiday

arrangements together.

Countrywide Holidays
Birch Heys
Cromwell Range
Manchester M14 6HU
Tel: 0161–224 2855
Countrywide holidays, which celebrated its centenary last year, offers a wide variety of walking and special-interest holidays for all ages and all levels of walking experience. Throughout England and Wales there are nine Countrywide-owned guest houses, all of which are situated in areas of outstanding natural beauty. Factsheets and brochures for all holidays are available on request.

The National Trust
36 Queen Anne's Gate
London SW1H 9AS
Tel: 0171–222 9251
The National Trust, through fully-bonded tour operator Arena Travel, offers holidays to the world's loveliest public and private gardens, including Madeira, Italy, Giverny (Monet's garden) and Canada. Details from:

Arena Travel
RHA Garden Holidays
Hamilton House
Cambridge Road
Felixstowe
Suffolk UP11 7EU
Tel: 01394 276276

Carefree Holidays Ltd
64 Florence Road
Northampton NN1 4NA
Tel: 01604 30382
Holidays for the over-55s in the UK and overseas for the able and less able.

Pre-retirement Association Holiday Courses
78 Capel Road
East Barnet
Herts EN4 8JF
Tel: 0181–449 4506
Organises retirement planning holidays at Barton Hall near Torquay, covering finance, health, hobbies and leisure. The PRA is a charity and has no link with insurance or finance houses.

CRUSE – Bereavement Care
CRUSE House
126 Sheen Road
Richmond
Surrey TW9 1UR
Tel: 0181–940 4818
Publishes *Holiday Ideas from CRUSE* (£2 plus p & p) to help bereaved people when they are on their own.

Major and Mrs Holt's Battlefield Tours
15 Market Street
Sandwich
Kent CT13 9DA
Tel: 01304 612248
This company arranges guided tours to First and Second World War and other battlefield areas and relatives' war graves in the UK and overseas.

Golden Rail Holidays
Ryedale Building
Piccadilly
York YO1 1NX
Tel: 01904 628992
Rail holidays, including special information for people with disabilities.

Shearings Ltd
Miry Lane
Wigan WN3 4AG
Tel: 01942 44246
Overseas and UK coach holidays.

Co-op Holiday Care
PO Box 53
Corporation Street
Manchester M60 4ES
Tel: 0161–832 7890
Arranges overseas, UK and long-stay holidays.

Golden Years
Airtours plc
Holcombe Road
Helmshaw
Rossendale
Lancs BB4 4NB
Tel: 01706 830130 or 01706 240033
   Short- and long-stay holidays in Europe. Details and brochures from travel agents throughout the UK.

Bakers Coaches
48 Locking Road
Weston-super-Mare
BS23 3DN
Tel: 01934 616000
Coach holidays.

Enterprise
First Choice Travel
Peel Cross Road
Salford
Manchester M5 2AN
Tel: 0161–745 7000
Winter sun holidays to Africa, Canary Islands, Balearics, etc., including long stay.

Aquasun Senior Sun
41 Crawford Street
London W1H 1HA
Tel: 0171–258 3555
Special holidays for over-60s to Malta, including long-stay.

Sun Island Holidays UK
Wroxall
Ventnor
Isle of Wight PO38 3BR
Tel: 01983 854532
Holidays in the Isle of Wight.

Scandinavian Seaways
Scandinavian House
Parkeston Quay
Harwich
Essex CO12 4QG
Tel: 01255 240240
Holidays and 'mini cruises' in Germany, Denmark and Scandinavia.

Leisurely Days
Enterprise (Owners Abroad)
Groundstar House
London Road
Crawley
West Sussex RH10 2TB
Tel: 01293 560777
Long-stay holidays overseas: Canary Islands, Cyprus, Spain and Malta.

The British Spas Federation
Central Information Services Unit
Thames Tower
Blacks Road
Hammersmith
London W6 9EL
Tel: 0181–846 9000
Contact this branch of the British Tourist Authority for a list of health-farms and hydros.

The British Resorts Association
8 Port Avenue
Southport, PR9 OUS
Tel: 01704 533133
Advice on British resorts.

Great British Cities
Castlegate House
Notts NG1 7AT
Tel: 0115 935 0727
City holidays.

H. F. Holidays
Imperial House
Edgware Road
London NW9 5AL
Tel: 0181–905 9556
Walking or special-interest holidays in Britain and overseas, many especially selected for the older holidaymaker and including Gentle Walking holidays and themed tours of discovery.

NADFAS Tours Ltd
Hermes House
80–89 Beckenham Road
Beckenham
Kent BR3 4RH
Tel: 0181–658 2308
Art holidays.

Portuguese Painting Holidays
Torres do Colegio
Monte Judeu
8600 Lagos
Algarve
Portugal
Tel: 00 351 82 67013
Tutored painting holidays in a luxury Portuguese manor house.

Warner Holidays,
PO Box 22
Havent PO9 1TA
Tel: 01705 492121
Holidays and weekend breaks, many tailor made for the over-60s.

Holidays for People with Disabilities

A number of organisations can assist with holidays for people with disabilities. These include:

The Holiday Care Service
2 Old Bank Chambers
Station Road
Horley
Sussex RH6 9HW
Tel: 01293 774535
The charitable Holiday Care Service is the UK's premier holiday information service for people with disabilities or the disadvantaged. It provides information about holidays in the UK and abroad for people with physical and mental disabilities, those on low incomes and those with other special needs; it also offers a booking service with discounted rates at UK accommodation.

Over 200 free information sheets are available (send a large sae), and books include:
The Holiday Care Guide to Accessible Travel UK (£9.95)
Providing Accessible Accommodation (£5)
Please phone for p & p information.

The Winged Fellowship
Angel House
20–32 Pentonville Road
London N1 9XD
Tel: 0171–833 2594

The Winged Fellowship is a charity which provides holidays and respite care for people with severe physical disabilities at five UK holiday centres and overseas. People with disabilities come alone or with a carer. One-to-one care is provided by trained staff and volunteers and there is 24-hour nursing cover.

Special-interest breaks range from riding to crafts or opera; outings are arranged each day to places of interest. A series of special weeks for Alzheimer's Disease sufferers and their carers is arranged each year. Phone for their 1995 brochure. Anyone can volunteer – no experience is necessary. More mature people are particularly welcome. Volunteers come for a week or two at a time, all year round; the Winged Fellowship pays board, lodging and travel within the UK, so all it costs is time!

Disabled Living Services
Redbank House
4 St Chad's Street
Cheetham
Manchester M8 8QA
Tel: 0161–832 3678

Disabled Living Services organises group holidays and outings throughout the year for people with physical disabilities, their families and friends. Door-to-door transport is available if they live within the Greater Manchester area.

Chalfont Line Holidays
4 Medway Parade
Perivale
Middlesex UB6 8HA
Tel: 0181–997 3799

Chalfont offers coach excursions and tailor-made breaks in the UK, as well as escorted air holidays to Switzerland, Holland, Malta or the Seychelles for people with disabilities.

BREAK
20 Hooks Hill Road
Sheringham
Norfolk NR26 8NL
Tel: 01263 823170

BREAK is a charity which provides holidays and respite care in a holiday environment for children and adults with learning disabilities or mental handicap from all areas of the country. It also organises special breaks for single people over 40.

The National Trust
36 Queen Anne's Gate
London SW1H 9AS
Tel: 0171–222 9251

The National Trust preserves historic buildings, gardens, parks, countryside, coastline and historic sites and also offers holiday cottages in England, Wales and Northern Ireland. It publishes a free booklet, 'Facilities for Disabled and Visually Handicapped Visitors'. The annual subscription allows free entry into National Trust properties.

Greater London Association for Disabled People
336 Brixton Road
London SW9 7AA
Tel: 0171–274 0107
Please send large sae for leaflet.

Holiday Services for Disabled Holidaymakers and their Families
38 Brunswick Street
Teignmouth
Devon TQ14 8AF
Tel: 01626 779424
This is a voluntary service for holidaymakers with disabilities seeking holiday accommodation in and around Devon and Cornwall, including information on sights and attractions, and advice or assistance. Please send sae for details of services and publications.

Disabled Traveller
PO Box 7
London W3 6XJ

Travelin' Talk
Box 3534
Clarksville
Tennessee 37043
USA
Tel: 001 615 552 6670
This organization can link you up with people with disabilities anywhere in the world you are planning to visit, so they can give you the benefit of their experience of getting around their home country.

Other charities provide information on holidays and, in some cases, have their own holiday homes or organise holidays for special groups. Some of these holidays may be for members only. These charities include:

Arthritis Care
18 Stephenson Way
London NE1 2HD
Tel: 0171–916 1500

The British Deaf Association
38 Victoria Place
Carlisle
Cumbria CA1 1HU
Tel: 01228 48844

The British Diabetic Association
10 Queen Anne Street
London W1M 0BD
Tel: 0171–323 1531

The British Red Cross Society
9 Grosvenor Crescent
London SW1X 7EJ
Tel: 0171–235 5454

MIND
22 Harley Street
London W1N 2ED
Tel: 0171–637 0741

Multiple Sclerosis Society
25 Effie Road
London SW6 1EE
Tel: 0171–381 4022

Parkinson's Disease Society
22 Upper Woburn Place
London WC1H 0RA
Tel: 0171–383 3513

Royal National Institute for the Blind
224 Great Portland Street
London W1N 6AA
Tel: 0171–388 1266

The National Deaf-Blind League
18 Rainbow Court
Paston Ridings
Peterborough PE4 6UP
Tel: 01733 573511

Tourist Boards

For general advice about travel in the British Isles, the appropriate tourist boards have many books, leaflets and brochures available, including advice for people with disabilities.

The English Tourist Board
Thames Tower
Blacks Road
Hammersmith
London W6 9EL
Tel: 0181–846 9000

The Scottish Tourist Board
23 Ravelston Terrace
Edinburgh, EH4 3EU
Tel: 0131–332 2433

The Wales Tourist Board
Brunel House
2 Fitzalan Road
Cardiff CF2 1UY
Tel: 01222 499909

Northern Ireland Tourist Board
St Anne's Court
59 North Street
Belfast BT1 1NB
Tel: 01232 231221

State of Guernsey Tourist Board
PO Box 23
North Esplanade
St Peter Port
Guernsey, GY1 3AN
Channel Islands
Tel: 01481 726611

The Irish Tourist Board (Bord Failte)
Ireland House
150 New Bond Street
London W2Y 0AQ
Tel: 0171–493 3201

The national tourist offices for other countries are mostly based in London. Telephone numbers are available from directory enquiries, the London telephone directory at the local library, or by contacting the relevant country's national airline.

Further Reading

Flying High is a booklet for older travellers and those with disabilities, price £2.50 from the Disabled Living Foundation (*address page 59*)

A Guide for Disabled People, 1995 (The Royal Association of Disability and Rehabilitation, tel: 0171–250 3222), £7 (including p & p). Details more than 1,000 specialised hotels, guest houses, self-catering properties, special centres and camp sites in the UK. It also lists voluntary and commercial organisations for people with disabilities, transport services and places to visit. A second book, *Holidays and Travel Abroad – Europe and the World*, is also available from them, price £5. Holiday factsheets, priced 75p each, are also available and cover subjects such as:

Holiday Insurance Cover
Sport and Outdoor Activity Holiday Courses
Planning and Booking a Holiday
Useful Addresses and Publications for the Disabled Holidaymaker.

Age Concern England (*address page 101*) publishes a factsheet (No 4), 'Holidays for Older People', which aims to give suggestions on where to go and how to get information on holidays for older people and those with disabilities. This includes information on locally organised holidays, financial help, commercial organisations, travelling abroad and holidays for people with disabilities and their carers. Its factsheet on travel concessions (No 26), 'Travel Information for Older People', contains important facts for any older person planning to travel in the UK or abroad.

chapter six

FINANCIAL MATTERS

*Benefits, Investments and
How to Find Good Financial Advice*

FINANCE IS A VAST SUBJECT. We are all affected by the need to understand it, whether we need to find a source of additional funds to live on or, at the other extreme, how to invest it most effectively to provide income, growth and tax efficiency.

Financial matters often cause stress and concern to older people, who may worry about not having sufficient money to live on or that, because it is the first time that they have a lump sum of money to invest, a wrong investment decision could cost them their 'nest egg'. Because of the apparent complexities and wide range of facts available it is often difficult to know where to find information or even to know what type of information is needed.

As each person enters retirement, the whole emphasis of his or her financial requirements change. Costs will generally be less, with the mortgage paid off, no work travel requirements and cheaper items such as travel fares and prescriptions. However, with the average person expecting to live a further 20 years or more, it is essential to plan ahead and understand what can be done to ensure continued financial security.

I have tried to keep this chapter as simple as possible. For the sake of clarity I have broken it into two broad categories: Benefits and Investments. First I examine the type of help and assistance that are available to those in need – including State pensions, war pensions, Income Support and Sick or Disability Benefit – and where to find it. The system of Social Security and other benefits is often complicated, and for many people the key is 'What could I claim, am I entitled to claim it and if so, how?' Although I cannot give detailed examples for each benefit to allow you necessarily to know whether you are eligible, I endeavour to explain what it is that is available, whom it is meant to assist and from where further information can be obtained if necessary. In the latter half of this chapter I consider some of the range of options that are important to those who are more financially independent, including an explanation of the types of investment and savings that are available and an indication of how to find a qualified and reputable advisor, and what protection is available for the inexperienced investor.

All the information is accurate at the time of writing; however legislation is constantly changing the rates of tax and allowances, as well as the types and levels of benefit. Neither I nor the publishers can accept any responsibility for errors or omissions arising from advice taken from the book. It should not be treated as a complete and authoritative statement of the law. Readers must take due care in ensuring to the best of their ability that any course of action on which they embark is suitable for their requirements; if in any doubt please do take professional advice.

Financial Assistance and Benefits

In this section I will consider the principal allowances and benefits that are available to the older person and to those in need of assistance who qualify for allowances and benefits. I also outline the organisations to contact for additional advice and help.

If limited provision or even no specific provision has been made for retirement, State Assistance is available to provide the basic necessities of life. The benefits available are essentially of two types:
1. Insured benefits, available by right if the requisite amount of National Insurance contributions has been paid. These include State Retirement Pension and State Earnings Related Pension.
2. Non-insured benefits, to which people may be entitled dependent upon their circumstances. Generally this involves means-testing. These include such benefits as Income Support.

Both of these categories are summarised below, together with a discussion of the help and benefits that are available for the sick and people with disabilities, and those who care for them.

Some people, particularly those who have had no previous dealings with the Social Security system, feel that applying for assistance is akin to relying on charity. The Department of Social Security claims that as of May 1993, 1,763,000 people aged 60 or over (single people or couples) were receiving Income Support because of their low income. It also estimates that in 1991 between 22 per cent and 33 per cent of pensioners who were entitled to Income Support, and between 5 per cent and 12 per cent who were entitled to Housing Benefit, did *not* claim. Research by the London Borough of Hounslow suggests that only two thirds of those who live in sheltered housing who are eligible for benefits are claiming them. Nationally this would mean 200,000 older persons in sheltered housing are living on less than they are due. As the legislation is regularly changing and has done so particularly in the last few years, it is in everyone's interest to review carefully what is available to ensure that they are obtaining the maximum financial benefits available to them.

Many forms of benefit are complicated and have a wide variety of rules and exceptions attached to them. At the end of each section below I have listed books and leaflets that can be referred to, as well as the names of organisations that are able to give advice. All of the leaflets are free of charge (unless otherwise stated) and are available from all Social Security offices (listed in the telephone book under Social Security or Benefits Agency, or for National Insurance matters, Contributions Agency) and most post offices and public libraries. Where leaflets or information is provided by a charitable organisation such as Age Concern, their address is given in the text or referred to with a page number. Leaflets on Housing Benefit and Council Tax Benefit are available from your local council. Anyone who is unable to find DSS leaflets locally should write (giving the leaflet titles and reference numbers to):

BA Publications
Heywood Stores
Manchester Road
Heywood
Lancs OL10 2PZ
or
Leaflets Unit
PO Box 21
Stanmore
Middlesex HA7 1AY

It is recommended that leaflets are obtained and, where necessary, you may contact the organisations mentioned therein for more advice.

There are also several free telephone numbers that can be called for more information about Social Security benefits and National Insurance:

Benefits Enquiry Line (BEL) – 0800 882 200. This is a confidential telephone service available for people with disabilities and their carers. BEL also provides a service through which forms and claim packs may be completed over the telephone and then sent to the applicant to be checked, signed and returned. Call free on 0800 441 144. For people with hearing or speech disabilities there is a textphone facility on 0800 242 355.

DSS Freeline (general information on benefits and Social Security advice) – 0800 666 555.

This same information service about benefits is also available for other ethnic groups in the following languages:
  Chinese 0800 252 451
  Punjabi 0800 521 360
  Urdu 0800 289 188
  Welsh 0800 289 011

The person you talk to will not, of course, have your papers or all the details of your situation to hand. Therefore the advice provided must not be taken as a decision on any matter about which you are enquiring.

Information and explanations are also available from local Social Security offices (or the Benefits Agencies as they are often called, being executive agencies of the DSS) or Citizens Advice Bureaux. All can be found in the telephone book, listed under Social Security, Health & Social Security or Citizens Advice, or by asking at your local library. The address of the local office of the Citizens Advice Bureau can also be obtained by writing to the CAB's central office:

Citizens Advice Bureau – National Association
Myddleton House
115–123 Pentonville Road
London N1 9LZ
Tel: 0171–833 2181

Scottish Association of Citizens Advice Bureau
82 Nicolson Road
Edinburgh EH8 9EW
Tel: 0131–667 0156

NACAB S. Wales
Andrews Buildings
Suite 3–27
67 Queen Street
Cardiff CF1 4AW
Tel: 01222 397686

NACAB N. Wales
134B High Street
Prestatyn
Clwyd LL19 9BN
Tel: 01745 856339

NACAB Northern Ireland Regional Office
11 Upper Crescent
Belfast BT7 1NT
Tel: 01232 231120

In addition, the charity Age Concern provides services and advice. They produce comprehensive factsheets which are referred to where applicable within this text. These are free as long as no more than five are required at any one time and if a large sae is sent. Age Concern also has local organisations throughout the country, whose addresses can be found in the local telephone book or from the local public library, or by contacting the central offices of Age Concern:

Age Concern England
Astral House
1268 London Road
London SW16 4EJ
Tel: 0181–679 8000

Age Concern Scotland
113 Rose Street
Edinburgh EH2 3DT
Tel: 0131–220 3345

Age Concern Wales
1 Cathedral Road
Cardiff CF1 9SD
Tel: 01222 371821

Age Concern Northern Ireland
6 Lower Crescent
Belfast BT7 1NR
Tel: 01232 245729

Help the Aged can also provide help and advice:

Help the Aged
Information Department
St James Walk
London EC1R 0BE
Tel: 0171–253 0253

Help the Aged's SeniorLine (Freephone 0800 289 404) is a free national service for senior citizens, their relatives, carers and friends, which offers advice on many topics including:

- welfare and disability benefits
- housing
- health
- support for carers
- mobility
- community alarms
- sources of local practical help
- other voluntary organisations.

Lines are open 10 a.m. to 4 p.m., Monday to Friday.

Help the Aged produces several useful leaflets that cover benefits generally:

'Can You Claim It?' – An annually updated leaflet that is a step-by-step guide to claiming Income Support, Housing Benefit, Council Tax Benefit and Social Fund Payments.

'Claiming Disability Benefits' – A leaflet giving details of benefits for people who are sick or who have disabilities, including Disability Living Allowance and Attendance Allowance.

Additional Information
Disablement Information and Advice Line (DIAL): Look in the telephone book for the local number or telephone DIAL UK on 01302 310123.

Further Reading
Your Rights 1995–96, Sally West (published annually by Age Concern), £2.95
This book is a guide to the State benefits available to older people, and contains advice on how to claim these benefits.
DSS leaflets which cover general matters:
FB 2, 'Which Benefit – A Guide to Social Security and NHS Benefits'
FB 32, 'Benefits after Retirement – What You Could Claim as a Pensioner'

State Retirement Pension (SRP)
The State Retirement Pension is a taxable weekly benefit payable to men when they reach 65 and women when they reach 60 (although this too will change to 65 within the next 20 years. The date for equalisation of retirement age is 2020; a transitional period will begin in 2010, to even out the changeover). It is possible to draw the pension even if work has not been given up completely, or alternatively it is possible to defer the pension for up to five years and thereby earn extra pension (or increments). If someone does continue to work after normal retirement age it is no longer necessary for him or her to pay National Insurance (NI) contributions.

Payment of the SRP can be made direct to a nominated bank or building society every four or 13 weeks, or can be collected weekly from the post office. If you are ill and/or are unable to collect your pension or any other benefit at the post office, you can sign on the back of each order or giro making it payable to a friend or relative. This person will be acting as an agent on your behalf.

If a pensioner has more permanent difficulty in collecting the money, because for instance he or she has had a stroke or is mentally ill, the local Benefits Agency

(Social Security) office can arrange an *appointee* (who is normally a close friend or relative). If the pensioner is already being looked after by the Court of Protection (*see Chapter 7* under Enduring Powers of Attorney) or has a legal representative, then those persons would become the appointee(s). Further details are available from DSS Form AP 1, 'A Helping Hand: How You Can Help Friends or Relatives Claim Social Security'.

The basic SRP is the same for men, for women who have paid sufficient of their own NI contributions at the standard rate, and for widows. Married women who are not entitled to SRP on the basis of their own contributions may get one on the basis of their husband's contributions, but only when he is already receiving a pension and the woman is over 60.

To receive a full-rate Basic Pension, persons must have 'qualifying years' for about 90 per cent of their working lives. A qualifying year is a tax year in which a person receives qualifying earnings (on which standard rate Class 1, 2 or 3 NI contributions have been paid) of at least 52 times the lower earnings limit for that year. If you are concerned that there may be gaps in your NI payment record, you can ask the local Benefits Agency (Social Security) office for advice. There are time limits within which contributions must be paid if they are to count for benefits, and there are higher rate penalties for contributions paid after a certain date. Further details are available on leaflet NI 48, 'National Insurance – Unpaid and late paid contributions'.

SRP is not paid automatically; it must be claimed. This can be done up to four months before retirement using Form BR 1, which should be sent to you automatically. If you do not receive one three months before retirement, ask the local Benefits Agency (Social Security office).

If you have paid standard rate NI contributions as an employee after 4 April 1978, it may be possible to claim an *Additional Earnings Related Pension*. If NI contributions were paid as an employee between 1961 and 1975 it may also be possible to claim a *Graduated Pension*.

If an individual is over 80, supports another adult or has children (for whom he or she is entitled to claim Child Benefit), it may be possible to claim an *additional weekly payment*. Also, anyone receiving Invalidity Allowance with an Invalidity Benefit within eight weeks of reaching pensionable age may be entitled to an additional Invalidity Payment. Further details are available on leaflet NI 184, 'Over 80 Pension'.

Further Reading
The DSS provide further information in the following leaflets:
FB 6, 'Retiring?'
NP 46, 'A Guide to Retirement Pensions'
FB 32, 'Benefits after Retirement'
All three provide general information on the range of benefits and services for people in retirement (FB 32 is to supersede FB 6 eventually), and NP 46 provides details of all aspects of retirement pensions.
DSS leaflet NP 45, 'A Guide to Widow's Benefits'

DSS leaflet NI 92, 'Giving up your Retirement Pension to Earn Extra'
Age Concern Factsheet No 18, 'A Brief Guide to Money Matters'
Age Concern Factsheet No 20, 'National Insurance Contributions and Qualifying for a Pension'

Special Circumstances

People Who Have Been Divorced
If you have been divorced and are not entitled to a full Basic Pension, your former spouse's NI record may be taken into account if it will provide a better pension, providing that you have not remarried before pensionable age. It is not necessary to wait until your former spouse is receiving his or her pension. For further information see DSS leaflet NP 46, 'A Guide to Retirement Pensions', and NI 95, 'National Insurance for Divorced Women'.

People Going into Hospital
If you need to go into hospital for in-patient treatment on the NHS, your pension will be reduced immediately if you live in a local nursing or similar home run by the council, and after six weeks if you do not live in a council-run home. The rates of reduction are varied, depending upon whether you have a dependent and whether you are claiming Income Support, or Housing or Community Charge Benefit. To find out the exact reductions, you need to contact your local Benefits Agency (Social Security) office. For further information see DSS leaflet NI 9, 'Going into Hospital'.

People Going Abroad
You can normally get your pension paid anywhere abroad. If you are making a trip for less than three months and you are receiving orders or giros which are normally cashed at the post office, it is possible to let them accumulate and cash them all at once. However, orders over three months old may not be cashed.

If you are going for between three and six months, it is possible to have your pension paid into a bank account. If you are going for more than six months, the pension can be paid to you while you live abroad.

If you are living abroad when the pension rates go up in the UK, you will receive the increased rate if you are living in a European Union (EU) country or in a non-EU country with which the UK has a reciprocal arrangement. If you are living in a non-EU country with no such arrangement, your pension will continue to be paid at the same rate as when you first left the country; it will not be increased.

For further details see:
SA 29, 'Your Social Security, healthcare and pension rights in the EU'
DSS leaflet NI 38, 'Social Security Abroad'
DSS leaflet NI 106, 'Pensioners or Widows Going Abroad'
Alternatively, you can write to (specify the country in which you are living or intend to live):

DSS Benefits Agency
Overseas Branch
Newcastle upon Tyne NE98 1YX

Further Information

Occupational Pensions Advisory Service (OPAS)
11 Belgrave Road
London SW1V 1RP
Tel: 0171–233 8080
OPAS is an independent voluntary organisation giving free help and advice to members of the public concerned about their pension rights on all matters about personal or company pension schemes. The OPAS service is available to anyone who believes that he or she has pension rights, including working members of pension schemes, pensioners, those with deferred pensions from previous employment, and their dependents.

War Pensions Schemes
You do not need to have served in wartime to receive a War Disablement Pension; nor do you need to have been a member of HM Armed Forces. This complex area is briefly described below, but it is worth discussing each case individually with one of the relevant organisations listed.

Anyone who has a disability as a result of service in HM Armed Forces (including the Ulster Defence Regiment, the Home Guard or the Nursing and Auxiliary Services) between 1914 and 1921 or at any time after September 1939 (and in certain cases any civilians whose disability is a result of enemy action or action to combat the enemy, and also merchant seamen who suffered a disability during a war) is entitled to a War Disablement Pension. Any widow, widower or dependent relative of someone who has died as a result of such an injury or disability is entitled to a War Widow's Pension (*see below*).

Pensions for disability or death caused by service in HM Armed Forces between 1 October 1921 and 2 September 1939 are the responsibility of the Ministry of Defence. For more information, write to the relevant address below:

Army
MoD
Army Pensions Office
Kentigern House
65 Brown Street
Glasgow G2 8EX

Royal Air Force
MoD
F2 (Air)
Building 56
RAF Innsworth
Gloucester GL3 1HW

Royal Navy and Marines
MoD
NPP (Acs) 3A
HMS Centurion
Grange Road
Gosport PO13 9XA

War Pensions are not taxable. Claims for War Pensions should be made in writing to:

War Pensions Agency
Benefits Agency
North Fylde Central Office
Norcross
Blackpool FY5 3TA

You should give your full name, service number, rank/rating, your branch of the Armed Forces, if applicable, and dates of enlistment and discharge. If you do not have all of the information available, provide all that you can.

There is also a War Pensions Helpline on 01253 858 858 which is available Monday to Friday. It offers general advice, for example to help you complete your claim form.

The War Pensions Schemes are separate from the Social Security Schemes. Therefore persons claiming War Pensions may also be able to claim other allowances, such as Attendance Allowance. Details are available from your local Benefits Agency (Social Security) office.

Further details are also available in leaflets MPL 153, 'How to Claim – War Pensions and other Support', MPL 154, 'Rates of War Pensions and Allowances', and MPL 158, 'Can I Claim? – War Pensions and other Support'.

It is possible for a person to claim War Pensions even if living abroad. Details are available in leaflet MPL 120, 'War Pensioners and War Widows Going Abroad'. Further advice and assistance are also available from the War Pensions Agency (for address and Helpline, *see above*).

War Disablement Pension (WDP)

There are no time limits for claiming WDP. Payment can, however, be made only from the date of the claim or the first contact was made with the War Pensions Agency. The amount paid depends upon the severity of the disability and the rank of the person claiming.

A doctor must assess your loss of physical ability or mental health resulting from your disability by comparing your conditions with that of a healthy person of the same age and sex. The most common claim is for deafness as a result of exposure to gunfire, but many other conditions are also recognised. Many prisoners of war suffer from dietary problems; troops who contracted tropical diseases or other similar diseases while operating abroad may still suffer the effects; others may experience arthritis in a joint which was injured or damaged by a fall.

People who are less than 20 per cent disabled will receive a lump sum gratuity instead of a pension. The loss of a middle finger, for example, involves a payment of about £4,000 at current rates. Since January 1993, less than 20 per cent deafness in each ear is excluded from the conditions that count towards a War Pension, as are all claims related to smoking, even though tobacco was issued to some troops until the 1960s.

WDP is paid tax-free and does not affect any Social Security benefits that you may receive. If you receive Income Support, Housing Benefit or Council Tax Benefit, the first £10 per week of your War Pension is ignored when entitlement to these benefits is worked out.

War Widow's or Dependant's Pension

A pension is also available for the widows, widowers, orphan children and close relatives of someone killed in the Armed Forces or who subsequently died of an injury sustained while in the Armed Forces.

A War Widow's Pension is payable on the death of a war pensioner who died as a result of war injury or if the widow's late husband was receiving a War Disablement Pension or Constant Attendance Allowance. The amount of the pension is determined by a means test, the rank of the person who has died and the age of the widow.

It is not possible for someone to claim a War Widow's Pension as well as a National Insurance Widow's Pension. However, the War Widow's Pension is usually paid at a higher rate.

Further details can be obtained from leaflet MPL 152, 'War Widows and Other Dependants', available from Social Security offices.

War Pensioner's Welfare Service (WPWS)

Additional assistance may also be available from the WPWS, which advises and assists war pensioners on pension matters or any other problems. The service works closely with local authority social services and other voluntary organisations that help ex-servicemen and -women with disabilities and their families. The address of the nearest WPWS office is available from your local Benefits Agency (Social Security) office or from the back of leaflet MPL 153, 'How to Claim – War Pensions and other Support'.

Useful Addresses

There are many ex-service organisations who help war-disabled people and their families. These include:

Royal British Legion and the Officers Association
48 Pall Mall
London SW1Y 5JY
Tel: 0171–973 0633
The Royal British Legion will help most ex-servicemen and -women with claims or appeals for War Pensions.

The Forces Help Society and Lord Roberts Workshops
122 Brompton Road
London SW3 1JE
Tel: 0171–589 3243
The Society helps, according to need, men and women who have served at any time in HM Armed Forces, and provides advice on obtaining benefits and services to which individuals may be entitled.

Further names and addresses of organisations which may help are given in Chapter 3 under the section headed 'Help for Ex-Servicemen and -Women'.

Income Support (IS)

Income Support is a Social Security benefit which is available to assist people whose total family income falls below a certain level which the Government thinks is the minimum that a person needs. It is intended to provide help with the weekly living expenses and may be paid in addition to other Benefits. It does not depend upon NI contributions that have been paid.

People over 60 are eligible if they:
a) reside in the UK
b) do not work nor have a partner working more than 16 hours a week and have a low income
c) do not have combined capital with their partner of in excess of £8,000.

To determine if you are eligible for IS, you will need to:
- calculate the minimum amount that the Government thinks you need each week to live on, which is called your *applicable amount*. It is made up of a basic personal allowance, depending upon whether you are single or married, plus special enhancements for certain categories such as pensioners, people with disabilities, or carers, and in some cases an added amount for certain housing costs such as mortgage interest or service charges. To obtain more information about the allowances and premiums, contact your local Benefits Agency (Social Security) office or Citizens Advice Bureau.
- calculate the amount of your net weekly income. The computation of net weekly income is complex. Certain types of income are ignored, such as Attendance Allowance, Social Fund payments, the special War Widow's Pension and also the actual income from your savings (but *see below*).
- add up the value of your savings (including property and investments). Savings of between £3,000 and £8,000 will reduce the amount of benefit available. Each £250 of savings in excess of £3,000 is treated as income of £1 per week. The value of your home (if you live in it) is excluded, as are personal possessions and the surrender value of any life assurance policies.

Once you have worked out your applicable amount, you should compare this with your income. If your income is less than your applicable amount (after taking into account your savings) you are entitled to Income Support. If your income is higher than your applicable amount, you will not be entitled to Income Support, although you may still be entitled to Housing or Council Tax Benefit.

Many people claim IS only to find that they are awarded a small amount each week. They therefore think that the bother of claiming is not worthwhile. However, apart from it being that person's right to claim, perhaps more importantly *it is a passport to other types of help*. For instance, if someone is eligible for IS he or she will also have their Council Tax paid and, probably, the rent or any interest on a mortgage or home loan. (For further information, *see* the section on Council Tax Benefit and Housing Benefit, *below*.)

In addition, he or she will obtain free NHS prescriptions, dental treatment, eye tests and vouchers to help with the cost of glasses, and assistance with the cost of travelling to hospital for NHS treatment. If that person lives in a private or voluntary nursing or residential care home where fees must be met from private means, he or she can receive IS to assist with those fees. There are special and quite complicated rules for working out how much is available. The local Benefits Agency (Social Security) office will be able to provide more information. Information is also available in DSS leaflet IS 50, 'Help for People Who Live in Residential Care Homes or Nursing Homes'. *See also* Counsel and Care's Factsheet No 6 (*details below*).

IS should be claimed from your local Benefits Agency (Social Security) office. You can get a claim form by writing, telephoning or sending in the tear-off slip from leaflet IS1, available from post offices. If you disagree with the amount of IS awarded you can ask for the decision to be reviewed and/or appeal to a Social Security Appeal Tribunal. If you wish to appeal, you must do so within three months of the original decision. It is advisable to seek assistance and advice on procedure from your local Citizens Advice Bureau.

Further assistance is given to help persons over 60 who receive Income Support with their heating costs when the weather becomes very cold. When the average temperature for your area has been or is forecast to be 0°C/32°F or colder for a seven-day period, you will automatically receive a giro through the post. (*See page 121*, Social Fund). No claim need be made. Your local Benefits Agency (Social Security) office will tell you if the temperatures are sufficiently low to enable them to make the payments, and they will put a notice in the local paper which will tell you which postcodes are affected. If you do not receive a giro within one month of the announcement, contact your local Benefits Agency (Social Security) office. For further information on how to keep warm and well in winter, phone the *Winter Warmth Line* (which is run by Age Concern and Neighbourhood Energy Action) free on 0800 289 404. In Scotland the telephone number is 0800 838 587.

Further Information
Age Concern Factsheet No 11, 'Preserved Rights to Income Support for residential and nursing homes'
Age Concern Factsheet No 25, 'Income Support and the Social Fund'
DSS leaflet IS 1, 'Income Support – See If You Are Entitled'
DSS leaflet IS 20, 'A Guide to Income Support'
DSS leaflet AB 11, 'Help with NHS Costs'
Help the Aged, 'Can You Claim It?'
Also contact Help the Aged's SeniorLine – a free advice line on 0800 289 404
Counsel and Care Factsheet No 14, 'Income Support for Older People at Home'
Counsel and Care Factsheet No 6, 'Claiming Income Support towards the Fees of a Registered Private or Voluntary Home'

Counsel and Care
Lower Ground Floor
Twyman House
16 Bonny Street
London NW1 9PG
Tel: 0171–485 1566 (10.30 a.m. – 4 p.m.)

For the Sick, Injured or Those with Disabilities
There are a wide range of benefits for people who are sick, injured or have a disability. For general information about the benefits available, refer to DSS leaflet F 28, 'Sick or Disabled?'

Invalidity Benefit
This benefit is tax-free and comprises several separate components.

Invalidity Pension is usually paid to people before retirement who are incapable of working for more than 28 weeks (after 28 weeks off work normal Statutory Sick Pay or Sickness Benefits end). Eligibility for Invalidity Pension is dependent upon enough full National Insurance contributions having been paid. An extra payment may be claimed depending upon the earnings of the claimant between April 1978 and April 1991, or if he or she first became incapable of work before 60 (men) or 55 (women). Invalidity Pension and the extra payments (Additional Invalidity Pension and Invalidity Allowance) are together known as **Invalidity Benefit**.

When a person reaches retirement age, it is possible to choose between Invalidity Benefit and the State Retirement Pension. Although the difference between the two is small, it is important to remember that Invalidity Benefit is tax-free, whereas Retirement Pension is taxable. No one may stay on Invalidity Benefit for more than five years after pensionable age, however, after which they can revert to the State Retirement Pension.

It is often difficult to decide whether it is better to remain on Invalidity Benefit or change to Retirement Pension. It is advisable to take advice from one of the independent bodies such as your local Citizens Advice Bureau, Age Concern or Help the Aged. It is possible that other benefits such as Income Support or Council Tax Benefit could be affected by your decision.

Further information is available from DSS leaflet NI 16A, 'Invalidity Benefit'.

Severe Disablement Allowance (SDA)
Severe Disablement Allowance is a tax-free benefit normally payable to persons of working age who have been unable to work for at least 28 weeks due to long-term sickness or severe mental or physical disability. SDA is normally paid to those who have not paid enough National Insurance contributions to receive Sickness or Invalidity Benefit, as your right to SDA does not depend upon National Insurance contributions.

To qualify for SDA a person must have a severe disability (at least 80 per cent disabled) and be under 65 when SDA is first claimed. Once claimed it can continue to be paid to any age.

If a person is claiming Income Support, this will be reduced by the amount of SDA received. However, as there may be long-term advantages in claiming SDA, I would recommend that it is always worth making a claim.

If anyone thinks they may be entitled to SDA, they should refer to their local Benefits Agency (Social Security) office or Citizens Advice Bureau. To claim use form SDA 1, which may be found in DSS leaflet NI 252, 'Severe Disablement Allowance'.

Attendance Allowance (AA)

Attendance Allowance is a tax-free weekly cash benefit for people with disabilities over 65 who require a great deal of personal care (such requirement starting after they turned 65) because of their physical or mental disability. Anyone who has needed care before their 65th birthday should claim Disability Living Allowance (*see below*).

AA is not means-tested, does not depend upon National Insurance contributions and can be paid in addition to other benefits, including Income Support. To get AA you must have normally needed help with personal care for at least six months. Exceptions are made for persons who are terminally ill and are not *expected* to live for more than six months; they can obtain the benefit quickly and easily, and do not even have to be receiving the care that they are deemed to need. There are general rules which allow an application to be made on behalf of a person who is terminally ill without him or her knowing the prognosis.

Two rates are available – a lower one of £31.20 per week for people who have such a severe physical or mental disability that they require looking after by day or by night, but not both, and a higher one of £46.70 for people with similar disability who need looking after both day and night or for those who are terminally ill.

For further information see DSS leaflet DS 702, 'Attendance Allowance'. The leaflet includes a reply slip to send for a claim pack. If you are in a position to claim, it should be sent off as soon as possible, as the benefit will normally be calculated from the date that the DSS receives the slip. The claim form is very lengthy, but normally a medical examination is not necessary. Once it is agreed that you may receive AA, it can be paid directly into your bank or building society account, or you will receive a book of orders to encash at a post office.

Further Information
Counsel and Care Factsheet No 11, 'Attendance Allowance for People aged 65 and Over' (*address page 110*)
Age Concern Factsheet No 34, 'Attendance Allowance and Disability Living Allowance' (*address page 101*)

Constant Attendance Allowance (CAA)

Constant Attendance Allowance is an extra allowance paid on top of War Disability Pensions or pensions for disability or illness caused by accident or disease at work. It is paid to people who need daily care and attention and whose disability for which they receive Industrial Injuries Disablement Benefit has been assessed at 100 per cent or whose war disablement pension is paid at the 80 per cent rate. There are four rates; how much is paid depends on how much attention is needed.

CAA and Attendance Allowance may not be claimed at the same time.

For people who are at the top or intermediate rate of CAA, there is also an additional allowance called Exceptionally Severe Disablement Allowance. This is paid to people who need constant care and attention. There is no need to claim for it, as each person claiming CAA is automatically considered.

Further Information

For more information see the following DSS leaflets:
NI 2, 'If You Have an Industrial Disease'
NI 6, 'Industrial Injuries Disablement Benefit'
NI 196, 'Social Security benefit rates', explains how much can be claimed for any of the above benefits, and what the qualifying circumstances are.
Also, Help the Aged, 'Claiming Disability Benefits'

Disability Living Allowance (DLA)

Disability Living Allowance is a tax-free benefit for people under 65 who need help with personal care or with getting around because of illness or disability. People disabled after they reach the age of 65 are not eligible for DLA and should claim Attendance Allowance. People aged between 65 and 66 may still claim if they started to need help before their 65th birthday.

DLA is not affected by any savings or (usually) income that the person claiming (or his or her partner) might have. It does not depend upon National Insurance contributions and it may be paid in addition to other benefits, including Income Support.

DLA may still be paid even if no one is actually providing all the care the individual needs. However, normally the person must have needed help for at least three months and be likely to need it for at least a further six months. Persons who are not expected to live for longer than six months have no need to go through the initial three-month waiting period.

There are two components of DLA:
1. help with personal care, and
2. help with mobility.

Both have different rates applicable to them.

DSS leaflet DS704 (*see below*) includes a reply slip to request a claim pack. This should be sent off as soon as possible, as the benefit will normally be calculated from the date that the DSS receives the slip. The claim form is very lengthy, but normally no medical examination is necessary. Any claim should be dealt with within six weeks; if there are delays or any hardship is suffered as a result of a delay, a complaint should be registered with the Customer Service Manager at the Disability Living Centre at which the claim is being dealt with. If the claim is turned down or is awarded on a lower scale than expected it is possible to appeal against the decision.

Further Information
For further information see the following DSS leaflets:
DS 704, 'Disability Living Allowance'
HB 6, 'Equipment and Services for Disabled People'
HB 6 is also available in Bengali, Chinese, Greek, Gujarati, Hindi, Punjabi, Turkish, Urdu, Vietnamese and Welsh.
For those living in Scotland, the Scottish Home and Health Department provides a leaflet entitled 'Help for the Handicapped in Scotland'.

Further Reading
The Disability Rights Handbook (Disability Alliance – *see below*), £8.95 including p & p; £5 to people on any means-tested benefit
From Claim to Appeal: A Guide to Disability Appeal Tribunals for disabled people and their advisors (Disability Alliance), £4 including p & p
Age Concern Factsheet No 34, 'Attendance Allowance and Disability Living Allowance' (*address page 101*)
Help the Aged, 'Claiming Disability Benefits'

Disability Alliance Educational and Research Association
Universal House
88–94 Wentworth Street
London E1 7SA
Tel: 0171–247 8776
Disability Alliance provides information about Social Security benefits to people with disabilities, and also to their families. They do this through the *Disability Rights Handbook*, which is updated every year. They also provide a list of other relevant publications and a telephone advice line; 0171–247 8763

Help for Carers
In addition to the benefits and allowances paid to those who are sick and have disabilities, there are a number of benefits that are available to carers. These benefits do not distinguish whether the person being cared for is a friend or a relative, whether you provide care on your own or jointly and whether it is for a few hours a week or full time.

Invalid Care Allowance (ICA)
ICA is a taxable weekly cash allowance which can be claimed by people of working age who are caring for a person with severe disabilities. The person being cared for must be receiving one of the following three allowances:

1. Disability Living Allowance (at either the higher or middle rate for help with personal care)
2. Attendance Allowance (at either of the two rates)
3. Constant Attendance Allowance (paid at more than the half-day rate under the Industrial Injuries or War Pensions scheme).

ICA is not means-tested and does not depend upon National Insurance contributions paid. It is, however, dependent upon the carer earning less than £50 per week after allowable expenses and spending at least 35 hours per week as a carer.

If the carer has other people to support, such as children or a spouse, he or she may receive more than the basic rate. If the carer is receiving Income Support, Housing Benefit or Council Tax Benefit, he or she will be entitled to a special Carer's Premium. It is as well to ask for advice in this situation, particularly with Income Support, as the rules become quite complex. For example, if a carer is receiving Income Support when he or she starts to receive ICA, the ICA will be taken off the Income Support; however, as a result of Carer Premium being added on, the carer will be better off.

ICA may be claimed, subject to certain conditions, irrespective of whether the carer is related to or living at the same address of the person being cared for.

To claim, a claim pack DS700 should be obtained from the local Benefits Agency (Social Security) office or Citizens Advice Bureau.

For further information see DSS leaflet FB 31, 'Caring for Someone'.

Home Responsibilities Protection (HRP)

If someone during their working life is unable to work because they have to stay at home to look after a sick, disabled or elderly person, they may be able to get Home Responsibilities Protection. HRP ensures that that person is not penalised for the fact that they are unable to pay sufficient National Insurance contributions to enable them to earn the basic Retirement Pension.

The rules for getting HRP are:
- the carer must be regularly engaged for at least 35 hours a week in caring for someone who receives one of these three benefits:
  the Disability Living Allowance care component (at the highest or middle rate)
  Attendance Allowance for a minimum of 48 weeks in the year
  Constant Attendance Allowance

or
- the carer must be receiving Income Support, and not be required to be available for employment because of the care duties at home.

If the carer receives Income Support he or she will receive HRP automatically. If the person being cared for receives Attendance Allowance or Constant Attendance Allowance, the carer needs to apply for HRP by obtaining form CF411 from a Benefits Agency (Social Security) office.

Further Information

For more information, see DSS leaflet NP 46, 'A Guide to Retirement Pensions' and leaflet FB 31, 'Caring for Someone'. Also see the notes that come with Form

CF 411, 'Home Responsibilities Protection' (from local Social Security offices). These notes explain how the HRP scheme works, and provide assistance in working out which years HRP may be needed for.

Council Tax Benefit (CTB)

Anyone receiving Income Support does not have to pay Council Tax. It is also possible to get help with Council Tax even if your income or capital is considered too high for you to get Income Support. The help is called Council Tax Benefit, and is worked out in a similar way to Income Support.

The amount of help individuals are entitled to depends upon the amount of money that they or their partner have coming in, the size of their family, their combined savings, the amount of Council Tax to be paid and whether other dependents share the same home.

To work out the amount of benefit to which you may be entitled you must:
- Work out the maximum Council Tax for which you can receive benefit – currently 100 per cent.
- Deduct amounts if there are people living in your home who are not children or your partner.
- Calculate your net applicable amount as for Income Support.
- Calculate your net weekly income in the same way as for Income Support.
- Add up the value of your savings in exactly the same way as for Income Support. The only difference is that the maximum amount of savings that you can have before CTB is no longer available is £16,000. If your savings are between £3,000 and £16,000 the benefit will be reduced accordingly.

If your income is the same or less than the applicable amount you will normally receive the maximum benefit. If your income is more than your applicable amount, the maximum benefit could be reduced by a 'taper' adjustment.

If you are receiving Income Support, CTB can be claimed at the same time. A form to claim CTB is included with the IS claim form. The office dealing with your claim will pass the form directly to the council. If you are not on Income Support but you believe that you might be eligible for CTB, contact the local council (or regional council in Scotland).

Further Information

DSS leaflet CT B1, 'Help with the Council Tax' (also available in Welsh)
DSS leaflet RR 2, 'A Guide to Housing Benefit and Council Tax Benefit'
A similar leaflet (referred to as CT B2) is also available in the following languages: Arabic, Bengali, Chinese, Greek, Gujarati, Hindi, Punjabi, Somali, Turkish, Urdu, Vietnamese.
Help the Aged, 'Can you Claim It?', or call their SeniorLine free on 0800 289 404.
Age Concern Factsheet No 17, 'Housing Benefit and Council Tax Benefit' (*address page 101*).

Second Adult Rebate

This is a special Council Tax Benefit which can be claimed in some cases when the individual responsible for paying the Council Tax has too high an income to receive CTB. It is called Second Adult Rebate and can be claimed by someone who is single but has another person(s) living in his or her home who meets specific conditions. This other person must be:
- aged 18 or older
- not paying rent
- not living as though married with the claimant
- not paying Council Tax him- or herself
- on a low income.

If the person living in the house is on Income Support, it is possible to claim a rebate of 25 per cent of the Council Tax. If his or her gross income is £111 or less per week, it is possible to get a rebate of 15 per cent of the Council Tax. A 7.5 per cent rebate will be obtained if the total gross weekly income of the second person is between £111 and £144.99 per week.

The rebate will not be given if:
- the person liable for Council Tax is receiving rent from someone living in the home
- the second adult is him- or herself liable to pay the tax as joint tenant or owner
- there is more than one person liable to pay the Council Tax.

If you wish to find out more or believe that you may be eligible, you should contact the local council or the Citizens Advice Bureau.

Housing Benefit

In the same way that people are eligible for Council Tax Benefit, so certain people who are tenants may receive help with their rent. This help is called Housing Benefit (or sometimes rent rebate or rent allowance) and is calculated in a similar way to Council Tax Benefit, except that net weekly rent, rather than weekly Council Tax, is used to determine the extent of the benefit.

The benefit is calculated in a complicated manner, but can basically by calculated by determining whether your income is less than the amount that it is deemed to require to live on.

If you are on Income Support, Housing Benefit may be claimed at the same time, as with Council Tax Benefit. The Benefits Agency (Social Security) office will pass the information to your local council. If you are not on Income Support but you believe that you might be in a position to claim Housing Benefit, you should go to the local council for assistance.

Housing Benefit is awarded for limited periods which are set by the council. A fresh claim must be made at the end of each period.

Further Information

DSS leaflet RR 1, 'Housing Benefit: Help with your Rent' – available from council offices

DSS leaflet RR 2, 'Guide to Housing Benefit and Council Tax Benefit' –

available from a Social Security office
Help the Aged, 'Can you Claim It?', or call their SeniorLine free on 0800 289 404
Age Concern Factsheet No 17, 'Housing Benefit and Council Tax Benefit' (*address page 101*)
Age Concern Factsheet No 21, 'The Council Tax and Older People'

Local Services
If you have a disability you might benefit from the special range of services provided by your local authority's Social Services Department. For instance, the Social Services Department may help with:

- bus and train fares
- special equipment and aids or adaptations to the home
- home helps
- day centres
- residential accommodation
- laundry
- holidays
- meals on wheels
- provision of telephone and television
- advice from a social worker.

Local councils will generally also provide a number of other services for the older person. For further information *see Chapter 3* of this book or ask at your local Citizens Advice Bureau or your local council's Social Services Department.

Also available from the local Benefits Agency (Social Security) office is the *Door to Door Guide*, for information about transport for people with disabilities, published by the Department of Transport. British Rail also produces a leaflet available from all stations, entitled 'The Railcard for Disabled People'. *See also Chapter 10 of this book.*

Some local transport services offer free or reduced price travel on buses or the London Underground. In addition, anyone over 60 can buy a British Rail Senior Citizens Railcard, allowing the holder to buy some tickets at a reduced price. Enquire from British Rail Information Offices, London Regional Transport or your local bus service company. *For further information, see Chapter 10 (page 189).*

Assistance with Home Repairs

Many older people, whose income is low, find it difficult to finance necessary repairs to their home. Although it can be difficult to find help, there are several sources which are always worthy of consideration.

The Local Authority should be able to give grants for certain qualifying types of work. Those with a low weekly income or those who have a disability qualify for grants. Applications should be made to the Local Authority, and assistance may be obtained from home improvement housing agency services, which exist in some areas. These agencies, which are sometimes called 'Care & Repair' or 'Staying Put', can help you work out exactly how much you may be entitled to and how much you would be expected to contribute. To find whether there is an agency in your area, contact the council's renovation grants section or the national office of Care & Repair at:

Care & Repair Ltd
Castle House
Kirtley Drive
Nottingham NG7 1LD
Tel: 0115 979 9091

Assistance for other types of work may be available from the Social Fund (*see page 121*) or from the Home Energy Efficiency Service (*see below*). Alternatively you may be able to obtain assistance towards smaller repair work from a charity or trust fund. You can find out about these from your local library, or alternatively from a local Age Concern group or Council for Voluntary Service. There is also an organisation called Charity Search (*address page 127*) which gives advice on any established charities which may be able to help.

If you are unable to obtain assistance from the above sources, you can always revert to obtaining a loan from a bank or building society. In some cases certain building societies are willing to provide interest-only loans to older people. If there is a Care & Repair or Staying Put in your area, they may be able to put you in touch with one of these building societies.

Further Reading
Age Concern Factsheet No 13, 'Older Home Owners – financial help with repairs' *(address page 101)*

Home Energy Efficiency

The Home Energy Efficiency Scheme (HEES) provides grants to cover the cost of making your home warmer by way of loft, pipe and hot water tank insulation, and draughtproofing. Run by the Energy Action Grants Agency, it is funded by the Energy Efficiency Office, Department of the Environment. Anyone over 60 who owns or rents their own home is eligible. For further information contact:

Energy Action Grants Agency
FREEPOST
PO Box 1NG
Newcastle upon Tyne
NE99 2RP
The Agency also has a Freephone number on which you can speak to the Enquiries Officer: 0800 181 667

Help with draughtproofing and insulation may also be obtained from local advice agencies or by writing to:

Neighbourhood Energy Action
St Andrews House
90-92 Pilgrim Street
Newcastle upon Tyne NE1 6SG
Tel: 0191 261 5677

For further information on heating, *see* Income Support (*above*) and Social Fund (*below*). There is also a factsheet (No 1), 'Help with Heating', available from Age Concern (*address page 101*)

Free NHS Prescriptions

All persons over retirement age automatically get free NHS prescriptions. Any person (or his or her partner) on Family Credit or Income Support receives free NHS dental treatment, wigs and fabric supports, prescriptions and vouchers for glasses. For further information *see Chapter 2* of this book.

People on a low income who are not on Income Support may, under certain circumstances, also receive some benefits free or at reduced cost. You will need to complete a Form AG1, which can be obtained from a Benefits Agency Office, Health Benefits Unit, GP surgeries and dentists, opticians and at NHS hospitals. The form should be sent to:

Health Benefits Division
Sandyford House
Newcastle upon Tyne
NE2 1DB

War and service pensioners may get additional assistance with glasses and dental treatment, and may receive assistance with other NHS charges for their pensioned disability.

Further Information
AB 11, 'Help with NHS Costs'
D 11, 'NHS Dental Treatment'
H 11, 'NHS Hospital Travel Costs'
P 11, 'NHS Prescriptions'
G 11, 'NHS Sight Tests and Vouchers for Glasses'
WF 11, 'NHS Wigs and Fabric Supports'
These leaflets, prepared by the Department of Health, are available at any GP's surgery and from some libraries; AB 11 is also available from some post offices; all are also available from:

The Health Publications Unit
No 2 Site, Heywood Stores
Manchester Road
Heywood
Lancs OL10 2PZ

Additional information is provided in Chapter 2 of this book.

Community Care

Community Care is the name given to the various kinds of care and support provided for people who need help and support because they are ill, frail or have a disability. It is designed to help people to live in as independent a manner as possible in their own homes; where this is not possible, it can offer alternative care facilities in a residential or nursing home. These services may be provided:
  by the National Health Service – through, for example, a family doctor
  the Local Authority's Social Services Department – through, for example, day centres, home care services and meals on wheels
  residential care homes or nursing homes
  voluntary or private organisations providing a large range of care.
In the context of Local Authority, I mean one of the following, whichever is applicable in your area:
  a County Council
  a Metropolitan Borough (or District)
  a London Borough.
From April 1993 significant changes were made to the way Community Care services are provided; these changes have had far-reaching effects, particularly for older people who previously went directly into residential care or a nursing home and claimed Social Security to cover the cost. The Council's Social Services Department now has a duty to assess what help should be given to people who need care services, and for making arrangements for this help. For instance, by making an arrangement for you to enter a residential or nursing home, the local authority takes legal responsibility for paying the fees, and will have a contract with the care home if it is not actually run by them. The local authority will collect from you as much as they deem you able to pay. Anyone who has savings of more than £8,000 will be expected to pay the full fees. For further information, see Social Fund – Community Care Grants (*pages 122–3*).

Who Is Entitled to Community Care Services?
The services are available for people who:

- are over pensionable age and have become frail
- have a substantial and permanent disability
- are blind, deaf or dumb
- have a serious mental illness
- are chronically ill
- are looking after someone in any of the above groups.

How Do You Get Community Care Service?
If you think you qualify for services, you or your principal carer can contact the local Benefits Agency (Social Services) office. An assessment is then carried out to find out about your needs and preferences, and to work out with you what help you may need. If you are then found to be eligible for assistance a summary of your needs will be agreed with you and a care plan will be drawn up, which may include just one service, such as meals on wheels, or a number of services.

Impact of the Community Care Act 1993

By the year 2000, it is estimated that there will be 1 million people over the age of 85 living in this country, of which over 25 per cent will need institutional care in some way. Since the Community Care Act 1993, many more people are being obliged to finance the cost of the care themselves. In most cases, anyone with savings of over £8,000 will not receive assistance towards the cost of residential care or nursing homes. This fact has not yet been registered by many older people, who believe that the State will automatically pay the bill. There are a number of private schemes which assist people to plan for the eventuality that they will require long-term care towards which the State will not contribute. (*See* Long-term Care Insurance, *pages 139–41*, and Raising Capital from your Home, *pages 144–7*).

Further Information

Age Concern Factsheet No 10, 'Local Authority charging procedures for residential and nursing home care'

Age Concern Factsheet No 11, 'Preserved Rights to Income Support for residential and nursing homes'

Age Concern Factsheet No 29, 'Finding Residential and Nursing Home Accommodation'

All are available from Age Concern (*address page 101*)

The Social Fund

The Social Fund was created to help people in need to be able to meet exceptional expenses that they could not provide out of regular income. There are two kinds of benefit: grants that are available by right (if the law says that a payment should be made, anyone who is eligible will receive it) in certain prescribed circumstances, and also interest-free loans and Community Care grants which enable certain priority groups to lead independent lives within the community, which are discretionary rather than paid by right. Grants do not usually have to be repaid, whereas the loans do.

The right to help from the Social Fund does not depend upon National Insurance contributions having been paid, but means-testing is used.

Payments by Right

These payments are grants and do not have to be repaid. They cover three areas:
1. cold weather payments
2. funeral payments
3. maternity payments.

I will only discuss the first two here, as the third is unlikely to be relevant for the readers of this book.

Cold Weather Payments

Cold Weather Payments of £6 per week are paid to persons receiving Income Support which includes one of the following premiums:

- a pension because the person or his or her partner is over 60
- a disability premium
- a disabled child premium because his or her child is getting either Attendance Allowance or is registered as blind.

The payments are made whenever the forecast for the local area shows that the temperature is likely to be 0°C/32°F or below for a period of seven days or more. The payments are automatically sent to each eligible person, so no claim has to be made. Your local Benefits Agency (Social Security) office will tell you if the temperatures are sufficiently low to enable them to make the payments, and they will put a notice in the local paper which will tell you which postcodes are affected. If, however, no payment is received within one month of the announcement of the cold weather, contact your local Benefits Agency (Social Security) office.

For further information see leaflet CWP 1, 'Extra Help with Heating Costs When It's Very Cold'. Available from all Benefits Agencies or Citizens Advice Bureau.

Age Concern also produces Factsheet No 1, 'Help with Heating'.

Help the Aged produces a free advice leaflet called 'Keep Out the Cold'. You can also obtain free advice through their SeniorLine on 0800 289 404.

Funeral Payments

Funeral Payments are limited to people with specified low-income benefits such as Income Support. Each benefit is to assist towards the cost of a simple funeral, and will include such things as the cost of an ordinary coffin, a car for the coffin and another for the mourners and the fees for the undertaker and the church or crematorium. Claims for a funeral must be made within three months after the date of the funeral; forms are available from Benefit Agency (Social Security) offices. The benefits are reduced if the savings of the person or partner of the person claiming are in excess of £500 for people aged under 60 and £1,000 for people aged 60 and over. Although the payment is not a loan, it is repayable out of the estate of the deceased.

For further information see DSS leaflet D 49, 'What to Do after a Death' (Funeral Payments).

Discretionary Payments

Discretionary payments from the Social Fund are determined by local Benefits Agency (Social Security) offices. There is no legal framework of entitlements; decisions about payments are taken by Social Fund officers acting under the directions and guidance issued by the Secretary of State. As a limited amount of money is made available by the Government, each DSS office is provided with a fixed amount which they are able to distribute. If, for instance, they pay all the available money out in the first six months of the year, all subsequent applications, regardless of their severity, may have to be turned down. As each area can apply the rules differently it is important to seek advice from an advice agency or your local Citizens Advice Bureau.

There are three types of payment:
1. Community Care Grants
2. Budgeting Loans
3. Crisis Loans.

Community Care Grants
These grants are intended to help certain groups of people who are facing special difficulty or hardship to lead independent lives in the community. Primarily they are aimed to assist individuals and families such as the elderly, handicapped, chronically ill or disabled. *For further information, see chapters 3 and 4 of this book.*

Grants may be awarded to help those establishing themselves in the community after they have come out of hospital, care or other institution. They may also be awarded to keep people within the community living in their own homes. In certain cases the grants may be awarded to ease exceptional pressures on families as a result of long-term illness or family breakdown.

The grants may cover the cost of a variety of household items such as furniture, bedding and clothes. In certain circumstances they may also cover removal costs, minor house repairs or travelling expenses – to attend a relative's funeral, for instance, or visit someone who is ill. Grants are not available for expenses that the local authority has a statutory duty to meet.

Community Care Grants are only available to people on Income Support or to those who expect to be on Income Support when they move into the community. If the person to receive the grant, or that person and his or her partner, has savings of over £1,000 (£500 for those under 60), the grant will be reduced by the extra amount of the savings.

The Community Care Grant is not a loan and does not have to be repaid.

To apply for a Community Care Grant, ask the local Benefits Agency (Social Security) office for Form SF 300.

Budgeting Loans
Budgeting Loans are interest-free loans that are available to people who have been receiving Income Support for at least six months. They are available to help spread large one-off costs for essential and expensive items over a longer period.

A loan might be made to allow the recipient to purchase essential household furniture, such as a cooker or bed, or to pay for essential repairs or removal expenses. Loans are not available for fuel bills or general housing costs (although certain exceptions are made when intermittent costs are not met by Housing Benefit or Income Support).

The minimum loan is £30 and the maximum that may be outstanding at any one time is £1,000. If the applicant for the loan (together with his or her partner) has savings of over £1,000 (£500 for those under 60) the loan will be reduced by the excess.

A Budgeting Loan is interest-free and repayable. The Social Fund Officer who approves the loan must ensure that the person receiving it can afford to repay it, usually by weekly deductions from the Income Support for up to 18 months. The rate of deduction (normally between 5 per cent and 15 per cent per week) is based upon an individual's income and general circumstances. If Income Support is stopped, the loan becomes immediately repayable.

Two important pieces of advice need to be heeded before applying for a Budgeting Loan:
1. Apply for a Community Care Grant rather than a Budgeting Loan.
2. If a Community Care Grant is not given for the item or service needed, seek advice from the local Citizens Advice Bureau before applying for a Budgeting Loan.

Crisis Loans

Crisis Loans are to help people with immediate short-term expenses that have arisen as the result of an emergency or a disaster. They may only be claimed if there is no other way of preventing serious risk or damage to the health or safety of your family. To claim the loan it is not necessary to be on Income Support or to receive any other form of benefit, although any money that the person may have is taken into account when the claim is assessed.

Loans have been given, for instance, in circumstances where people have lost their money, lost their belongings in a fire or have been stranded away from home.

The loans can cover both living expenses (usually for up to 14 days) or something that is needed urgently such as household equipment or travel costs. Loans are not available for such things as holidays, mobility needs, televisions, telephones or motor vehicle costs (except for emergency travelling expenses).

The loan is interest-free but repayable, either by weekly deductions from benefit or in some other way. The rate and period of repayment are based upon available income and other general circumstances.

To apply for a Crisis Loan you should contact the local Benefits Agency (Social Security) office, or the nearest one if you are away from home at the time of need.

For further information on the Social Fund, see the following DSS leaflets:
SFL 2, 'How the Social Fund Can Help You'
SB 16, 'A Guide to the Social Fund'

Counsel and Care produce a leaflet called 'The Social Fund for Older People'. Their address is on *page 127* of this chapter.

Reviews and Appeals

If someone has applied for a Community Care Grant, Budgeting Loan or a Crisis Loan and is not happy with the decision, he or she can ask for the Social Fund Officer to look at the application again. You must ask in writing within 28 days of the decision having been made on the original application for this review to take place.

If a satisfactory reply is not received to the review, it is possible to ask the Inspector of the Independent Review Service for the Social Fund to look at your application. This should be done within 28 days of the review decision by the

Social Fund Officer. The Inspector is independent of the DSS. The local Benefits Agency (Social Security) office should be contacted if you wish to apply to the Inspector.

If someone has applied for a Funeral Payment and is not happy with the decision, it is possible to appeal. Also if a person thinks he or she should have had a Cold Weather Payment, he or she can appeal. To appeal it is necessary to write to the local Benefit Agency (Social Security) office within three months of the decision, giving reasons why an appeal is justified.

Further information on reviews and appeals:
Leaflet NI 246, 'How to Appeal'
Leaflet NI 260, 'A Guide to Reviews and Appeals'
Leaflet IRS/1, 'Your Social Fund Request – Still not satisfied?'
Copies of leaflet IRS/1 may be obtained by writing to the

Independent Review Service
4th Floor
Centre City Podium
5 Hill Street
Birmingham B5 4UB

Money Advice and How to Deal with Problems
Anyone who is on Income Support can obtain free advice on how to manage money. This advice could be of help to those who often find themselves in financial difficulty. A discussion can be arranged at home or at the local Benefits Agency (Social Security) office. The objective will be to find a way to balance income and outgoing. If required, assistance can also be given in negotiating on the person's behalf with people to whom he or she owes money.

For further assistance or for those in debt, refer to Chapter 7 (the section headed 'Debt'). In it is an explanation of what can be done if someone is in severe financial difficulty. Two organisations, National Debtline and Money Management Council, are available to help. Their addresses and telephone numbers are provided (*see page 164*).

Further information is provided in *Thinking about Money*, a free booklet published by Help the Aged in association with the Birmingham Settlement. It aims to show a person how to assess the present financial situation and how to stretch limited resources by preparing a balanced personal budget.

Credit Unions
These are self-help money co-operatives which are run almost entirely by volunteers. They are organised by groups of people who must have a common bond, which is either social (they belong to the same local organisation, church or club), communal (they live in the same small area) or work-related (they share the same workplace). Their purpose is to provide a means to obtain credit at low cost. The members of a Credit Union will save together; members who have saved regularly then qualify for a loan which might have an annual interest rate of less than

half of the APR of a high street lender. It is possible for a member to borrow up to five times their savings (with a current maximum of £5,000), although they must continue to save whilst repaying the loan.

Credit Unions have a wide appeal, although less than one in 300 people belong to one (compared to more than one in 3 in countries such as Canada and Ireland). They are as suitable for people on middle incomes, as reflected by the fact that one third of the police in the West Midlands belong to a scheme, as for those on low incomes.

Recent recommendations by the Department of Trade and Industry could mean that a more prosperous future lies in store for the 400 unions that currently exist within the country. Proposals include the raising of the ceiling on loans from £5,000 to 1.5 per cent of the total liabilities of the union, and the broadening of the definition of the common bond that must exist between the members. One of the restrictions on expansion has also been the lack of suitably trained volunteers; the National Consumer Council has proposed that official training systems are established, and is intending to lobby local authorities to provide funding to get unions started.

A compensation fund is also being set up, which will require that each credit union will pay a proportion of its funds (1–2 per cent) into the scheme, which will be run by a limited company. It will guarantee that 75 per cent of a member's savings will be reimbursed in the event of the failure of a Union.

Further information about Credit Unions and how to set them up, or which ones might be in your local area, is available from:

Association of British Credit Unions Ltd
Unit 307
Westminster Business Centre
339 Kennington Lane
London SE11 5QY
Tel: 0171–582 2626

National Federation of Credit Unions
Unit 1.1 & 1.2
Howard House Commercial Centre
Howard Street
North Shields
NE30 1AR
Tel: 0191–257 2219

Charities

There are a number of other organisations which may also be available to help anyone who is in severe financial difficulty. Most will expect that anyone approaching them has already tried the normal statutory sources and family connections.

There are many charities. It is necessary to identify the ones most relevant to you by way of background or individual needs. For instance, if you have a disability it will be better to identify a charity that is associated with that particular disability or with the disease that causes the disability.

There are a large number of charities that are set up to look after members of a particular group and their families. These include trade and professional organisations, welfare societies tied up to a particular religion such as Jewish Care (*see below*), or those for people with a professional or similar background such as the Distressed Gentlefolk's Aid Association (*see below*). Finally there are national charities whose objectives are specifically identified with the needs of the elderly or those with disabilities, such as Counsel and Care for the Elderly (*see below*).

Some of these organisations provide continuing support for an individual, while others provide only a one-off grant. However, once a decision is made to approach them, it is advisable to see if a doctor or local social worker can support your application.

Charitable and other organisations that might assist you include:

Charity Search
25 Portview Road
Avonmouth
Bristol BS11 9LD
Tel: 0117 982 4060
Charity Search is a free advisory service for elderly people in genuine financial difficulties, introducing them to charities that might help them.

The Association of Charity Officers
c/o RICS Benevolent Fund Limited
First Floor
Tavistock House North
Tavistock Square
London WC1H 9RJ
Tel: 0171–383 5557
The Association keeps a directory of about 250 member charities, many of whom are professional and trade benevolent funds. They will try and assist enquirers to locate sources of help.

Counsel and Care for the Elderly
Lower Ground Floor
Twyman House
16 Bonny Street
London NW1 9PG
Tel: 0171–485 1566 (10.30 a.m. – 4 p.m.)
Counsel and Care is a national service for elderly people. It provides information and advice to older persons and those concerned with their care and welfare on nearly any relevant matter. It also provides, if possible, lump sum grants to improve the quality of life of older people.

Distressed Gentlefolk's Aid Association
Vicarage Gate
London W8 4AQ
Tel: 0171–229 9341
This charity assists people of a professional or similar background in one of two ways. It helps them to stay at home or in a private home when they do not have the means to do so under their own resources. It also runs a number of homes offering both residential and full nursing facilities.

Jewish Care
221 Golders Green Road
London NW11 9DW
Tel: 0181–458 3282
Jewish Care offers many assistance programmes including residential and nursing homes and sheltered housing schemes for Jewish people.

Society for the Assistance of Ladies in Reduced Circumstances
Lancaster House
25 Hornyold Road
Malvern
Worcs WR14 1QQ

National Benevolent Institution
61 Bayswater Road
London W2 3PH
Tel: 0171–723 0021
Provides assistance to older professional and semi-professional persons.

Independent Living 1993 Fund
PO Box 183
Nottingham NG8 3RD
Tel: 0115 942 8191
The Fund is designed to help people who have very severe disabilities to stay in their own homes. Anyone under 65 who receives at least £200 per week from the Social Services is eligible to apply.

INVESTMENTS AND OTHER FINANCIAL ADVICE

The need for careful financial planning does not cease when you reach pensionable age, as the average person is expected to live for at least 20 more years. Things may seem fine at the time of retirement, with reduced cost of living and regular outgoings. Most people will have contributed sufficiently during their working life to receive some form of pension, and may have even accumulated some capital by the time they retire. However, if you live for a long time, the effects of inflation may effectively reduce your income.

Unfortunately, living longer does not necessarily mean staying as healthy. It is more likely as you grow older that you will need more care as a result of illness or disability. Government statistics reveal that over 70 per cent of people over the age of 80 have some form of disability and one in five over 80 have some form of senile dementia. In the year to April 1993, over £6.5bn was spent by the Government on caring for people over the age of 65. It is perhaps not surprising that Government policy is such that you are now expected to meet the cost of care yourself.

In this section I examine the options that face people in deciding how to invest and how to cater for their current and future needs. I will also look in general terms at certain types of investment and at different types of plans and schemes to provide flexibility and maintain security in old age. Finally I consider how an investor should seek out the right advisors and what protection and compensation schemes are available to them.

None of the companies or types of investment mentioned in this book should be considered to be recommended as to its suitability. The inclusion of a name or product of any company in this book is not an endorsement by myself of that company or product. Each individual wishing to invest or make a decision on savings must use the necessary due care and diligence before taking advice and proceeding with an investment. Although I can advise on what precautionary steps to take before investing, it must be remembered that a type of investment or saving plan suitable for one person may be totally inappropriate for another. Once the assistance of an authorised advisor has been sought, and he or she has been provided with all of the relevant information about your affairs, he or she will supply advice. The final decision on the type of savings plan or investment then lies with the person whose money is being invested. If you remain in doubt, see another advisor.

The Choice Facing Investors

Generally the desire to receive a regular income is the most important consideration for anyone who has retired or is about to retire, while at least maintaining their capital base. Investing for income is in many ways more difficult than investing for capital. With the latter a broad-based approach with a wide enough spread of exposure is likely to produce the required returns given enough time. It is much harder to produce a high yield with good prospects of growth in both income and capital without taking undue risks.

Before deciding what type of investment is most likely to meet his or her requirements, an investor must consider five fundamental points:
1. taxation
2. risk
3. inflation
4. returns
5. future requirements.

Taxation
A saver or investor must choose a scheme of investment or saving that is appropriate to his or her tax position.

Risk
No investor should accept a higher level of risk than they can comfortably cope with and afford. For instance, although the stock market, which provides a higher risk than a bank deposit, may produce good returns over a long period of time, it does fluctuate and if money is needed in a hurry, the investor might have to sell when the market is down.

Inflation
An investor who is concerned about the risk to his or her capital, and at the same time requires income, might decide to invest all of his or her capital into a Building Society or National Savings account. Although both the investor's criteria are met by this action, if there is inflation at the same time there is no growth allowed for in the capital to combat its effects. Even with inflation at a 25-year low, an annual income that is sufficient in 1996 will almost certainly not suffice in 2006.

Returns
An investor who forgoes risk will generally expect a lower return than one who accepts an element of risk. However, in the early 1990s the Building Societies cut the rate on their monthly income accounts (still the most popular home for older people's savings) by over two thirds. Although the net return may still be higher than the rate of inflation, monthly income from these accounts fell dramatically

and has not yet risen to the type of levels seen previously. This has meant that many people who rely on their income from this type of saving are suffering additional hardship.

Future Requirements

If an investor is aware of or concerned with any future event that might require a sizable financial commitment, it is often better to plan specifically for it in advance.

The information contained below is a summary of some of the investment options available. It is followed by a section outlining some of the types of scheme that have been put together by financial institutions specifically for the older generation. The information is not intended to and should not take the place of considered professional advice which takes into account the actual requirements and the current financial situation of the investor.

Investment in Shares (directly or by other means)

Shares in Companies

Shares are issued by companies to allow that company to finance expenditure. By owning a share, the investor is entitled to participate in the performance of the business. Although the owner or shareholder may participate in profits by receiving dividends (a sharing of a portion of the current profits, paid at the discretion of the directors) and in an increasing share price, there is no guarantee how the company will perform or that dividends will be paid. The investor will buy the shares from a stockbroker at a given price, quoted for that day. The share price might rise (principally if the company performs well) or it might fall. Although the investor can never lose more than he invests (assuming he avoids the very high-risk areas of option and futures trading) it is possible to lose the whole value of the investment if, for example, the company is put into liquidation.

The value of shares fluctuate, sometimes wildly. One of the primary principles to be followed by an investor when making any form of investment is the need to spread the risk. If an investor puts all of his or her money into only one or two shares (a course of action that is strictly *not* recommended), the overall performance of the portfolio is purely tied to those shares; even though the overall market is increasing strongly, his or her shares might be falling in value.

The larger investor is able to spread the risk by investing in a wide range of shares.

For the smaller investor there are more suitable means of investing in the performance of companies. Investment trusts and unit trusts, explained below, provide a vehicle by which an investor can participate in the stock market without being exposed to the type of risk that is involved in investing directly into shares. The reason for this is that indirectly the investor has a wide spread of investment. However, neither type of trust is without risk, and some more specialist trusts carry a higher degree of risk than others. Investment in this manner is more suited to the long term.

Investment Trusts

Investment trusts are companies formed purely to deal in other companies' shares. They issue shares themselves which may be bought and sold easily through stockbrokers. An investment in one of these companies represents an indirect investment in the wide range of companies that they have invested in. However, investment trusts are allowed to borrow money and invest in other companies with this money. This 'gearing' tends to enhance the value of the shares in a rising market and depress the value in a falling market. Therefore, the share price of investment trusts can also be very volatile.

Often there are economies in the world that are more attractive than the UK markets. Investment trusts (and unit trusts) are the most economical and risk-averse way of investing in these economies without incurring too great a direct exposure. Emerging market, Pacific Rim, South American, European and US funds are some of the huge variety that are available.

Unit Trusts

Unit trusts also invest in shares in the same way as investment trusts. However, rather than buying shares in a company traded on the Stock Exchange, the investor purchases units in a group of investments that are actively managed by a fund manager. Usually twice a year the unit holder will be allocated a dividend, called a 'distribution', based on the units held. Either a cheque will be paid or the managers will buy more units for the holder, depending upon whether he or she holds 'Income' or 'Accumulation' units. Unit trust prices are quoted in newspapers and do not have to be bought through the Stock Exchange; you may simply contact the managers direct. The names, addresses and telephone numbers of the managers are always quoted above the prices in the financial section of the newspapers.

A special type of unit trust is the Equity-income unit trust, designed specifically for investors interested in income. Investing in them does mean giving up some capital security. One of the oldest, Prolific High Income Fund, has a record of 20 years of rising dividends, with the exception of one year when the dividend remained constant with the previous year. Some of the large trusts produce annual yields of over 9 per cent, although their scope for generating capital growth is limited. However, the gap between the best and worst performing trusts can be huge. A recent survey by Premier (*see below*) revealed that while the top dozen trusts had increased their payouts by 25 per cent over the previous four years, the bottom dozen had decreased by 16 per cent.

Two companies have useful information on equity income trusts:

Premier Unit Trust Brokers
54 Baldwin Street
Bristol BS1 1QW
Tel: 0117 927 9806

Premier produce regular surveys of income unit trusts, tracking their performance and including recommendations.

Hargreaves Landsdown Asset Management Ltd
Embassy House
Queens Avenue
Clifton
Bristol BS8 1SB
Tel: 0117 976 7767
HL produce two 20-page booklets entitled 'Equity Income' and 'Investing in your Fifties'.

Personal Equity Plans – PEPs

PEPs allow individuals to invest up to £6,000 every financial year into equities, unit trusts, investment trusts, corporate bonds, convertibles and preference shares in the UK and European Union provided certain conditions are adhered to. In addition to this general PEP, it is also possible to invest £3,000 into a 'single company' PEP.

All income from dividends and interest earned within the PEP is tax free, and the proceeds are free of Capital Gains.

PEPs must be administered by a manager, who will charge for doing so. The exception is unit trusts, where it costs no more to hold the unit trust in a PEP than outside one; unit trusts do charge in the normal way, which may mean an initial 6 per cent charge and an annual 1.5 per cent charge. It is possible to have a 'self-select' scheme, where you instruct the manager what to buy. If this is what you want, check the charging structure as some have a low dealing charge but an annual fee, whereas others only charge for the administration in reclaiming tax on dividends.

Chase de Vere
63 Lincoln's Inn Fields
London WC2A 3JX
Tel: 0171–404 5766
Chase de Vere publish an annual guide to PEPs, costing £9.95, refundable if you buy a PEP through the firm.

Fixed Income Investments
The safest schemes for savings and investment come from the Banks, Building Societies and National Savings.

Banks and Building Societies

Both have a wide range of savings schemes. Regular interest is paid on capital but there is no chance of making a capital gain.

Interest is normally credited to an account after deduction of tax. It is possible, and advisable, for a non-taxpayer to request that the interest is credited gross. To do this it is necessary to complete Inland Revenue Form R85 available from all banks, building societies and tax offices.

The rates and terms of deposits vary widely. The larger the sum invested and the longer the period this sum is committed for, the greater may be the rate of interest. However, all investors should consider with what regularity the interest will be paid and also for how long they are willing to lock their money into an account. Although money can always be withdrawn from a long-term savings account, there is normally a financial penalty for doing so.

Further Information

Willis Owen Trading as The Building Society Shop
98–100 Mansfield Road
Nottingham NG1 3HD
Tel: 0115 947 2595
The Building Society Shop give free advice in the selection of the highest paying building society accounts. As Independent Financial Advisors they also advise on all aspects of personal investment – from investing capital to maximise income to selecting the best long-term care policy.

National Savings
All National Savings schemes, including even Premium Bonds, offer total security for the capital invested. There are many types of product available; the full range is detailed in the National Savings product leaflet available at most Post Offices. Income Bonds are more suitable for investors who pay no tax, whereas National Savings Certificates and Index-linked Certificates are more suitable for higher rate taxpayers.

Tax Exempt Special Savings Accounts – TESSA
Introduced in the early 1990s by the government, TESSAs enable people to place up to £9,000 over five years (£3,000 in the first year, £1,800 in the subsequent four years) into a deposit account where after the five-year qualifying period the gross interest may be paid free of tax. Net interest may be withdrawn during the five year period, but withdrawal of capital will disqualify the TESSA.

Government Stock (Gilts) and Bonds
Gilts are fixed-interest loan notes issued by the UK Government to finance their expenditure. They are somewhere between National Savings schemes and shares in companies; like National Savings they are backed by the Government, but like shares their value can rise and fall. Bonds are the same fixed-interest investments which are also issued by governments (including HM Government), local authorities and by companies, and are rated according to the quality of the borrower. Bonds issued by third world countries and high-risk companies (junk bonds) should be avoided by all but the most experienced investor.

Fixed-interest bonds should not be confused with the many other types of investment that have appropriated the word bond into their title (*See* Income and Growth Bonds, *below.*)

Gilts and bonds are loans generally issued for a fixed term with a fixed interest rate. The interest rate the gilt or bond pays – called the 'coupon' – relates to its nominal value: for example Treasury 8 per cent 2010 will pay £8 for every £100 invested every year until it is repaid in 2010. As interest rates increase and decrease, the capital value of the gilt also fluctuates because the fixed-interest rate is always based on the nominal value of the gilt. Therefore, a gilt issued for maturity in 2000 with an interest rate of 12 per cent might be quoted at £118, as opposed to a nominal value of £100. This indicates that interest rates are currently lower than 12 per cent (as the capital value of the gilt is higher than £100). If the gilt was bought at £118, the gross yield would approximate to 10 per cent.

There are other types of bond which are index linked, have variable interest rates (floating notes) or even do not pay interest (zero coupon). However, at the end of the day a standard bond or gilt is one of the more vulnerable investments in a period of high inflation. As inflation rises, so do interest rates. The holder of the gilt or bond will then lose out on both capital and income. This can partially be offset by investing in index-linked or variable-rate instruments.

Gilts can be bought through a stockbroker or through the Post Office. The Post Office will not give advice as to which gilts to buy, but the National Savings leaflet 'Government Stock' gives general information on gilts.

Insurance Scheme Investments

Income and Growth Bonds
Income and growth bonds consist of portfolios of Investment Bonds held in a range of Equity, Fixed Interest and Cash Funds managed by leading investment institutions. In many respects they are similar to unit trusts, although care should be taken when investing in them because no basic rate tax is reclaimable on the dividends paid (despite the fact that they are paid 'net') and liquidation of the bonds may lead to a tax liability at one of the higher rates of tax.

With-Profit Bonds
With-Profit Bonds are issued by life assurance companies and offer regular payouts to investors of about between 6 per cent and 8 per cent net of basic rate tax. The bonds are invested in the with-profits funds of life companies. Their advantage is that the capital value is guaranteed on death and the bonds provide regular payouts. However, income levels are not guaranteed and there can be penalties upon encashment.

For more information, contact:

Towry Law
Baylis House
Stoke Poges Lane
Slough
Berks SL1 3BR
Tel: 01753 554400

Towry Law was established over 30 years ago to advise individuals on personal financial planning. They produce a free booklet called 'Over 55? How to make your money work harder & pay less tax in retirement'.

David Aaron Partnership
Shelton House
High Street
Woburn Sands
Milton Keynes
MK17 8SD

Both companies produce reports on with-profit bond investments.

Guaranteed Equity Funds – GEFs

GEFs allow individuals, who consider that the inherent risk in investing directly in shares or unit and investment trusts to be too great, to invest into equities.

In return for accepting a guarantee that the price of the original investment will not fall below a certain level and that the price of the fund will move in line with a pre-selected Index (such as the FTSE 100 Index), the investor forgoes most of the dividend income from the underlying investments and also the potential to perform better than the market. However, each GEF should be looked at carefully; some are better if markets rise in a straight line but lose out if the market has begun to fall when they are to be sold. Others can guard against this by averaging out returns in a predetermined period before they mature.

BESt Investment
4 New Bridge Street
London EC4V 6AA
Tel: 0171–936 2037
BESt produces a monthly report on GEFs and GIBs (*see below*), priced £10.

Guaranteed Income Bonds – GIBs

GIBs provide a fixed guaranteed income over a period with a guaranteed return of capital. Although the rate will usually be a little lower than long-term deposits in a Building Society, the overall yield will remain constant. GIBs provide no hedge against inflation.

Guaranteed Acceptance Policies

Some companies are now selling 'guaranteed acceptance' policies, which are aimed at pensioners and the over-50s. These policies, which are generally non-profit whole-life plans, offer a fixed amount of lifetime insurance cover without the insured needing to undergo any form of medical examination or answer any medical questions. They are protection plans rather than savings plans, and are aimed at people who believe that they are either too old for a normal policy or that the medical will be too detailed and onerous for them. They have been very popular in recent years.

However, if a person is in reasonable health he or she should have no problem taking out an ordinary non-profit whole-life policy, which would give much better value for money.

Annuities

To buy an annuity one pays an insurance company a lump sum, in return for which they will pay a guaranteed income for life or for a specified period.

Annuities therefore play an important part in retirement planning because most individual or small company policies must be converted into an annuity at or after retirement in order to provide the pension income for life. However, when an annuity is purchased, the money used to purchase it will be lost to you and your dependents. If someone aged 85 has £150,000 in investments, the net annual income generated would be approximately £4,500. To earn the same income from an annuity might require a capital outlay of, say £40,000. However, in the first case the £150,000 capital will continue to increase in your own name, whereas any increases in the capital value of the annuity have been factored into the payments to be made to you and will accrue solely to the benefit of the company from which the annuity was purchased.

It is possible to buy escalation annuities which increase by a fixed per cent per annum or inflation-linked annuities. The purpose is that the buying power of the income paid is not constantly diminished with time and inflation. These types of annuity are more expensive, and pay less income per £1 of annuity purchased in the early years. Joint life pension annuities may also be purchased, which allows for an income to be paid to the spouse of the annuitant on his or her death.

When a person is due to retire, the pension company will provide that person with a quotation showing the maximum tax-free cash which is available and the annuity payable. This offer does not have to be accepted because there may be a better annuity rate from another company. In some cases the difference may be significant enough to increase your pension by up to 25 per cent. This Open Market Option allows a person to shop around for a better annuity; there is normally no charge for exercising this option.

Since 1994 the rules governing annuities at retirement were changed to allow greater flexibility to the individual. At the time annuity rates had fallen to their lowest for 30 years, penalising people who were retiring and had to buy annuities. Flexible annuities have now been introduced which mean that people who retire can postpone the purchase of their annuities until they are 75. In the mean time they can draw income from their pension funds, which must be at a rate 'broadly equivalent' to that provided by annuities. One advantage of this is that if the person dies before an annuity is purchased, the value of the pension is returned to his estate. In most cases, annuities 'die' with the annuitant.

For further information contact:

The Annuity Bureau Ltd
Enterprise House
59/65 Upper Ground
London SE1 9PQ
Tel: 0171–620 4090
The Annuity Bureau specialises in annuities market and provides accurate and up-to-date annuity quotations with completely independent advice and service on the purchase of all annuity types. It will send to you free of charge an information pack called 'You and your Annuity'.

Annuity Direct
32 Scrutton Street
London EC2A 4RQ
Tel: 0171–375 1175

'With Profit' Endowment Policies

The maximum age for endowment policies is 65, so they are more suited to those about to retire and in good health who wish to save for a capital sum which will be received tax free after 10 years. The policies are generally low risk, except anyone wanting to sell or surrender the policy before maturity will lose a substantial portion of the terminal value of the policy. Any policy surrendered within the first four years is unlikely to recoup even the value of the money invested in it.

If it is necessary to dispose of them early, it is best to try and sell them through a recognised broker rather than surrender them. It is usually a requirement that the policies have been paid up for more than five years. Your financial advisor will put you in touch with one of these brokers.

Other Useful Contacts

Towry Law Group
Baylis House
Stoke Poges Lane
Slough
SL1 3BR
Tel: 01753 554400

Money Management Council
PO Box 77
Hertford
Herts SG14 2HW
Tel: 01992 503448

Money Management Council is an independent educational charity set up in 1985 to promote education and better general understanding in personal and family finance. Its committee members are drawn from the financial institutions, consumer organisations and the world of education. It operates through help/advice agencies, the financial institutions and the media. It has an extensive reference library of resource materials and produces its own free factsheets on a variety of topics (*see below*). The council also leads money sessions on adult education courses. It does not offer an individual counselling service.

Factsheets

All are free, but a large (A4) stamped addressed envelope is appreciated.
'You and your Money (a general introduction)'
'Savings and Lump Sum Investment'
'Where Can I get Financial Advice?'
'Don't Leave your Money to Chance'
'When Someone Dies'
'Personal Budgeting'
'Independent Taxation (how married women and their husbands can benefit)'
'Watch Out for Fraud'
'Planning your Finances Before You Retire'

Further Reading
Investing for Beginners by Daniel O'Shea (Financial Times Business Information), £11.50
Managing a Lump Sum – A free booklet from Help the Aged which explains in simple language the different types of investments available, explains some investment jargon and the choices open to anyone wishing to invest or save.
Approaching Retirement (Consumers Association), £6.95
Which? Way to Save and Invest (Consumers Association), £12.99
These organisations also produce free publications on their respective types of savings and investments:

British Bankers Association
10 Lombard Street
London EC3V 9AT
Tel: 0171–626 8486

Building Societies Association
3 Savile Row
London W1X 1AF
Tel: 0171–437 0655

Association of British Insurers
51 Gresham Street
London EC2V 7HQ
Tel: 0171–600 3333
For information on insurance-linked schemes.

Association of Investment Trust Companies
6th Floor, Park House
16 Finsbury Circus
London EC2M 7JJ
Tel: 0171–588 5347

Department for National Savings
Marketing and Sales Information Dept
Charles House
375 Kensington High Street
London W14 8SD
Information also available from major post offices.

The Stock Exchange
Public Affairs Department
The London Stock Exchange
London EC2N 1HP

Association of Unit Trusts and Investment Funds
65 Kingsway
London WC2B 6TD

Types of Specialist Product Put Together for the Older Person

Insurance as Part of an Overall Financial Plan
Throughout our lives we tend to take out insurance, whether it is because we are compelled to, such as for our car, or to obtain peace of mind in case of disaster or loss. Everyone must balance up the cost of insurance against the impact of not being insured in case of an event which would trigger a claim.

Older people have in recent years been specifically targeted for certain types of insurance. Companies now specialise in offering insurance to those aged 50 and over for a wide range of cover, which includes long-term care, health, travel, car and household insurance. Often the rates from these companies are far more competitive that from standard sources, because insurers have identified that the over-50s are exceedingly good risks.

Long-term Care Insurance

Twenty-five per cent of people over the age of 85 are in residential care homes. Since the Community Care Act in 1993, anybody entering a residential care or nursing home who has savings of more than £8,000 (generally including the value of their home) will have to meet the cost themselves. This can produce one of the largest expenses of their life, and can create genuine financial problems. The latest figures available reveal that the average annual cost of care in a residential home is £17,000, with the cost in London-based homes exceeding £22,000. Over 60 per cent of those currently in residential care have to meet part or all of the cost themselves.

The problem of financing long-term care is a potentially explosive issue of which many people are unaware or choose to ignore. In the last few years a number of the large financial institutions have put together schemes which allow older persons to plan for the possibility of entering residential care or requiring assistance while remaining at home. As yet these have not proved to be a success with the public, with only 5 per cent planning to provide for care in old age. However, within the next few years it is expected that the take-up on these schemes will increase significantly as people become aware of their benefits.

In principal there are two types of scheme:

Pre-Funding Schemes provide protection against a future need for long-term care. They can be taken out on a regular or single premium basis, with benefits being paid for as long as needed once a claim is accepted. The disadvantage of these plans is that if care is not required the premiums will have been paid for nothing. This has been addressed by some schemes, which incorporate some life insurance cover into the scheme to pay a lump sum to the estate of the deceased. The benefit of the scheme is that it allows peace of mind to those who may need care because they know that at least some, if not all, of the cost has already been taken care of when the need arises. In general a claim can be made when the insured person is no longer able to perform a number of daily living functions without the aid of a third party. Typically these might be washing and bathing, feeding, using the lavatory and general mobility about the house or getting into or out of bed.

Immediate Funding Plans are lump sum plans purchased by someone about to enter care. They are like an annuity and pay a guaranteed level of fees for however long they may be required. The worse that someone's health is, or the older the person, the higher the level of fees paid per £1,000 of premium invested. As with the pre-funding schemes, a capital guarantee can be incorporated into the plan in the event that someone dies relatively soon after taking out the scheme.

Scottish Amicable European

Scottish Amicable European
3700 Solent Centre
Parkway Solent Business Park
Whiteley
Fareham
Hampshire PO15 7AW
Tel: 0171–338–0066

Scottish Amicable European has a unique lump sum solution to the problems of providing for long-term care – a solution which combines care protection, investment of capital and, where appropriate, inheritance tax planning. It also benefits from the tax advantages of Scottish Amicable European's location in Dublin's International Financial Services Centre.

MORTON-WILSON LIMITED
SPECIALISTS IN RETIREMENT CARE

Morton-Wilson Limited
Bridge House
Severn Bridge
Bewdley
Worcs DY12 1AB
Tel: 01299 400488 and also at:
Spinney Grange
Barton Road
Carlton
Nuneaton
Warwicks CV13 0RL
Tel: 01455 291538

Morton-Wilson Limited is a firm of specialist investment advisors who have made a special study of the financial and legal aspects of entering long-term care; they are recognised in the Financial Press as being one of the very few specialist advisors in this field. The company already assists many clients who are in residential care and so has first-hand knowledge of the problems that can arise. They provide a booklet free of charge, 'Financial Considerations on Entering Long Term Care'.

Two types of policy are provided: for those planning now for the practical help they may need in the future should long-term care needs arise, and for those who require long-term care immediately.

Eagle Star Life Assurance Company Ltd
Eagle Star House
Bath Road
Cheltenham
Glos GL53 7LQ
Tel: 01242 221311

Eagle Star have a specialist Care Fees Payment Plan designed to assist paying for long-term care. In return for a lump sum payment it guarantees a series of payments designed to meet care fees as they become due.

Kleinwort Benson
Private Bank
PO Box 191
10 Fenchurch Street
London EC3M 3LB
0171–956 6600

Specialising in a residential care scheme, and in managing the affairs of the elderly.

Asset Financial Planning
FREEPOST (BS2614)
PO Box 106
37 Broad Street
Bristol BS99 7YJ
Tel: 0117 926 3822
Asset, part of National Westminster Insurance Services, has a financial planning service that was devised in conjunction with Age Concern. They are able to advise on a range of topics concerning the elderly, in addition to providing healthcare plans.

Nursing Home Fees Agency
Old Bank House
95 London Road
Headington
Oxford OX3 9AE
Tel: 01865 750665
The NHFA advises potential residents of care homes and their relatives on how best to provide for long-term care fees from resources available, with an aim to protect capital and preserve the ability to pay fees. They will also advise on a care home resident's entitlement and eligibility for state benefit.

Further Reading
'Financing long-term care', a booklet produced by Age Concern (*address page 101*)

Health Insurance

For those who want pure medical insurance that excludes long-term care there are a number of options for the older person from the specialist healthcare companies. However, because of the risk of an increased number of claims, the premium costs tend to rise disproportionately to the rest of the market, regardless of the length of membership of a scheme without claim. BUPA says that the average claim for someone over 60 is on average about 40 per cent higher than the average claim for someone under 60. In 1994 one of the leading insurers raised premiums for the over-60s by 18 per cent, while their average increase for other subscribers was 4 per cent. This level of increase, combined with the loss of higher rate tax relief that was previously available to people over 60, has made the cost prohibitive to many people.

Schemes to take into account a 'no claims' record are being considered by a number of organisations. One way for reducing the level of premiums paid is to accept a higher excess figure, or to look around for schemes which accept lower premiums from people in good health, such as Commercial Union's Health-Wise policy. However, one of the disadvantages of switching schemes is the possible invalidation of claims for conditions or illnesses which had previously been treated or diagnosed.

The Private Health Partnership
8 Manor Square
Otley
West Yorkshire LS21 2NJ
Tel: 01943 851133

An impartial consultancy service on private medical insurance schemes and long-term care schemes. They charge a fee of £10 for detailed consumer information and advice.

WPA (Western Provident Association)
Rivergate House
Blackbrook Park
Taunton
Somerset TA1 2PE
Tel: 01823 623330
WPA, a not-for-profit organisation, offers a range of health insurance schemes for the over-60s. These schemes qualify for tax relief at the rate of 25 per cent.

Commercial Union Assurance Company Ltd
Third Age Initiative
Leon House
11th Floor
High Street
Croydon CR9 1AW
Tel: 0171–283 7500
In conjunction with WPA, Commercial Union provide a 'Health-Wise Insurance' specifically designed for people over 60 who are in good health. A regular medical check-up is required, but the subscriber will be part of a low-risk group, which should mean lower subscriptions. There is no upper age limit for joining.

Private Patients Plan
Senior Health Plan
FREEPOST
PPP House
Upperton Road
Eastbourne
East Sussex BN21 1BR
Tel: 0800 335 555
Medical insurance with guaranteed acceptance; no age limit and no medical check-up required.

Saga Private Healthcare Plan
Saga Services Ltd
FREEPOST CU1121
Folkestone
Kent CT20 1BR
Tel: 0800 484 184
Provide specialist health insurance for the over-60s. Saga also provide a convalescent care scheme in conjunction with Prime Health Ltd, which will provide help, in the form of cash or care, to someone who is convalescing after a period in hospital.

Exeter Friendly Society
Beech Hill House
Walnut Gardens
Exeter EX4 4DG
Tel: 01392 498063
Provide over-50s medical insurance.

Household and Motor Insurance

Older people are more security-conscious and careful with their homes. They are less likely to be burgled because they spend more time at home. They are also less likely to be involved in a motor accident resulting in a claim. Insurance statistics show that while one in five under-30s claims on a household policy, only one in 10 over-50 policy holder claims. Government statistics reveal that while 35 per cent of drivers are over 50, they represent less than 20 per cent of reported accidents involving men and 15 per cent of those involving women.

The over-50s are also likely to be more honest in their claims. According to research carried out by the Centre of the Study of Public Order at Leicester University, 90 per cent of all fraudulent claims are made by those under 45.

A number of major companies, such as Sun Alliance, now offer a discount on household insurance for the over-50s. Others such as Direct Line have raised their maximum no-claims discount from 65 per cent to 70 per cent.

Whatever your individual requirements, it does pay to shop around. All policies should also be reviewed each year to ensure that they are adequate and not vastly in excess of requirement. The names of some specialist companies which will be able to assist include:

SUN ALLIANCE
INSURANCE UK
TOGETHER WE MAKE SOME ALLIANCE

Sun Alliance Insurance UK
National Quotation Centre
Linden House
Horsham
West Sussex RH12 1BT
Tel: 0800 300 800
or contact your nearest branch (details in the Yellow Pages) quoting reference P310XX

Sun Alliance offers special insurance for the over-50s. 'Motorist 50+' rewards the mature careful driver with an average saving of £50 on an annual premium when switching from a previous policy. Sun Alliance is also the largest household insurer in the UK, with a wide range of cover at highly competitive prices. Special discounts are given to the over-50s who, Sun Alliance believes, take better care of their homes.

Age Concern Insurance Services
Garrod House
Chaldon Road
Caterham
Surrey CR3 5YZ
Tel: 01883 330330
Provide a wide range of general insurance for the older person.

CGA Direct
FREEPOST
Horsham
West Sussex RH12 1ZA
Tel: 0800 525 200
Insurance for the older person.

Saga Services Ltd
Saga Group
Middelburg Square
Folkestone
Kent CT20 1AZ
Tel: 0800 484 184
Provide specialist insurance for the older person, covering household, accident, life and motor vehicle.

Severnside Associates
79a Gloucester Road
Bristol BS7 8AS
Tel: 01984 632285
Car, household contents and buildings insurance. Also commercial mortgages, re-mortgages and loans, both secured and unsecured.

Direct Line Insurance
Tel: 0181–686 2468

Retirement Insurance Advisory Service
Tel: 0800 552 100
Car insurance for more mature drivers.

Life Insurance

A number of organisations specialise in providing life cover for older persons, in some cases guaranteeing that no medical check-ups will be required (*see page 135*, Guaranteed Acceptance Policies). By the nature of the potential risk that the insurer is taking on, it may be better for someone in good health to apply for a better rate with a company that does require a check-up.

If you do have life assurance, ensure that it is written in trust. By using this basic form of tax planning the funds paid out on death will not form part of the estate for inheritance tax purposes. Always check with your financial advisor before making any decisions on how to set up the trust and obtain maximum flexibility from it. *For further information see pages 168–70* (Legal – Inheritance Tax Planning).

General Accident
Lifecover Plus
FREEPOST (LE5732)
Leicester LE4 5ZA
Tel: 0800 616 155

The Equitable Life
FREEPOST
Walton Street
Aylesbury
Bucks HP21 7BR

Equity & Law Life Assurance Society plc
20 Lincoln's Inn Fields
London WC2A 3ES
Tel: 0171–242 6844

Friends Provident Life Office
Pixham End
Dorking
Surrey RH4 1QA

Scottish Equitable Life Assurances
28 St Andrew Square
Edinburgh EH2 1YF
Tel: 0131–556 9101

Raising Capital from your Home

The principal asset of many people is their home. This has probably been acquired throughout their years of working when they had a reasonable disposable income. After retirement they are often faced with a conundrum: just as they are beginning to face up to a life of leisure, their income drops (often considerably and particularly in later years if there is no inflation linking with their pension) and their most valuable asset remains in bricks and mortar producing no income.

Many elderly homeowners find themselves in the unenviable position of having insufficient income on which to live while the principal value of what they own is locked up in their house. The only apparent option to many would be to sell their home to raise 'income producing' capital.

However, over 20 years ago a scheme was devised which allows homeowners to release regular income from the capital tied up in their home while remaining *in situ*. These plans are called Home Income Plans. They are made up from several alternative types of scheme, all of which purport to achieve the same objective. Recent experience has shown that some types of plan are less safe and secure than others, although all the poor quality schemes which were sold in the late 80s and which relied on high performing bonds backed by stock market investments have now been banned. As a result of the negative image of Home Income Plans, a group of the main specialist providers of Home Income Plans throughout the UK have collectively launched a Code of Practice called **SHIP** – Safe Home Income Plans.

The Code requires companies to provide a fair, simple and complete presentation of their plans, and as a further safeguard stipulates that the solicitor of a person entering a plan must sign a certificate before proceeding with the Plan to acknowledge that the essential features and implications of the chosen SHIP Plan have been brought to their attention. Any plan offered by the companies affiliated to SHIP guarantee that there are no circumstances in which plan holders will lose their homes, and that if the circumstances of the plan-holder changes, they still have the opportunity to move house. All companies that are bound by the SHIP Code will carry a SHIP logo. Further details of the Code are available from:

SHIP Campaign
Hinton & Wild (Home Plans) Ltd
374 Ewell Road
Surbiton
Surrey KT6 7BB
Tel: 0181–390 8166

Most plans involve either raising a loan against the value of the home, or selling all or part of the property. From the proceeds of the money raised an annuity is bought which can provide guaranteed income for life. Both types of plan are acceptable; which is more suitable depends upon the circumstances of each individual. Anyone considering any plan must consider whether they will retain security of tenure in their house for the reminder of their life, whether they will have the freedom to move house if they wish and whether they will receive a cash sum or assured regular income. There is generally a minimum age for people to be able to participate in the plans. This varies from plan to plan and may depend upon whether the individual is single or married; it is generally between 65 and 80. The property should ideally also be worth at least £40,000 to be able to take advantage of any of the plans.

There are two main types of safe home income plan:

Home Reversion Schemes

Under this scheme the house (or a part of it) is sold to the 'reversion' company, but you (and any surviving partner) retain the legal right to live as tenants for life. You will receive a percentage of the value of the home outright which in turn can be turned into income for life by the purchase of an annuity. This scheme is not a loan, and once you have sold some or all of your property you cannot buy it back. Typically the amount received will be less than 45 per cent of the value, so it is more frequently recommended when the value of the home exceeds £75,000. From these schemes it is possible to link the income generated from the capital raised to the value of the property in future years.

If you retain some of the house, you are able to benefit from any future rise in house prices on that portion.

Mortgage Annuity Schemes

This plan entails a loan (ideally fixed rate interest-only) being taken out against the security of the home. The loan is used to purchase an annuity which repays the interest on the loan and provides a guaranteed income for life. The loan needs to be repaid (from the sale proceeds of the house) when you or your surviving partner dies. There are variations of the scheme which can be entered into. Interest can be rolled up, which can be dangerous when the interest is not fixed and rates rise; also some of the capital sum can be protected against the possibility of the borrower's early death by he or she taking out insurance policies.

Generally the amounts available under the scheme are small as a proportion of the value of the house because of the length of time the plan provider must wait to receive the capital back. Each person considering a Home Income Plan should consider the implications carefully and should obtain proper advice. They should also check whether the companies are registered by the PIA (Personal Investment Authority).

Useful Contacts

Age Alliance
6 Allerton Hill
Leeds LS7 3QB
Tel: 0113 237 0666
Age Alliance assists retired homeowners to raise a tax-free lump sum without risk by selling part or all of their property equity.

Home and Capital Trust Limited
31 Goldington Road
Bedford MK 40 3LH
Tel: 01234 340511
Home and Capital Trust, a member of SHIP, specialises in providing a cash lump sum through the sale of all or part of the property.

Allchurches Life Assurance Ltd
Beaufort House
Brunswick Road
Gloucester GL1 1JZ
Tel: 01452 526265
SHIP member.

Carlyle Life Assurance Co Ltd
21 Windsor Place
Cardiff CF1 3BY
Tel: 01222 371726
SHIP member.

Stalwart Assurance Co Ltd
Stalwart House
142 South Street
Dorking
Surrey RH4 2EU
Tel: 0800 378 921
SHIP member.

The Cash Plan
c/o Johnson Fry plc
20 Regent Street
London SW1Y 4PZ
Tel: 0171–321 0220

Roll Up Loans

There is a further type of loan that is beginning to become available. It involves borrowing a lump sum and rolling up the interest with the principal of the loan. Nothing is repayable until the property is sold, although you can obviously pay some or all of the interest if you choose to do so. These schemes are called Roll Up Loans. At times when interest rates are very high, the amount outstanding on the loan can double every four or five years. In addition, you need to ensure that if the amount of the loan grows to such an extent that it is nearly equal to the value of the house, that you are not forced to sell the house.

For further information contact:

Western Trust and Savings Ltd
The Moneycentre
Plymouth PL1 1SE
Tel: 01752 261161

Further Reading

Using your Home As Capital, Cecil Hinton (Age Concern), £4.50
Updated every year, this explains the different types of Home Income Plan available, the advantages and disadvantages, and also provides a checklist of matters you should consider before taking up a plan.
Age Concern also produce two factsheets:
No 12, 'Raising Income or Capital from your Home'
No 24, 'Housing Schemes for Older People where a Capital Sum is required'. This sheet provides information for many of the older people who want to move home, own their own property or have other assets such as savings, but often do not have enough to buy outright and cannot find suitable rented accommodation.

WHERE CAN YOU FIND FINANCIAL ADVICE?

It is important to ensure that anyone seeking financial advice receives the very best professional advice. However, where can one find a reliable advisor who will give investment advice that is entirely suitable for your needs?

As a simple rule of thumb, a potential investor must consider that the more they are prepared to risk with their investment, the more important it is to seek professional financial advice. For instance, if one is placing money on deposit in a bank it is sufficient to identify the best rate of interest for the amount being deposited. However, if one wishes to invest in the stockmarket or to buy an annuity, one needs to have advice on all of the different options and types of investment that are available.

Independent financial advisors (IFAs) fall into two categories; those who are remunerated by commission, and those who charge fees. Although the quality of the advice should be the same, someone who earns commission is perhaps less likely to recommend products which do not pay commission or only pay a little. There is also less likely to be a conflict between the advisor's need to earn a living and the quality of the advice that he or she gives to the client.

There are many sources of professional advice on finance. The key sources are provided below:

SIB Securities and Investments Board
Gavrelle House
2–14 Bunhill Row
London EC1Y 8RA
Tel: 0171–638 1240
The SIB, which is responsible for controlling the five Self Regulatory Organisations (SROs) listed below, has a comprehensive list of all authorised firms and individual advisors. It also produces a number of free booklets, including:
'The Background to Investor Protection'
'Investment Businesses: what to do if you need to complain'
'The Central Register'
'Compensation for Investors'
'How to Spot the Investment Cowboys'

Money Management Fee-based Advice Register
Financial Times Business Information
Greystoke Place
Fetter Lane
London EC4A 1ND
Tel: 0171–405 6969
Publishers of *Money Management* magazine, they keep a list of fee-based advisors. The complete list costs £1,000, but if you simply want a list of fee-paying advisors in your area state your postcode and a shorter list will be sent free of charge.

Registry of Financial Planning
Institute of Financial Planning
Hereford House
East Street
Hereford HR1 2LU
Tel: 01432 274891
The registry is a free list of IFAs, indicating which are fee based.

IFA Promotion Ltd
4th Floor
28 Greville Street
London EC1N 8SU
Tel: 0171–831 4027
IFAP is a commercial company which promotes independent financial advisors. Over 15,000 firms around the country are registered with IFAP. One can telephone 01483 461461 for a free list of independent financial advisors in one's home or work area. IFAP will also send out a free factsheet called 'Look at how your IFA is paid' and a booklet, *Your Guide to Independent Financial Advice* which details, among other things, the type of question that should be asked by an individual seeking advice for an IFA and what the investor should be looking for.

Self Regulatory Organisations (SROs)

PIA
Personal Investment Authority
Hertsmere House
Hertsmere Road
London E14 4AB
Tel: 0171–538 8860

First recognised in July 1994, PIA was created to regulate business primarily done with or directly for the private investor. It has already taken over much of the work that was previously carried on by FIMBRA and LAUTRO (*see below*) which, at time of going to press, are likely to be de-recognised by the end of 1995. It will also take business from IMRO where such business involves significant amount of retail investment business. By the end of 1995 a large number of investment firms will come under the jurisdiction of the PIA. They will have a complaints procedure for anyone who has bought an investment (including life assurance, personal pensions and unit trusts). They also produce a leaflet, 'How to Complain'.

IMRO
The Investment Management Regulatory Organisation
Broadwalk House
Appold Street
London EC2A 2LL
Tel: 0171–628 6022

IMRO regulates investment managers, including unit trust managers and trustees. Where the organisations are involved in a substantial amount of selling to the general public, the responsibility will now fall under PIA.

SFA
The Securities and Futures Authority Ltd
The Stock Exchange Building
Old Broad Street
London EC2A 2LL
Tel: 0171–256 9000

SFA is responsible for the regulation of those who advise on and deal in shares dealt on the Stock Exchange as well as trading in futures and options. It also covers advisors whose secondary activities are advising on and dealing in unit trusts, futures, investment management and similar investments.

FIMBRA
Financial Intermediaries, Managers and Brokers Regulatory Association
Hertsmere House
Hertsmere Road
London E14 4AB
Tel: 0171–538 8860

FIMBRA regulates the independent intermediaries advising on life assurance, pensions, unit trusts, stocks and shares and financial management. This was the most important organisation for most investors, but by the end of 1995 will have been replaced by PIA.

LAUTRO
The Life Assurance and Unit Trust Regulatory Organisation
Centre Point
103 New Oxford Street
London WC1 1QH
Tel: 0171–538 8860

LAUTRO regulates the marketing of life assurance, pensions and unit trust products. By the end of 1995 it will have been replaced by PIA

Ombudsmen

Banking Ombudsman
70 Grays Inn Road
London WC1X 8NB
Tel: 0171–404 9944

Building Societies Ombudsman
35–37 Grosvenor Gardens
London SW1X 7AW
Tel: 0171–931 0044

The Investment Ombudsman
6 Fredericks Place
London EC2R 8BT
Tel: 0171–796 3065

Recognised Professional Bodies

In addition to the SROs, there are a number of other organisations called Recognised Professional Bodies (RPBs). These regulate, for example, insurance brokers, solicitors and accountants who have obtained authorisation to give advice on investments through their professional body.

The names, addresses and telephone numbers of the five main RPBs are given below.

ACCA – Chartered Association of Certified Accountants
29 Lincoln's Inn Fields
London WC2A 3EE
Tel: 0171–242 6855

IBRC – Insurance Brokers' Registration Council
15 St Helens Place
London EC3A 6DS
Tel: 0171–588 4387

ICAEW – Institute of Chartered Accountants in England and Wales
PO Box 433, Chartered Accountants Hall
Moorgate Place
London EC2P 2BJ
Tel: 0171–628 7060

Institute of Chartered Accountants in Scotland
27 Queen Street
Edinburgh EH2 1LA

Law Societies

Law Society of England and Wales
113 Chancery Lane
London WC1 1PL
Tel: 0171–242 1222

Law Society of Scotland
The Law Society's Hall
26 Drumsheugh Gardens
Edinburgh EH3 7YR
Tel: 0131–226 7411

Other Organisations

BIIBA British Insurance and Investment Brokers' Association
BIIBA House
14 Bevis Marks
London EC3A 7NT
Tel: 0171–623 9043
Provides a list of brokers and consultants.

Types of Advisor

In the past few years, as financial markets have become more complicated and individuals have tended to become more wealthy with more substantial net assets, more people have sought or have tried to seek impartial and expert advice. With the distinctions made after the Financial Services Act 1986 it has become easier to identify the type of advice that one is seeking.

There are now two types of advisor:

The 'tied' agent is tied or linked to a particular company or group of companies which sell financial products. He or she acts on behalf of the seller of the product and will offer advice based on this product range; he or she need not compare the quality of the products with others in the market place.

The Independent Financial Advisor (IFA) is totally independent and therefore by definition should also be impartial. He or she acts on behalf of the buyer of the product (the investor) and should be in a position to offer the best advice from the whole market place; when advising he or she should compare the products of a number of companies before identifying the best product for a client. IFAs are legally bound to obtain specific information about the individual's financial and general circumstances; therefore the more information they have, the better can be the quality of the advice.

All Independent Financial Advisors (IFAs) must be authorised by the PIA. Many insurance brokers, accountants and solicitors will have obtained authorisation through their own professional organisations, called Recognised Professional Bodies (RPBs).

There is no right answer to the question of 'tied' or 'independent' advice; both may give entirely suitable advice. However, the investor should always be clear which he or she is dealing with, and accept that if the advisor is 'tied' the investor will be investing money only in the company to which the advisor is tied.

Having decided which is preferred, the investor should ensure that the advisor is registered with PIA. He should meet the broker or salesperson face to face; it is easier to understand something explained in a meeting than over a telephone, where written examples cannot be shown. After the meeting a written summary of what is being offered should always be requested; if there is anything which remains unclear, answers should be obtained in writing. The broker or salesperson must be fully briefed on all of the investor's circumstances; he or she must, by law, give advice suitable only to the circumstances of the investor.

The advice received by an investor will not come free; both types of advisor are likely to be paid commission on the sale of the investment products. Some may charge the investor a fee, a proportion of which you may get back if the advisor then receives commission from an insurance firm. It is always worth remembering that some forms of investment and types of company pay more commission than others, and since 1 January 1995 all recommendations have to come in writing and must show how much in pounds and pence the salesperson will be making from selling the product. This recommendation must also show what a policy holder will receive if they cash in a specific insurance-related plan early; this allows investors to see how much of their contributions disappear in charges (which do not include just the salesperson's commission) over the first five years and over subsequent years. This Reduction in Yield (RIY) can be significant; an RIY of 1.9 per cent would mean that a policy with annual growth of 8 per cent would yield net 6.1 per cent. This reduction may not sound much, but over a longer period may amount to tens of thousands of pounds.

After 1995 investors now receive far more information than needed to be made available previously, and in addition to the information included in the written recommendation itemised above, a written record of the reasons why a recommendation is made has to be provided to the potential investor either during their meeting or soon afterwards. In addition, all illustrations that are provided must be based on the customer's actual age and circumstances, rather than on general circumstances. The result of this change in legislation means that consumers should receive advice which meets their needs, which they understand and which will result in an investment which delivers the benefits that they are expecting.

Before deciding whether an advisor is suitable, the following questions at least should have been asked and satisfactorily answered:

Questions to Ask an Advisor
1. Are you independent or tied?
2. By which body are you authorised? What are your professional qualifications? These are becoming increasingly important, and by the end of 1995 every independent advisor will be required to hold the Financial Planning Certificate from the Chartered Insurance Institute.
3. How long have you been in the business of providing financial advice, in what areas do you specialise and how many clients do you have?
4. What research facilities do you have to compare investment and insurance products?
5. (If the advisor is fee based): How much will the advice cost per hour, and will all commission be refunded to the customer? How many hours are likely to be needed?
6. (If the advisor is commission-based, how much will the advisor receive (although it is a legal requirement that this information is shown on any recommendation given), and will non-commissionable products (such as National Savings) be recommended?

Questions to Ask Yourself about an Advisor
1. Does the Advisor appear to know what he is doing, and does he show sufficient specialised knowledge about the investments he is recommending?
2. Does the Advisor show that she is interested in my business and would my interests come before her own?
3. Do I feel comfortable with the Advisor, do I understand his charges and will he provide continuity of service?
4. Is the Advisor legitimately carrying on business?

Stockbrokers

The stockbroker is still the main person who actually handles the buying and selling of equities and gilts, whether it be for a private individual or a large pension fund. However, as a new breed of client has sprung up after the Government's privatisation, so stockbrokers have begun to offer a wider range of services.

Advisory Services

There are different levels of advisory service which are basically split into non-discretionary (when you wish to discuss your own ideas with a broker, and you have the final decision) and discretionary (when the broker takes full responsibility for all decisions). The broker will have to know something about you before he or she can make any decisions on your behalf.

Execution-only Services

These services mean that you can buy or sell shares over the telephone or by post. The cost is obviously cheaper than an advisory service. Commission is normally in the region of 1.5 to 2 per cent for the first few thousand pounds, with a minimum charge of between £10 and £25. The commission rate on larger orders can be negotiated down. If you do not know the broker, it is likely that he or she will want the shares that you are selling or the money before you actually buy new shares before he or she will 'deal' for you.

Many banks and building societies allow you to buy and sell shares 'over the counter'.

Nominee Services

Most brokers offer nominee services, which mean that nominees hold investors' shares on their behalf. This takes away the problems of paperwork and share certificates for the investor, and makes the broker certain that everything will be ready when the certificates and paperwork have to be passed over within a few days of executing the sale.

Further Information

Association of Private Client Investment Managers (Apcims)
112 Middlesex Street
London E1 7HY
Tel: 0891 335 521
Apcims will send a 44-page free brochure with an introduction to share buying and thumbnail sketches of its 120 member firms.

General Investor Protection
The Financial Services Act 1986 has ushered in a formidable body of legislation that is designed, among other things, to protect the interests of private investors and ensure that they receive impartial professional advice. This has been done by enforcing stringent controls over companies operating within the financial

services industry.

Enforcement of the regulations is controlled by the Securities and Investment Board. This organisation delegates authority to various bodies called Self Regulatory Organisations (SROs). A list of these, with telephone numbers and addresses, was given in the previous section.

It is the SROs' responsibility to ensure that all their members comply with the complex Conduct of Business Rules. The SROs themselves have recourse to the appropriate body in case of complaint.

The current legislation restricts the type of business that companies can carry on, and ensures that they are professionally qualified to carry out the businesses for which they do receive authorisation. For an investor to be sure that an investment advisor is registered, he or she can contact the SIB and check its Central Register, which contains a computerised database of 40,000 investment firms. The Register contains details of the firm's authorised status, whom the firm is regulated by, whether it is authorised to handle clients' money or merely give advice, and what types of investment business it is permitted to engage in. The public can gain access to the Register by writing to, visiting or telephoning the SIB on 0171–929 3652. Their address is:

Securities and Investments Board
Gavrelle House
2–14 Bunhill Row
London EC1Y 8RA

Alternatively, investors can contact the PIA, which is now the SRO which is most likely to be dealing with an investment advisor giving advice to the general public.

Compensation

The act of investing nearly always means that one has to let someone else handle one's money. This means that advisors give advice, may receive cheques from the investor for the investment and also may receive the proceeds of the sale of the investment. There are rules in place to ensure that the investor's money is duly segregated from the business' own funds, but, even if reasonable precautions are taken, there is always a very remote chance that something may go wrong; the money might be lost as a result of fraud or due to the company going bankrupt without having protected its clients' money properly.

When this happens there are compensation schemes in place for people who have lost their money as a result of the investment company undertaking their business improperly. However, for these schemes to be operative it is essential that the investment company is either recognised by the Securities and Investment Board (SIB) or is a bank, building society or life insurance company which have their own compensation schemes, governed by the Deposit Protection Board and the Policy Holders Protection Scheme respectively. In the previous sections 'Where Can You Find Financial Advice' and 'Investor Protection', we have looked at the role of the SIB and its Self Regulatory Organisations (SROs) such as PIA and IMRO, and have given their addresses and telephone numbers. Further information can be obtained from them about the scope of compensation available if one of their members goes bankrupt.

Remember: Investment can be a risky business; no one will pay an investor compensation if the investment falls in value or inflation erodes the real value of the return.

The Investors Compensation Fund

This Fund is carried out by a company separate from the SIB. It may be able to help an investor if all of the following apply to his or her position:
 – the investor is a private investor
 – the investment firm is fully authorised
 – the firm is unable to pay out investors' claims
 – the firm owes the investor money, or is holding shares or other investments on his or her behalf
 – the investor's claim arises out of business regulated by the Financial Services Act.

If you are uncertain about the definitions used, the SIB will be able to assist if you write to them or telephone on 0171–929 3652.

In addition, they produce an explanatory booklet, 'Compensation for Investors', which they will send to you free of charge.

There is a ceiling of £50,000 on the amount any individual can claim. A claimant would receive the first £30,000 of his or her claim in full and 90 per cent of the next £20,000. Therefore anyone claiming £50,000 would receive a maximum amount of £48,000.

Banks and Building Societies

In the event of a bank or building society failing, there are compensation schemes which protect 75 per cent of the money lodged in a bank up to £20,000 (£15,000 in total per bank) or 90 per cent of the money lodged in a building society up to £20,000 (£18,000 in total per building society).

chapter seven

LEGAL AND TAX MATTERS

Help with Understanding Powers of Attorney, Wills, Getting Out of Debt, Taxation

THIS CHAPTER CONSIDERS the implications of various legal and taxation problems that need to be considered as people grow older.

Within the last three years the Law Society has focused a campaign on improving and developing legal services to meet the needs of older people. Practitioners have been encouraged to develop links with local organisations such as Age Concern, in order not only to promote their services but also to understand issues with which they may be unfamiliar. An early idea that has developed from these meetings is the need to ensure that offices are friendly to older people; this encompasses the need to have facilities such as ground-floor meeting rooms, disabled access and even the possibility of arranging home visits, and also considers communication at the level of the receptionist's level of courtesy to older people and correspondence being written in larger typeface.

On the service side, the Law Society campaign has focused on areas of work in which the lawyer will most typically become involved, such as will making, powers of attorney, community care and financial services. The need for much of this work is evident because the Law Society's Will Power campaigns in recent years have shown that *only about one in three people makes a will.*

Many people are unaware of the legal complications that may arise after the death of someone who has failed to make a will. Indeed, problems can arise even if a will *has* been made without consideration of changes in legislation (taxation, etc.) or the existing circumstances of the person making the will.

Even less consideration is given to the implications of a sickness or accident temporarily or permanently incapacitating someone to the extent that he or she is powerless to make or carry out even normal day-to-day decisions and actions.

POWERS OF ATTORNEY

A Power of Attorney is a legal document that can be given to an older child, a partner or any third party. It provides them with the legal authority to manage the financial and general affairs of the donor (the person making or giving the

Power) in the event of sickness or incapacity. The Power of Attorney is conferred by completing a special legal document, which is available from stationers who supply legal forms or from any solicitor. Normally the document should be completed with the help of a solicitor. Typically the charge from a solicitor for assisting in the preparation of a straightforward Power of Attorney would be between £20 and £40 (plus VAT).

There are two types of Powers of Attorney. The first type, the *ordinary Power of Attorney*, is satisfactory in most circumstances but is invalidated in the event of the donor no longer having the mental capacity to manage his or her own affairs. The shortcomings of this have been recognised and in March 1986 legislation was passed under the Enduring Powers of Attorney Act 1985. This Act overcomes the problems that the older legislation did not cover. An *Enduring Power of Attorney* is a power of attorney which enables an Attorney, subject to certain conditions and safeguards, to be appointed against the possibility of the donor becoming mentally incapable of handling his or her affairs, provided that it is registered (*see below*).

An Enduring Power of Attorney allows the donor, while still mentally capable of deciding for themselves, to select who should act for them in the case of loss of mental capability. The Enduring Power of Attorney may give:

A General Authority
A general power authorises the Attorney to carry out any transactions on the Donor's behalf which the Donor is legally able to delegate to the Attorney.

A Specific Authority
A specific power enables the Attorney to deal only with those aspects of the Donor's affairs which are specified in the Power.

Subsequent legal protection is provided to ensure that the Powers conferred are not abused by the Attorney.

A General or Specific Authority with Restrictions and Conditions
A combination of the two authorities above authorises the Attorney to deal with all the Donor's property and affairs except specified aspects.

It is advisable for anyone wishing to provide an Enduring Power of Attorney to consult with a legal advisor before completing it. Although it is possible for any person of whatever age to issue an Enduring Power of Attorney, consideration should also be given to restricting its Powers. For instance, the Donor may wish to exclude the right of the Attorney to sell the house in which the Donor resides, or to make gifts to him- or herself and his or her family without restriction, or even to direct that the Attorney is not to act until the Power is registered.

It is also possible to appoint a number of Attorneys under different Powers to carry out specific duties or actions on behalf of the Donor.

A Donor may revoke or cancel the Enduring Power of Attorney at any time while he or she remains mentally capable; but it may not be cancelled or revoked once it has been registered unless and until the Court of Protection confirms the revocation.

When the Attorney who has been appointed under an Enduring Power of Attorney believes that the Donor is becoming confused or mentally incapable, he or she must apply to register the Enduring Power with the Court of Protection before he or she can act or continue to act under it. The Attorney must give notice of intention to register, in a prescribed form EP1 (which is available from the Public Trust Office, which carries out the administrative functions on behalf of the Court of Protection) to the Donor and to at least three near relatives of the Donor. The order of priority of the notification is laid down within Schedule 1, Part 1 of the Act. The order of priority must be complied with, class by class, and initially goes:

1. The Donor's spouse
2. The Donor's children
3. The Donor's parents
4. The Donors brothers and sisters, whether of whole or half blood
5. The widow or widower of a child of the Donor.

If there is more than one person in a particular class of relative entitled to receive notice, then all persons in that class must be given notice.

Immediately (within three days) after notification has been given to the Donor and the prescribed relatives, an application must be made to the Court of Protection, in prescribed form EP2, accompanied by the original of the Enduring Power and a fee of £50.

In the event that the circumstance arises in which anyone considers that the affairs and property of someone else may need protection because of his or her mental incapacity, *and no attorney has been appointed*, an application can be made to the Court of Protection for assistance. If the Court is satisfied that there is a genuine need, it will appoint a Receiver (who will deal with the day-to-day management of the patient's financial affairs). The Receiver may be a relative, a friend or even an official from the local authority. Although the day-to-day responsibilities of an attorney and a Receiver towards a patient should be identical, the Receiver is ultimately responsible to the Public Trust Office, from which his or her specific powers have been conferred and to which he or she must submit annual accounts. There are also fees payable, as the Protection Division of the Court are required to cover their operating costs from fees received from patients' estates. The scale of fees is laid down by Parliament; details are available from the Protection Division (*see below*). Finally, although the Receiver will be a diligent and suitable person, he or she may not be the person who necessarily understands the affairs of the patient as well as someone who might originally have been chosen by the patient and provided with a Power of Attorney before the need for the appointment of a Receiver was apparent.

The Court of Protection
Stewart House
24 Kingsway
London WC2B 6JX
Tel: 0171–269 7000

The Court of Protection is an office of the Supreme Court. Its function is to protect and manage the property and financial affairs of people who, because of mental disorder, are unable to manage for themselves.

If there are any objections to the registration, the Court will arbitrate. The Court's control is regulated by the Mental Health Act 1983 and the Court of Protection Rules Act 1984.

The Protection Division of the Public Trust Office, on behalf of the Court, deals with the management of the affairs of the person under protection in conjunction with a Receiver appointed by the Court. Generally, in the case of an Enduring Power of Attorney, the receiver will automatically be the Attorney selected by the Donor.

Considering how many people over the age of 65 suffer from senile dementia, the Act with its in-built safeguards offers a very helpful way of administering the affairs of elderly people who are unable to do so themselves.

The Public Trust Office produces excellent booklets called *Handbook for Receivers*, which offers guidance to Receivers appointed by the Court of Protection, and *Enduring Powers of Attorney*. The latter explains clearly the procedure for making and registering Enduring Powers of Attorney. Both are free. The Public Trust Office is located at the same address as the Court of Protection (*see above*).

The best way to find a suitable solicitor is through the recommendation of friends or relations. However, if you do not have a solicitor or anyone to recommend one, it is possible to ask the local Citizens Advice Bureau or at the local library; failing this you can contact The Law Society for their help. They will provide a list of the names of solicitors in your area.

The Law Society
113 Chancery Lane
London WC2A 1PL
Tel: 0171–242 1222

Further Reading
Age Concern England (*address page 101*) produces a factsheet (No 22), 'Legal Arrangements for Managing Financial Affairs'.
Help the Aged (*address page 182*) produces a free booklet, 'Enduring Powers of Attorney'. This booklet simplifies the complexities of appointing a Power of Attorney or acting as one.
As Scottish law differs in some respects, readers living in Scotland should contact Age Concern Scotland (*address page 101*) for Factsheet No 22, available free on receipt of a 9-inch x 6-inch sae.

Where to Complain Against a Solicitor

If you are dissatisfied with the performance of a solicitor, ensure that you have tried everything reasonable to make the solicitor's firm sort out the problem themselves. Ensure you keep all copies of correspondence, because if the matter is not settled in an amicable manner it may be used as evidence against the solicitor.

If you are not satisfied as a result of your own actions, or you wish to discuss your problems, you can telephone the Solicitors Complaints Bureau helpline on 01926 822007. This is a free service, staffed by solicitors who are supposed to offer independent advice. They can send you a copy of their free booklet *What to do, Where to go and When to complain*. In the booklet there is a complaints form which can be completed and sent to the Bureau at:

Solicitors Complaints Bureau
Victoria Court
8 Dormer Place
Leamington Spa
CV32 5AF

If you feel that your case has still not been handled fairly, you can complain to the Legal Services Ombudsman. The Ombudsman is not a lawyer. He or she must be contacted within three months of your being informed of the SCB's final decision. Write to:

Legal Services Ombudsman
22 Oxford Court
Manchester M2 3WQ
Tel: 0161–236 9532

THE WILL

Most family lawyers will advise: 'There is only one way to make sure that your money is distributed in the way that you want after you die and that is to make a Will.'

A Will is a formal expression of how the testator (the person making the Will) wishes his or her property to be divided up when he or she dies. A little time spent in the preparation of a Will to make intentions clear can result in a significant saving in time, hardship and money for the beneficiaries. Few actions can produce greater benefit for so little cost and effort, even though *more than two thirds of adults never make out a will*.

The Law Society commissioned research that found various reasons why so few people make a Will. Some people have never thought or have not wanted to think about it; others have not got around to it and many simply assume that their partner will automatically inherit everything. One in 10 did not want to think about dying, or believed that making a Will was inviting premature death.

Cost should never be a barrier to drawing up a Will; lawyers make far more money from unravelling both badly drawn up Wills or those situations when no Will has been prepared at all, than they do in drawing them up professionally in the first place.

Once a Will is drawn up it should be reviewed periodically. Changes in a person's financial or family circumstances may affect the original Will.

Discussing the implications in drawing up a Will does seem a difficult subject for many people to broach. However, a Will that is properly made can give complete peace of mind to those who make them, in that they know that their affairs are settled and that their assets and property are being distributed according to their wishes. This is discussed further in Chapter 12.

If a Will is not made and a person dies intestate, the estate (the net personal assets of the deceased) will be divided by strict rules of law. This can cause difficulty for even the smallest estate, resulting in confusion and possible hardship for relations while the estate is being unravelled; it certainly causes unnecessary cost and the possible loss of capital and income for the beneficiaries.

Confusion is caused by the fact that agreement has to be reached over who should administer the estate; complications are caused by the need to divide the estate under the intestacy rules. Inheritance tax may end up being paid unnecessarily, as well as the assets being distributed in a way that would not necessarily have been approved of by the deceased.

For instance, if the deceased was married with children, under the intestacy rules the surviving spouse will receive only £75,000 plus the personal and household effects. The remainder is divided equally – half to the children and the balance held in trust. The surviving spouse only has a life interest in the amount held in trust; he or she is able to receive an income but not to have access to the capital. In cases where there are no family and the deceased has not made a Will, all of the estate will automatically pass to the Crown; none will go to friends or charities that may have been selected by the deceased.

Once the decision has been made to make a Will, it is essential for the person preparing it to receive legal advice. It is possible for a layperson to prepare a 'home made' will him- or herself (the printed forms are available from newsagents) but this is not recommended. You are not able to rely on covering every eventuality, or even having a Will that can stand up to scrutiny when it needs to be proven after your death.

A solicitor will charge a fee (which should be negotiated in advance) and can advise on the best ways of structuring the Will, taking into account numerous possibilities and provisions that would not necessarily be apparent to the layperson, in order to make the best provisions for the family and, if applicable, planning for inheritance tax. If a high street solicitor draws up a simple Will the cost will be about £50 (*see also below*).

Once a Will is drawn up, for it to be valid under UK law it must be signed in front of two witnesses. The witnesses need not, and probably will not, read the contents of the Will, but must sign the document themselves to evidence that it has been signed in front of them. They should observe the other's signature. Neither witness should be a beneficiary under the terms of the Will.

An important part of the Will is to ensure that there are correct executors to carry out the terms of the Will and manage the estate. It is better to have two executors rather than one. Often a professional is appointed to handle the complex matters and inheritance tax, and a member of the family is appointed to ensure that the duties are discharged promptly and efficiently. Banks, accountants and solicitors all have specialist executor departments; all will charge for the service provided, with banks in particular being the most expensive, charging around 5 per cent of the value of the estate. It will normally be cheaper to use a provincial firm rather than one of the main London firms; however, cost should be measured against the quality of service to be provided.

In all cases permission should be sought from the persons appointed as executors under the terms of the Will, as no one is bound to act as an executor.

Preparing a Will correctly can secure significant tax savings. (For information on inheritance tax and tax planning, *see below*). Therefore a regular review is important to take the fullest advantage of changing legislation. Changes can be made to a Will at any time by adding a supplementary *codicil* to the original Will. The codicil must be signed and witnessed in the same way as the original Will, although not necessarily by the same witnesses. *The original Will must never be altered by way of insertion or deletion.* A Will may also be revoked by making a new Will, which must specify that it revokes all previous Wills and codicils. A Will may also be invalidated by marriage, divorce or remarriage, unless it has been prepared in anticipation of the event.

Another method by which the fullest advantage may be taken of all available tax reliefs is to leave the executors the discretion to override dispositions in the Will. This can be done by providing the executors with restricted powers that enable them to change conditions of the Will solely to avoid unnecessary taxation. These imposed restrictions on the discretion of the executor can be included in the Will in such a way as to include or exclude as much as the testator wishes. It is normal to include restrictions to prevent the executor from having control over the primary distribution of the estate.

Once a Will is made it should be lodged with a bank or lawyer. A copy, also stating where the original is kept, should always be filed with the testator's personal papers.

In any situation where explanations are needed about official documents or help or general advice are needed on any legal or administrative matter, contact the local Citizens Advice Bureau. They will also advise on local solicitors who could help.

Age Concern publishes a leaflet, 'Instructions for my next of kin and executors upon my death', which can be left in a convenient place to tell your family where all your important documents are, including your Will. The leaflet is available for the price of a sae from Age Concern (*address page 101*).

A postal Will-writing service is available from Age Concern England. Users of this service are asked to complete a short questionnaire, which is then sent to a solicitor who will draft the Will and send it to the client within 14 days. If the answers to the questionnaire indicate that the person's circumstances are more complex than can be properly handled by means of a postal service the solicitor will advise a personal consultation with another will-maker. The service costs from £50 for individuals.

The Will Registry
357–361 Lewisham High Street
London SE13 6NZ
Tel: 01303 248644
The Will Registry offers to prepare a single Will for as little as £27.95. It will store Wills for as little as £9.95 per year.

Further Reading
Age Concern Factsheet No 7, 'Making your Will' (*address page 101*), free if an sae is sent with each request

If your tax affairs are quite complex, it might be necessary to seek the help of an accountant. The Institute of Chartered Accountants will provide a list of appropriate local members. Always ask an accountant for an indication of the fee, preferably in writing, before making a commitment.

The Institute of Chartered Accountants
Moorgate Place
London EC2 2BJ
Tel: 0171–920 8100

Further Reading
Don't Leave your Money to Chance (Money Management Council; *address page 164*), free with sae
Your Guide to Making a Will (Help the Aged, *address page 182*). This is a comprehensive free booklet which also comes with supplementary booklets *Records of Personal Assets* and *Preparing to Make or Change your Will*, which provide a checklist of information you will need before preparing a Will.
Wills and Probate (Consumer's Association, Castlemead, Gascoyne Way, Hertford SG14 1LH), £9.95. Written for the layperson, this includes excellent advice on the preparation of a Will.
Inheritance Tax Planning - Leaving it to your Family (KPMG Peat Marwick, 1 Puddle Dock, London EC4V 3PD), free

DEBT

Although this is not strictly a legal issue, debt has become a major problem in recent years. The easy credit and boom years of the 1980s have combined to create a situation during the early 1990s in which many elderly people are facing severe financial hardship, often for the first time in their lives. The hardships may be the result of over-commitment, of unexpected unemployment or disability, or merely of the inflation of the 1970s and 1980s and the low interest levels of the 1990s eating away at the fixed income which makes up the pension of many retired persons.

Excessive debt invariably generates severe stress and worry. Worse still, the situation will generally snowball unless properly managed and contained. If you are in this situation, or have friends or relatives who are, it is essential to discuss the problem and look at the various ways in which it might be alleviated. The Social Fund (*see Chapter 6*) can provide a small amount of assistance (never more than £1,000), but is primarily aimed at providing loans for items that are difficult to budget for. This is generally inadequate except for the most desperate and needy cases.

The Citizens Advice Bureau or a Money Advice Centre, if there is one in your local area, will provide further advice. If necessary, free advice can also be obtained from a legal aid solicitor.

Other organisations committed to helping people in debt:

Money Management Council
PO Box 77
Hertford
Herts SG14 2HW
Tel: 01992 503448

The Money Management Council is an independent impartial charity that promotes education in and better understanding of personal and family finance. The Council does *not* offer an individual advice service but it does produce a series of factsheets that are circulated to advisory/help agencies, and direct to members of the public. This material is addressed primarily at people who are financially inexperienced.

Leaflets are available free from the above address, but the Council asks that you do send along an A4-sized sae.
Factsheets:
No 1, 'You and your Money (A General Introduction)'
No 3, 'Where Can I Get Financial Advice?'
No 7, 'Personal Budgeting'

National Debtline
The Birmingham Settlement
318 Summer Lane
Birmingham B19 3RL
Tel: 0121–359 8501

National Debtline is a national telephone helpline for people with debt problems. It offers expert advice over the telephone to callers in England and Wales on all aspects of debt. The aim is to enable callers to deal with their debts with the assistance of a self-help information pack, which is sent to individuals free of charge. The service is free, confidential and independent. The Debtline also provide booklets that are free to people in debt (for professionals and advisors there is a £2.50 fee):
Dealing with your Debts – For People with Mortgages
Dealing with your Debts – For People Who Pay Rent
Opening hours are 10 a.m. to 4 p.m. Monday and Thursday, 3 p.m. to 7 p.m.

Tuesday and Wednesday. There is a 24-hour answering machine.

Office of Fair Trading
Field House
15–25 Breams Buildings
London EC4A 1PR
Tel: 0171–242 2858
The OFT produces a range of free advisory publications on consumer rights, credit and debt. A full set of current publications or a publications list is available free of charge from: OFT, PO Box 2, Central Way, Feltham, Middlesex TW14 0TG (tel: 0181–398 3405). Their list includes the following publications:
Debt: A Survival Guide
Creditwise
Moneyfax 3
No Credit?

TAXATION

Taxation principles remain unaffected by the age of the taxpayer. There are, however, additional allowances available to older persons. These allowances, combined with the general need of the older person to maximise income, means there are special considerations to be borne in mind when reviewing tax and the best way to manage finances (*see Chapter 6*).

Professional Advice

Tax and related affairs can easily become quite complex. It might therefore be necessary to seek the help of an accountant or lawyer. The Institute of Chartered Accountants will provide a list of appropriate local members. Always ask an accountant for an indication of the fee, preferably in writing, before making a commitment.

The Institute of Chartered Accountants
Moorgate Place
London EC2 2BJ
Tel: 0171–920 8100
A further body which has been set up is the Society of Trust and Estate Practitioners (STEP), which is the professional body for the Trust and Estate profession in the UK and worldwide. STEP was founded with the aim of bringing together the senior practitioners in the field, cutting across professional boundaries. The organisation currently has over 1,400 members, all of whom must have had five years first-hand experience in trust-related work.

Society of Trust and Estate Practitioners
46 Farlington Avenue
Haywards Heath
West Sussex RH16 3EY
A membership directory is available free.

**Belgrave International Trust and
Taxation Consultants**
PO Box 602
Town Mills
Rue du Pré
St Peter Port
Guernsey GY1 4NL
Tel: 01481 700220
STEP member.

Income Tax

Income tax is calculated over a tax year which runs from 6 April to 5 April. During the tax year every individual is allowed to earn a certain amount of income before he or she has to pay any tax; this figure is known as a tax allowance. The total taxable income received by an individual is calculated, and his or her tax allowances are deducted. The remaining amount is the figure on which tax is calculated. The lowest rate of tax for the year 1995/6 is 20 per cent and the highest is 40 per cent.

The basic allowances are personal allowances which are given to each person; an additional allowance is available for married couples. The basic allowance increases for people over 65 and under 75, and increases again for those of 75 and over. If married, and the elder of the couple is over 65, the married couple's allowance is increased; if either is over 75 it is increased again. The full amount of these higher allowances is given only if the individual's total income less certain deductions does not exceed a set figure for the tax year. The amount of allowance will be reduced by £1 for every £2 the total income exceeds the limit, although it will never fall below the level of the personal allowance.

Since April 1995 the married couple's allowance is restricted to 15 per cent tax relief, which means that if the husband is over 75 he will receive an allowance of £3,035. However, his tax bill will be reduced by no more than £455.25 (that is, 15 per cent of £3,035) regardless of the rate of tax he pays.

The age allowances apply to people if they reach the relevant age at any time during the tax year. Therefore, even if your 65th or 75th birthday is on the last day of the tax year (5 April), you can still get the age allowance for the full year.

Additional allowances are available for married persons, blind persons and for widows in the tax year that their husbands die and in the following year, assuming that the widows do not remarry during that period. You do not need to make a special claim, but you should let your Tax Office know when your husband dies.

Almost all income is taxable, but there are notable exceptions. These are:
- certain types of Social Security Benefit. These include benefits paid for illness or disability, such as Attendance Allowance, Disability Living Allowance, Income Support, or War Pensions.
- certain types of investment income. These include income from National Savings, TESSAs, and Personal Equity Plans, although all are subject to certain regulations.

- prizes and winnings, which are all tax-free, including those from Premium Bonds and the National Lottery.

Most types of investment income have tax deducted at source, meaning that the interest or dividend is paid after deducting tax at 20 per cent. A non-taxpayer may prefer to select investments that do not deduct tax at source. It is also possible to request a bank or building society to pay interest gross, but only to someone who is not a taxpayer. There is a special form (R85) for this purpose, which is obtainable from banks, building societies and tax offices. There are estimated to be about five million retired people who could register to have their income paid gross from a bank. Many have not done so.

If tax is deducted at source, it is possible to reclaim it at the end of the year by filling in a tax form if you are a non-taxpayer. The Inland Revenue estimates that four million retired people have not reclaimed tax that they are owed, amounting to about £800 million.

Retirement pensions are normally all taxable. An exception to this is the amount by which a pension awarded on retirement through disability caused by industrial injury or work-related illness exceeds the pension which would have been paid if retirement had been on ordinary ill-health grounds. This amount is not treated as taxable income.

Tax Tips

Certain types of the investments identified above are tax-free not only for the income that they generate but also for the potential capital gains. If you have savings and you pay tax, it is worth considering investing in these types of schemes (National Savings, TESSAs, etc.) to get tax-free interest. However, each investment should be made based on its own merits, so do take advice (*See Chapter 6*).

Married couples often have the possibility of saving tax by moving investments between them. If one partner has all or most of the income, consideration should be given to moving the source of the income to the other partner so that they fully benefit from their personal allowances and lower-rate tax bands. The benefits to be derived from the age allowances (explained above) should also be fully utilised.

If you do not pay tax, you can request your bank or building society to pay you interest gross. As mentioned above, Form R85 enables you to register for gross interest and is available in every bank or building society. If you cannot register because your income is high enough to pay some tax, or because you have a joint account with someone who pays tax, you may still reclaim the tax overpaid. Just fill in form R95 (found in leaflet R111) as soon as the tax due reaches £50. Otherwise you have to wait until the end of the tax year.

Further help and advice can be obtained at your local Tax Enquiry Centre, which is in the telephone book under Inland Revenue, or from the local Citizens Advice Bureau. For those living in London, free advice on tax is available from the charitable trust TaxAid, which commonly advises on things such as:

– tax deducted from pensions

– tax codes and allowances
– tax returns
– wills and inheritance tax
– tax assessments and demands
– communicating with the Inland Revenue.

TaxAid provides free tax advice and assistance to people who cannot afford to pay for professional help from an accountant. Simple advice can be given on the telephone, while for more complex matters TaxAid can arrange a free appointment at its offices with a qualified accountant or solicitor, who will normally be a volunteer. (At present meetings are in London only).

TaxAid does not advise on Council Tax or State Welfare Benefits.

TaxAid
Linburn House
342 Kilburn High Road
London NW6 2QJ
Tel: 0171–624 3768 (weekdays 9 a.m. to 11 a.m.) for an appointment.

Further Reading
Age Concern Factsheet No 15, 'Income Tax and Older People' (available free with sae, *address page 101*)
'Independent Taxation – A Guide for Widows and Widowers' (free leaflet IR 91 from your local Tax Office)
Two other free leaflets available from Inland Revenue are:
IR 80, 'Income Tax and Married Couples'
IR 121, 'Income Tax and Pensioners'
'Check your Tax' (free and updated annually; available from Help the Aged, *address page 182*)
Which? Way to Save Tax (Consumers Association, Castlemead, Gascoyne Way, Hertford SG14 1LH), £11.95
Widows' Benefits and Tax, Paul Lewis (Saga Publishing Ltd, The Saga Building, Middelburg Square, Folkestone, Kent CT20 1AZ), free to Saga club members

Inheritance Tax
Inheritance Tax is payable on the estate of the deceased at the time of his or her death, and on any transfer from the estate that has been made within a certain time before death (currently seven years). The estate comprises all assets of the deceased, including the home and its contents, the car, savings and investments, jewellery and other similar items. The rules covering inheritance tax are quite complex, so it is worth taking expert advice if an estate is large. Further information can also be obtained from the local Tax Enquiry Office or Citizens Advice Bureau.

In its most simple form, the value of an estate in excess of £150,000 is subject to tax at 40 per cent. This rate is applicable for 1995/6. Any transfers made within seven years of death will be taxed at the rate prevailing at the time of death, subject to a 'tapering relief' which reduces the liability by up to 80 per cent for transfers made between six and seven years before death. However, any gifts made within the seven years preceding death, and which are outside the standard exemptions, will be included in full in valuing the estate for inheritance tax purposes. These gifts are included first in the NIL rate band when the liability is being calculated. Therefore the reduction of up to 80 per cent only comes into effect when these gifts exceed the £150,000 allowance. This fact is often ignored and can distort the extent of the liability that was expected to arise on the estate.

The executor of an estate is responsible for paying tax before distributions are made to beneficiaries under the will. (For more information *see Chapter 12*).

There is no tax payable on assets transferred between husband and wife or on bequests to a UK-based charity. However, leaving everything to your spouse is not always sensible, because the value of both of the estates will be accumulated on his or her death, losing one of the exemptions on the first £150,000. If you have substantial assets, apart from your house, you should consider leaving what you can to children or other beneficiaries, so that you make use of the £150,000 which is free of tax when you die. If your main asset is your home, then there is not much you can do about avoiding tax, because even if you give it to your children but continue to live in it, it will still be taxed as though you continued to own it. However, if you are married you can separate the ownership of the house into two parts; one will be yours and the other will belong to your spouse, and each of you can then leave your own half to your children or other beneficiaries. You are not allowed to make a formal agreement that the person surviving will live in the house for the rest of his or her life, but must rely on the goodwill of your children or beneficiaries.

Transfers of assets made to beneficiaries more than seven years before death are free of tax. Certain gifts, including gifts into and out of some trusts, will be taxed at only half the death rate. Other gifts may also escape the tax if they do not need to be included in the value of the estate – such as maintenance for children under 18 or in full-time education, and wedding gifts of up to £5,000 to children, £2,500 to grandchildren and £1,000 to others. There is also a £250 small gifts exemption and a £3,000 annual exemption for gifts made by any one person.

If nothing was given away in the previous year, the annual exemption is increased to £6,000 for the current year. These limits apply separately to husbands and wives. Finally, lifetime gifts that are made out of income each year may be exempt from tax provided they do not affect the donor's standard of living in any way.

If a person's death can be linked to an accident, illness or wound suffered while on active service in the armed forces during wartime or service 'of a warlike nature', then his or her estate is completely exempt from inheritance tax. The service injury does not have to be the only cause of death, as long it is a contributory cause. The exemption has to be claimed after death by the personal representative (*See Chapter 12*, under Administering the Estate), who should write for a Certificate of Exemption from Inheritance Tax under section 154 of the Inheritance Act to:

Personnel and Logistics (Legal Services)
Room 604
Ministry of Defence
Neville House
Page Street
London SW1P 4LS

Saving of Inheritance Tax

In recent years, the financial services industry has created a number of schemes which claim to reduce future inheritance tax bills. These schemes, some with grandiose names such as 'retained interest plans' and 'discounted gift schemes', invariably involve some form of life assurance policy written under trust. They are complex to understand, so no one should enter into them without taking expert professional advice first and gaining a full understanding of the implications of the advice. Remember that if the scheme is not sound, it is your heirs who will suffer and not the person who sold the scheme to you in the first place.

However, if you have taken out life assurance as a normal precaution for your heirs, it should be written under trust so that the funds paid out on death do not form part of the estate for inheritance tax purposes. There are also other benefits to doing this. If a spouse dies with a mortgage protection policy designed to pay off the outstanding house loan but which is not written under trust, the surviving spouse will be left without funds to pay it quickly and will be saddled with an additional, unnecessary tax burden.

One plan that has been conceived by a London firm of solicitors can save up to £60,000 in tax for married couples but allows the survivors continued access to the assets of the deceased. It revolves around a Will-writing technique called the Loan Plan. For further information contact:

Speechly Bircham
Bouverie House
154 Fleet Street
London EC4A 2HX
Tel: 0171–353 4825/4992

Further Reading

Booklet IHT1, *Inheritance Tax* (Capital Taxes Office, Minford House, Rockley Road, London W14 0DF)
Inheritance Tax and Capital Gains Tax, Paul Lewis (Saga Publishing Ltd, The Saga Building, Middelburg Square, Folkestone, Kent CT20 1AZ), free to Saga club members
The Smart Investors Guide to the Use of Trusts, David Aaron (available from David Aaron, Shelton House, High Street, Woburn Sands, Milton Keynes MK17 8SD), £3. This booklet endeavours to take the mystique out of trusts, providing examples of the common situations in which they can be used to your advantage.

chapter eight

SPECIAL EQUIPMENT FOR DAILY LIFE

Small Gadgets and More Sophisticated Equipment to Make Life Easier

AS PEOPLE GROW OLDER they may find that ordinary, routine tasks may not be so easy to manage. A vast range of equipment is available to help make these tasks easier, from small items such as electric tin openers and gardening tools to larger devices such as stairlifts and adjustable beds.

The range of equipment is enormous and by no means only for the very frail or those with disabilities – there are plenty of ingenious devices for people who are just realising that certain activities are slightly harder to manage than they used to be.

EQUIPMENT IDEAS

There are literally hundreds of labour- or effort-saving gadgets. I list just a few of them below in order to illustrate the vast range that is available, some so simple, others more sophisticated. The local Social Services Department will advise on funding for adaptations that might make life easier or safer in the home, for example handrails for the bathroom and stairs. Many of the other kitchen gadgets, cutlery, gardening equipment and other goods are available from the shops or mail-order catalogues listed at the end of this chapter.

In the Kitchen

Among the helpful kitchen gadgets available are the following (*see* Household and General Equipment later in this chapter [*pages 180–1*] for suppliers):

KITCHEN PREPARATION

- slicing guides for cutting bread, fruit or vegetables
- a special rubber grip for opening bottles and jars, or a conical rubber twisting slot for one-handed opening
- mesh baskets for boiling foods in the pan (no need to lift the heavy pan to drain)
- special potato peelers, tin openers and butter spreaders

- excellent designs for taps to make them easier to operate
- kettle and pan stabilisers
- a variety of tongs, grips and reachers
- a range of 'tippers' for pouring

- from cartons, bottles, kettles and teapots
- special stands for hot water bottles (to assist filling)
- easy-grip handles for electric plugs

EATING AND DRINKING

- beakers with holders, cups with spouts and high-sided plates for single-handed eating
- combination easy-grip cutlery which acts as knife, fork and spoon in one
- non-slip mats and trays, and trays for one-handed carrying

General

A booklet, 'Equipment and Services for People with Disabilities, is prepared by the Department of Health and The Central Office of Information. It is full of information about what equipment may be obtained from doctors, health services, social services, charities and government bodies. The booklet may be obtained from The Health Publications Unit (*see page 119*).

Disabled Living Centres (*see page 179*) are demonstration and information resource centres concerned with the practical aspects of daily living. They offer impartial information and advice, and a permanent display of tools for daily living.

Mangar International
Presteigne Industrial Estate
Presteigne
Powys LD8 2UF
Tel: 01544 267674

Mangar International Ltd is independent, British and acclaimed for its innovative designs and superior quality. Mangar equipment – such as bathlifts, floorlifts, lifting cushions and emergency lifts – is powered by very low air pressure to help people lift and transfer during their everyday living. Mangar Lifts enable the elderly to cope independently or with minimum assistance at home wherever possible.

Stairlifts and Lifts

Installing a stairlift can be the difference between staying in one's own home or having to move house. The lift can be installed on straight or curved staircases and may have a swivel seat for easy access, or may even be designed to carry a person in a wheelchair.

You should seek expert advice from, say, the Social Services Department, and should check the manufacturer's safety record on design, construction, installation, operation and maintenance against the relevant British Standards before committing to any stairlift.

Stannah Stairlifts Ltd is the world's leading manufacturer of stairlifts. Both standing and seated models are available in an attractive range of fabrics and colours to suit straight, curved or even spiral staircases. All products are fully approved to relevant British Standards and are comprehensively guaranteed.

For further information about Stannah Stairlifts write or telephone for a free information pack.

Stannah Stairlifts Ltd
Dept 7679
FREEPOST
Andover
Hants SP10 3BR
Tel: 0800 715 116

Gimson Stairlifts
62 Boston Road
Leicester LE4 1AZ
Tel: 0800 622 251

Beds and Chairs

Several companies make adjustable manual or electric beds which can be adapted to the needs of older people, either for a better and more comfortable sleep or for people who are bedridden.

Adjustable beds can raise the feet or the knees or allow for sitting up to read, eat or work. Alternatively, back rests can be used for a more upright position – there is even one which resembles the top half of an armchair.

Theraposture is an established family company which makes electric adjustable beds and seat-lift chairs in its own purpose-built factory. All its equipment enables elderly or infirm people to remain independent in their own homes. Beds can be adjusted up and down, and the head and foot can be adjusted for lying down or sitting upright. Automatic chairs can lift or sit someone down gently, or recline to facilitate a restful sleep. Theraposture can provide free, 'no obligation' home demonstrations and brochures.

Theraposture Ltd
Warminster Business Park
Bath Road
Warminster
Wilts BA12 8PE
Tel: 01985 847788

Additional equipment for the bedroom can make life easier: a lifting pole by the bed to facilitate getting in and out, 'over-bed' tables (on wheels), powered, inflatable mattress-raisers (*see* Mangar International, *page 172*), and a selection of commodes.

Chairs have been designed that perform a number of functions. They can gently lean incline to help you stand up or lower you into a seated position, or recline (with or without a footrest) for reading, resting or sleeping. Some even incorporate heat and massage treatment.

Everstyl Reclining Armchairs
91 South End
Croydon
Surrey CR0 1BG
Tel: 0181–760 5178
Everstyl recliners can be used as armchairs, recliners and beds. Manually or electrically operated, they have an infinite selection of positions that offer much-needed relief for aches and pains. Fully independent movement of the back and legs means that anyone can find a position that suits. There are three woodstains to choose from and a wealth of fabric and leather coverings. Free colour catalogue on request.

Adjustamatic Beds
2 Lumley Road
Horley
Surrey RH6 7RJ
Tel: 01293 783837

EEZEE-Rise
Body Therapy
72 Babbacombe Road
Torquay
Devon TQ1 3SW
Tel: 01803 322533
This company sells reclining chairs and beds.

Concern for Comfort
Abacus House
Manor Road
London W13 0AS
Tel: 0181–810 9508
For mobility equipment, beds and chairs.

Everstyl Reclining Armchairs
91 South End
Croydon CR0 1BG
Tel: 0181–760 5178

Relief of Pressure Sores

Pressure sores, or bed sores, caused by periods of immobility can be very painful and difficult to heal. A number of specially-designed beds can alleviate the problem and provide comfort; fleeces, cushions, pads and rings can also help considerably.

In the Bathroom

It is vital that the bathroom is both safe and hygienic. A simple handrail or grabrail can be installed to prevent slipping or falling; these are available in a number of shapes and sizes.

Baths with built-in seating are available, but it is also possible to adapt an existing bath with a number of bath stools or chairs, some of which have a lifting facility (*see* Mangar International, *page 172*) or a 'swivel' action for further ease and safety. Special shower seats are also available.

A number of items are available to facilitate personal care, such as long-handled bath brushes, combs and hairbrushes, and wall-mounted dispensers for toothpaste, creams, etc.

Many older people find that the lavatory seat is too low. Raised seats are available, some with a gentle rising action and some with back rests or arm supports.

Special support frames can be fitted around the lavatory for assistance. A number of rails in different shapes and sizes can also be installed.

Parker Bath Developments
Stem Lane
New Milton
Hants BH25 5NN
Tel: 01425 622287

Dolphin Special Needs Bathrooms
Bromwich Road
Worcester WR2 4BD
Tel: 01905 748500

Miscellaneous Helpful Tools
See Household and General Equipment later *in this chapter (pages 180–1) for suppliers.*

- key-turners that fit on to keys to provide a proper handle for frail fingers
- large-numbered playing cards, card shufflers and card holders
- clear, flat magnifiers
- easy-grip pens
- needle threaders

- special stands for help putting on stockings or tights
- long-handled shoe horns
- handreachers, some with magnetic ends for picking up pins and needles, with or without counter-balancers
- electric plugs with handles for a better grip
- footrests and 'leg loungers'

Walking trolleys are ideal for people who are not so steady on their feet: they combine a walking frame with a tray or trolley to enable people to move things around the house.

Alternatively, a multi-purpose lifter such as the *Mangar Booster* can be used. It can lift up to 20 stone in weight and can be used to pick up and carry luggage or equipment, or help to transfer people from chair to bed, floor to chair, etc. (*see* Mangar International, *page 172*).

In the Garden

- kneeler seats

- long-handled weeders, trowels, forks, flower-pickers and pruners (in lightweight materials)

The Disabled Information Trust (tel: 01865 750103) can supply gardening equipment for people with disabilities.

The Society for Horticultural Therapy
Goulds Ground
Vallis Way
Frome
Somerset BA11 3DW
Tel: 01373 464782

The Society for Horticultural Therapy can supply gardeners who have special needs with a list of useful mail-order tools and equipment, as well as a problem-solving service and list of publications which can assist them.

COMMUNICATION AND HEARING EQUIPMENT

(*see also* Hearing, *Chapter 2, pages 29–31*)

Before buying equipment through advertisements or shops do consult a doctor. NHS hearing aids are more effective and less obtrusive than they have ever been. If you do choose one of the many commercially available hearing aids, check its claims and take advice before you buy it, and make sure it is covered by British Standard BS6083.

For guidance, Sound Advantage is part of the Royal National Institute for Deaf People (RNID) and provides a one-stop shop for the special needs of the deaf and hard of hearing. It sells a wide range of assistive products that can help make life easier and more enjoyable. They include listening products to help people hear conversations in crowded rooms and public places, TV and radio devices, alerting products (including flashing lights for the telephone or doorbell, smoke detectors and alarm clocks), and special telephones, including textphones. A variety of free factsheets and a full product guide are available from:

Sound Advantage
1 Metro Centre
Welbeck Way
Peterborough PE2 7UH
Tel: 01733 361199
For books, literature and information on hearing aids:

Breakthrough Deaf-Hearing Integration
Birmingham Centre
Charles W. Gillett Centre
998 Bristol Road
Selly Oak
Birmingham B29 6LE
Tel: 0121–472 6447
Please send stamped addressed envelope.

The Sequal Trust
Ddol Hir
Glyn Ceirlog
Llangollen
Clwyd LL20 7NP
Tel: 01691 718331
The Sequal (Special Equipment and Aids for Living) Trust is a totally independent, non-manufacturing national charity which aims to assist people with severe physical disabilities by providing special electronic/electrical equipment. It helps people by assessing their requirements, raising funds and providing equipment on permanent free loan.

Telephones

The Chronically Sick and Disabled Persons Act 1970 gives local authorities a duty to provide a telephone for certain people with disabilities, or help them to get a telephone. Each local authority will have its own guidelines on what it will provide – this may include installation (and sometimes rental) of special phones with signalling handsets for people with hearing difficulties, and inductive couplers to eliminate background noise.

People on Income Support may be able to get a loan from the Social Fund (*see pages 121–5*). For further advice and information contact the Social Services Department or DIEL (address below).

DIEL is the Advisory Committee on Telecommunications for Disabled and Elderly People and produces an information pack on telephone services for use by the elderly or people with disabilities and their helpers. This includes information on installation and rental charges, billing services for visually impaired people, telephones for hard of hearing people and telephone systems for people with limited dexterity or mobility. Copies of the information pack are available from:

DIEL
Second Floor
Room 2/3
Export House
50 Ludgate Hill
London EC4M 7JJ
Tel: 0171–634 8700

Typetalk is a telephone relay service developed jointly by the RNID and BT. It is designed to give deaf, deafened, deaf-blind, hard of hearing and speech-impaired people access to a public telephone network which matches the quality of service currently enjoyed by hearing people. Calls are relayed to and from people using text transmissions (i.e. typing on a screen) throughout the UK to hearing people worldwide. Typetalk is open 24 hours a day, seven days a week, 365 days a year, and users pay virtually the same as a hearing person would for the same call had it been dialled direct. Users can claim a rebate from BT by telephoning their local office (telephone number on the telephone bill). Further information and free leaflets from:

Typetalk
Pauline Ashley House
Ravenside Retail Park
Speke Road
Liverpool L24 8QB
Tel: 0151–494 1000
Text: 0800 500 800

Age Concern England (*address page 101*) publishes a leaflet (No 28), 'Help with Telephones'.

For the Blind and Partially Sighted

Royal National Institute for the Blind (RNIB)
224 Great Portland Street
London W1N 6AA
Tel: 0171–388 1266
The RNIB produces six brochures full of useful products for the kitchen, home, office and 'out and about'. The brochures, called 'Daily Living', 'Clocks and Watches', 'Braille', 'Mobility', 'Learning', and 'Games and Puzzles', are available by calling 01733 371555.

FOOTWEAR

It may be difficult for older people to find footwear which is both comfortable and stylish in soft materials with wide fittings. They should not be tempted to wear a favourite pair of slippers all day, as this can exacerbate foot problems. (*See* Feet, *Chapter 2, pages 32–3*). Several specialist mail-order companies make broad-fitting, quality footwear.

Cosyfeet
5 The Tanyard
Leigh Road
Street
Somerset BA16 0HR
Tel: 01458 447275
Cosyfeet is a leading footwear company whose mail-order catalogue is aimed mainly at the housebound elderly. It specialises in wider, deeper, roomier slippers, sandals and shoes.

GENERAL EQUIPMENT DISTRIBUTORS

A great many of the items I have listed are available commercially; the local Social Services Department may be able to assist people with disabilities. Your GP will have a list of equipment that may be prescribed or may be available from the Department of Health. Alternatively, you should talk to your district nurse, health visitor or social worker.

There are many organisations that distribute a range of equipment. The Disabled Living Centres Council is the national organisation of 35 independent Disabled Living Centres in the UK which provide assessment, advice and information on daily living. The majority of Centres also have a large range of equipment on display; trained advisors are able to offer impartial advice and so help avoid costly mistakes. Equipment includes children's equipment, clothing and footwear, continence management, communication equipment and help with eating and drinking, hoists and lifting, mobility, personal care, seating and sleeping. For information on the nearest Centre, contact:

The Disabled Living Centres Council
286 Camden Road
London N7 0BJ
Tel: 0171–700 1707

The Disabled Living Foundation
380–384 Harrow Road
London W9 2HU
Tel: 0171–289 6111

The Disabled Living Foundation (part of the DLCC) responds to over 30,000 letters and telephone calls a year about where people can obtain equipment, footwear and clothing and on all aspects of independent living. It has a permanent exhibition of equipment and aids, from small gadgets to wheelchairs, which can be seen by appointment in London.

Disability Action

The Northern Ireland Information Service for Disabled People
2 Annadale Avenue
Belfast BT7 3JR
Tel: 01232 491011
This is a lobbying body and information unit.

Disability Scotland Information Service
5 Shandwick Place
Edinburgh EH2 4RG
Tel: 0131–229 8632
For information on equipment and an advisory service.

Disability Wales
Wales Council for the Disabled
(Cyngor Cymru I'r Anabl)
Llys Ifor
Crescent Road
Caerphilly
Mid Glamorgan CF8 1XL
Tel: 01222 887325

The Disability Information Trust
Mary Marlborough Centre
Nuffield Orthopaedic Centre
Headington, Oxford OX3 7LD
Tel: 01865 227592
The Disability Information Trust is a registered charity supported by the Department of Health. It is an unrivalled source of independent and authoritative information on products and ideas to assist people with disabilities in their daily living. Its main activity is to assess and test a whole range of disability equipment and publish the results in its series of books, *Equipment for Disabled People*. Full details of all products are included along with descriptive comments, photographs, specifications, manufacturers and prices. In addition, much advice is offered in the form of points to consider before any purchase is made. Most aspects of daily living are included; the series comprises 14 titles, from outdoor transport to home management. A free descriptive leaflet is available on request.

REMAP GB
Hazeldene
Ightham
Sevenoaks
Kent TN15 9AD
Tel: 01732 883818
REMAP can design, manufacture and supply aids and equipment free of charge for people with disabilities whose problems cannot be solved with standard commercial equipment. This is made possible by volunteers all over the country who contribute their time and skills. Leaflets are available free of charge; their handbook (£5 including p & p) details helpful organisations, engineers and therapists throughout the UK, and features illustrations of the equipment they have made.

The British Red Cross Society
9 Grosvenor Crescent
London SW1X 7EJ
Tel: 0171–235 5454
The Red Cross has 1,000 depots across the UK carrying stocks of items for short-term loan. Charges are modest and may be waived in cases of hardship. In addition, its range of services includes therapeutic beauty care, mobility aids, medical loans, escort and transport services, first-aid duties and training, a home-from-hospital scheme, and specially organised holidays.

HOUSEHOLD AND GENERAL EQUIPMENT

The following companies supply a variety of goods – details of their prices and/or catalogues are available on request.

The Special Collection
The Special Collection
J. D. Williams
53 Dale Street
Manchester M60 6ES
Tel: 0161–237 1200 (dept SCL2007)
The Special Collection catalogue offers a wide selection of carefully selected clothes for men and women with special needs. The clothes are designed to make dressing simple and are made in fabrics that are easy to care for. Diagrams throughout the catalogue highlight the easy dressing features, which include velcro fastenings, generous arm holes and long front zips. Catalogues available on request.

Home and Comfort
PO Box 25
Wellesbourne
Warwick CV35 9TY
Tel: 01789 470055
Mail-order goods including bath handles, hearing amplifiers, extending shoe trees, etc.

CC Products
152 Markham Road
Charminster
Bournemouth BH9 1JE
Tel: 01202 522260
Manufacturers of a 'portaloo' for long journeys.

Homecraft Supplies Ltd
Farnham Trading Estate
Farnham
Surrey GU9 9NN
Tel: 01252 714182
Homecraft produces a catalogue of special products for older people, from household and kitchen items to ramps and wheelchairs.

Keep Able
Fleming Close
Park Farm
Wellingborough
Northants NN8 6UF (Catalogue only, shops in London, Northants and the West Midlands)
Tel: 01933 679426
Large range of small items and larger goods and equipment for the house and garden, available from shops or by catalogue.

Chester-Care
Low Moor Estate
Kirkby in Ashfield
Notts NG17 7JZ
Tel: 01623 757955
Mail-order catalogue of small and larger household items for independent life at home.

Infratech
2 Dukes Court
Wellington Street
Luton
Beds LU1 5AF
Tel: 01582 455239
Products to enhance the volume of the television for the hearing impaired.

Clover
21 Francis Street
Leicester LE2 2BE
Tel: 0116 270 5671
Shop selling goods and clothes.

Parker Hilton Ltd
Parker Hilton House
Primrose Street
Tyldesley
Manchester M29 8BQ
Tel: 01942 891818
Manufacturers of a portable jigsaw carrier

The Boots Company plc
Nottingham
England
Boots chemists distribute their own catalogue of household aids, including bedroom, bathroom and mobility equipment, at their local outlets.

Dressense
Hampden House
Hampden Road
Chalfont St Peter
Bucks SL9 9DP
Tel: 01753 892728
Mail-order clothes.

Further Reading
Directory of Aids for Disabled and Elderly People, Ann Darnbrough and Derek Kinrade (Woodhead-Faulkner, 1986), £14.95

chapter nine

KEEPING SAFE

*Home Protection, Basic Safety Guidelines
and Where to Turn for Help*

IT IS IMPORTANT that older people know that their homes and they themselves are safe at all times – safe from accidents in the home or from criminal acts. Accidents do happen but most can be avoided by taking precautions. Crime statistics do make disturbing reading but, in fact, figures show that elderly people are less likely to be attacked or robbed than any other age group. By taking reasonable precautions and avoiding danger there is no reason why older people should not live their lives with complete confidence and security.

WHO CAN HELP?

Help the Aged offers the most comprehensive help in the form of advice and literature about the risks and prevention of fire, burglary and break-ins and accidents in the home, as well as fundraising for the provision of home safety equipment. This chapter includes information from Help the Aged's range of free advice leaflets:
'Security in your Home'
'Safety In your Home'
'Fire'

Help the Aged
Information Department
St James Walk
London EC1R 0BE
Tel: 0171–253 0253

SeniorLine (free): 0800 289 404 (10 a.m. to 4 p.m. Monday to Friday)
Age Concern produces Factsheet No 33, 'Feeling Safer at Home and Outside', full of invaluable advice (*address page 101*)

Royal Society for Prevention of
Accidents (ROSPA)
Cannon House
The Priory
Queensway
Birmingham B4 6BS
Tel: 0121–200 2461

The ROSPA publishes two leaflets:
RSDR 167, *Older and Wise – Road Safety for Older People* (£1.90)
HS 55, *Home Safety Factsheet – Safety of Older People* (£1.90)
    See also pages 186–7.

Help in an Emergency

Community alarms are a boon to people living on their own, enabling them to call for help even if they cannot reach a telephone. All that is needed is a telephone line and an electric 13-amp power point. A special button on the telephone or on a pendant will alert control centre staff who can speak to the user (even if he or she cannot reach the telephone) and send whatever help is necessary. These alarms are not just for use in an emergency: staff at the control centre can also provide friendly advice and assistance.

Help the Aged's Community Alarms Department is the largest provider of alarms to elderly people in the country, having supplied over 27,000 alarms so far. It runs a national alarms scheme throughout the UK. Advice can be given on whether the local authority has an alarm scheme, what it will cost and whom to contact. If there is no local scheme, or if you cannot afford the scheme, the charity may provide an alarm. The charity also sells alarms, arranges monitoring from 200 centres around the UK and publishes *The Guide to Community Alarms* (£1.95 post paid). Contact their Community Alarms Department at the address or telephone numbers provided above.

Age Concern recommends the *ComCare Messenger*, a monitoring service which incorporates an emergency button, visual ringing telephone, remote control pendant or clip, high-speed dialling, adjustable volume and ring tone, hand-free operation and activity monitor which will check up you if you do not use the phone during the pre-arranged period of your choice. For costs and further information contact Age Concern/ComCare free on 0800 300 123.

Security in the Home

Most break-ins are not the work of professional burglars. Many are carried out by opportunists: petty thieves who see an open window or insecure door.

Remember that if you are going out even for a few moments you should check that all doors and windows are securely locked. If going away on holiday you must be sure to cancel all deliveries – milk on the doorstep for a few days is a true give-away. You should also ask neighbours to keep an eye on your home and to report anything suspicious.

Garden tools should be locked away – a ladder can be very useful for the opportunistic burglar. And no holidaymakers should display their home address on the outside of their luggage – why advertise a departure to burglars who are lurking at the airport or ferry terminal? Companies such as Homesitters and Housewatch (*addresses page 90*) can offer security and peace of mind to anyone who will be away from their home for a period of time.

Closed and locked windows are an effective deterrent to burglars – they will rarely break a window and risk the noise or danger of cuts. Keys should be removed from locked windows and kept out of sight and reach.

A front door should be made of solid wood, with a strong frame, a good lock and at least one dead lock, a door viewer and a security chain. Back and side doors are equally vulnerable.

Extra security in the form of intruder alarms and exterior lighting can help fight crime and make the house more secure. Your local Crime Prevention Officer (at local police stations) should be able to discuss alternatives and give you advice.

Crime Concern
Signal Point
Station Road
Swindon
Wilts SN1 1FE
Tel: 01793 514596

Crime Concern is a national organisation responsible for supporting and developing crime prevention activity. It can offer advice on many different aspects of crime prevention and general information, leaflets and a publication list on application.

Marking Possessions

Valuables are more likely to be found by the police if a record is kept of serial numbers and property is marked with the owner's postcode. This can be done by etching, die-stamping or using a security marker which can only be read under an ultra-violet light. Local Crime Prevention Officers or Neighbourhood Watch Groups can give details of where to get this marking equipment. They will also advise on where a window sticker can be obtained to warn thieves that property is marked. In addition, a full list of valuable items with descriptions and colour photographs can greatly assist in the safe return of stolen property.

A 40-page handbook entitled *Practical Ways to Crack Crime* and its shorter version *The Family Guide* are useful Home Office publications available free of charge in a range of different languages. Telephone Crime Prevention on 0171–373 2193 (24 hrs) to request copies.

Neighbourhood Watch schemes are self-help groups which work in partnership with the police. They aim to prevent crime and are able to offer valuable neighbourly help and advice. Ask your local Crime Prevention Officer if there is a scheme locally and, if not, why not help to set one up?

If the house is burgled...
- Do not touch anything.
- Contact the police straightaway.

VICTIM SUPPORT SCHEMES
(SEE ALSO CHAPTER 3, PAGE 54)

If your home is broken into or you are robbed on the street it can be traumatic experience. Victim Support Schemes can help and advise people who have suffered such experiences. They can provide support and understanding to people who need to get over the shock and regain their self-confidence. Ask at your local police station for the nearest branch or contact:

The National Association of Victim Support Schemes
39 Brixton Road
London SW9 6DZ
Tel: 0171–735 9166

Victim Support Scotland
14 Frederick Street
Edinburgh EH2 2HB
Tel: 0131–225 7779/8233

The Criminal Injuries Compensation Board
300 Bath Street
Glasgow G2 4JR
Tel: 0141–331 2726
Anyone who has been injured as a direct result of a crime may be eligible for compensation. *A Guide to The Criminal Injuries Compensation Scheme* sets out who can apply and what injuries qualify. Victims may need the services of a solicitor or advisor, but the Board will not cover the cost of this.

SOS Talisman
TALISMAN Ltd
Gray's Inn Corner
Ley Street
Ilford
Essex IG2 7RQ
Tel: 0181–554 5579
A private company selling personal alarms.

Aid Call plc
Linhay House
Ashburton
Devon TQ13 7UP
Tel: 01364 654321
A private company selling medical/panic personal alarms with transmitters to a central monitoring centre.

Response Electronics plc
Unit 1
First Quarter
Longmead Industrial Estate
Blenheim Road
Epsom
Surrey KT19 9QN
Tel: 01372 744330
A private company selling intruder alarms – telephone for the showroom nearest you.

Racal Chubb Products
PO Box 197
Wednesfield Road
Wolverhampton WV10 0ET
Tel: 01902 455440
Chubb is Britain's number one home security company, making door and window locks and other security products such as door chains, hinge bolts and door viewers. Phone for information on their product range and pocket security guide.

Burglar Alarms

Be sure that they conform to British Standard 4737. Other BS numbers apply to intruder alarms for consumer installation – be sure that it bears the Kite Mark. If in doubt, telephone the British Standards Institution on 0181–996 7372.

Banham Burglary Prevention Services
233 Kensington High Street
London W8 6SF
Tel: 0171–937 4311
For locks, grilles and gates, window locks, safes, burglar alarms and intercoms.

Jaguar Alarms
Januar House
191 Old Oak Road
London W3 7HH
Tel: 0181–743 1356
A private company selling intruder alarms.

Someone at the Door?

It makes sense to be cautious when the doorbell goes and you should not be embarrassed about refusing to let someone in – it is *your* home. Use the door viewer to see who it is and, if you do not know them, put on the chain before opening the door. If the caller has a good reason for being there, he or she will not mind being asked for an identification card.

If you are still not happy, ask for the name and the telephone number of the organisation the caller claims to represent, keep the chain on the door and telephone the organisation. If you do not have a telephone, just send the caller away. You can always ask him or her to return when you have a friend or neighbour there. If you are still suspicious, dial 999 and ask for the police.

STAYING SAFE AND ACTIVE

It is important that older people are safe from everyday accidents, most of which can be prevented. A few important practical steps can avoid the most common domestic accidents:

- Even in familiar surroundings, good lighting can help prevent a fall, particularly on the stairs.
- If climbing the stairs is difficult, handrails on both sides can help.
- Sturdy shoes with rubberised soles and non-slip heels can aid stability.
- Lifting heavy objects or bags should be avoided – ask for help.
- Rearrange the furniture so that you can move about freely and without bumping into things.
- Make sure there are no trailing flexes or rucked up carpets to trip over.

The Royal Society for the Prevention of Accidents (ROSPA) has as its sole objective the promotion of safety for all age groups in all environments. It is Europe's largest safety organisation and provides comment, advice, information, educational materials and training. It is a charity whose income is derived from membership fees and the sale of its services. ROSPA publishes safety in the home booklets, leaflets and audio-visual aids which are listed in a catalogue and available from the address given on *page 183*.

Royal National Institute for the Blind
224 Great Portland Street
London W1N 6AA
Tel: 0171–388 1266

The RNIB publishes a selection of leaflets on eye safety such as 'Protect your Eyes from Injuries at Home'.

Taking Medication
Some points to remember:

- Keep all medicines out of reach of any young children who may visit.
- Make sure you understand the instructions on the label – ask the pharmacist if you are in any doubt. The right amount at the right time will help you get better: anything else may be harmful.
- Ask the pharmacist about pill dispensers, as these can help to organise your daily requirements.
- Some caps on bottles are childproof – and often fairly adultproof, too! The pharmacist can help if you have problems.
- Return unused medicines to the pharmacist.

FIRE

One of the most important investments anyone can make in the home is a smoke alarm. Even a small fire can be destructive and traumatic. A smoke alarm can detect the first whiff of smoke and avoid a great deal of damage.

Basic smoke alarms can be purchased at comparatively low prices. Choose one bearing the British Standard Number BS5446 and the Kite Mark. Smoke alarms can be fitted in any room where a fire might start (but not in the kitchen or bathroom, as steam or ordinary cooking fumes can trigger the alarm) and at the bottom of each staircase. B & Q stores sell smoke alarms and offer a 10 per cent discount to members of the 'B & Q over-60s club' (*see page 203 for details*). The instructions will advise on the best site for an alarm. The alarm will indicate when its batteries need to be changed.

British Gas will carry out a free gas safety check on gas appliances if:

- you are over 60 years of age and live alone or with someone who also qualifies
- you are a registered disabled person of any age and live alone or with someone who also qualifies
- you receive a State Disability Benefit and live alone or with someone who also qualifies.

The check will consist of a basic examination and includes any necessary adjustments and materials up to a cost of £2.50 plus VAT. If as a result of the check any additional work needs to be done it will have to be paid for, so ask for an estimate first. If you receive Income Support ask at your local Department of Social Security office to see if you are entitled to any financial assistance before ordering the work to be done.

A free booklet, 'Advice for Older People', gives information about the free gas safety check and special adaptors which can be fitted free of charge to some gas fires and cookers to make the controls easier to use. Also, 'Help yourself to Gas Safety' is available free of charge from your local British Gas showroom (the telephone number is in the telephone book under 'Gas').

Smokers

Smokers should use plenty of deep ashtrays and be sure to put them in places where they cannot be knocked over. If you or someone you live with smokes, make sure all cigarettes are stubbed out properly, particularly before emptying the ashtray into a bin, and check that no cigarettes are still burning in an ashtray before you go out or go to bed. Everyone should now be aware of the great dangers of smoking in bed.

In the Kitchen

When cooking with fats and oils, due care must be taken never to leave pans unattended and to lower the temperature if they start spitting. If a frying or chip pan catches fire, *never* pour water on it. Turn off the heat and smother the flames with the pan lid or a damp cloth or blanket and leave it to cool for at least half an hour. It is best to call the fire brigade even if the fire appears to be out. If you are thinking of buying a fire blanket, make sure you choose one bearing the British Standard number BS6575.

Heaters

Ensure heaters are used away from bedclothes, furniture or curtains and that they are not in a position where they could be knocked over. Sitting too close to a heater should always be avoided, as clothing could catch fire. Paraffin heaters should always be filled out of doors and never filled or moved when alight.

Electricity

All electrical equipment should be checked regularly by a competent electrician for safety. A list of approved contractors can be found at most Electricity Board shops or local reference libraries. Fuses should be checked for the correct rating and flexes checked to make sure that they are not too long or worn.

Avoid placing a flex under carpeting, as this damages the flex. Do not overload power points by using multiple adaptors. If any piece of electrical equipment cuts out continually or gives off a strange smell, or if the plug feels warm, switch it off immediately and have it checked.

chapter ten

MOBILITY AND GETTING AROUND

*Transport Schemes and Special Vehicles
to Help Older People Stay Mobile*

ONE OF THE WAYS of maintaining independence for as long as possible is to keep fit and mobile, and mobility around the home is as important as being able to get out and about.

Walking sticks and frames, in a wide variety designs and grips, are available by prescription or commercially. Whichever you decide on, you should always check it bears the British Standards Kite Mark. Stairlifts, walking frames that double as trolleys for transporting things around the house or with seats or shopping baskets attached, and other useful mobility aids are discussed in Chapter 8.

Help the Aged (*see page 182*) produces a leaflet called 'Mobility' (sponsored by Stannah Stairlifts – *see page 173*) which advises how conditions that sometimes restrict mobility can be prevented, alleviated or even cured, how to remain mobile and the range of help and advice that is available.

Age Concern (*see page 101*) produces Factsheet No 26, 'Travel Information for Older People', which gives information and advice on travel and financial assistance relating to travel, and on mobility and other possible difficulties.

For further details on the provision of equipment, first check to see what is available through the local Social Services Department. Certain equipment is available on loan from the British Red Cross Society (*address page 180*) or for sale from The Disabled Living Centres Council (*address page 179*). For information about white sticks for people with loss of sight, contact the RNIB (*address page 187*).

MOTORING

Most driving licences are valid until the driver is 70; thereafter licences must be renewed every three years. Unless there has been a change in the driver's medical circumstances the new licence will be granted automatically. If you are in any doubt about your eligibility to drive you should talk to your GP. Any change in medical circumstances must immediately be reported to the Driver Vehicle Licensing Centre at:

DVLC
Swansea
SA6 7JL
Tel: 01792 72151

Contrary to many insurance companies, Sun Alliance actually rewards mature drivers. If you are aged over 50 and a careful driver, you could cut the cost of your car insurance. New Motorist 50+ policyholders enjoy an average saving of £50 on their annual premium when they switch from their previous policy. The nearest branch can be found in the Yellow Pages, or details can be obtained from the address below (please quote reference number P310XX):

Sun Alliance Insurance UK
National Quotation Centre
Linden House
Horsham
West Sussex RH12 1BT
Freephone: 0800 300 800

SUN ALLIANCE
INSURANCE UK
TOGETHER WE MAKE SOME ALLIANCE

People who are unable to walk or cannot walk more than a short distance, and either drive a car or are driven by someone else, can ask their local Social Services Department (see telephone book under Social Services for the local council or borough) about the national Orange Badge Scheme, which entitles badge holders to be exempt from certain parking restrictions. Only persons who satisfy the criteria for Mobility Allowance are eligible for the Orange Parking Badge, but that does not necessarily mean that you must be in receipt of Mobility Allowance in order to obtain a Badge. Many places have parking spaces specially reserved for cars displaying the Orange Badge on the windscreen; bearers may also stop for a limited time in places where parking is not normally allowed. Further details are also available in a leaflet from:

The Mobility Unit
Room S10/20
Department of Transport
2 Marsham Street
London SW1P 3EB
Tel: 0171–276 5252/5256/5257 or 0171–276 4973

The Mobility Advice and Vehicle Information Service (MAVIS)
Department of Transport TRL
Crowthorne
Berks RG11 6AU
Tel: 01344 770456

The MAVIS provides driving ability assessment, advice on driving, car adaptations and a range of car options for people with disabilities both as drivers and passengers. Twenty adapted vehicles are available to test drive, with a variety of equipment and accessories for demonstration. A free information service is also available.

The Disability Information Trust
Mary Marlborough Centre
Nuffield Orthopaedic Centre
Headington
Oxford OX3 7LD
Tel: 01865 227592

The Disability Information Trust is a registered charity which is supported by the Department of Health. It is an unrivalled source of independent and authoritative information on products and ideas to assist people with disabilities in their daily living. The Trust assesses and tests a wide range of disability equipment that comes onto the UK market, and publishes the series of reference books, *Equipment for Disabled People*. The books offer advice, guidance, product specification, comment, manufacturers, prices and photographs. It is available from most libraries; a free leaflet can be obtained on request.

The Mobility Information Service
National Mobility Centre
Unit 2a, Atcham Estate
Shrewsbury SY4 4UG
Tel: 01743 761889

The MIS provides driving assessments for people with disabilities, and general advice on mobility problems and benefits. It produces publications covering various aspects of mobility, including information on specific vehicle road tests from the point of view of a driver with disabilities.

BUS TRAVEL

Fare concessions are available on buses; these vary from one local authority to another. In some, travel is free at certain times or available at reduced rates for women over 60 and men over 65. For further information on concessionary rates and bus passes look for information at the local library or Citizens Advice Bureau, or contact the local Age Concern group (*address page 101*).

Coach Travel

Coach travel can work out cheaper than the train, and is often more convenient, with direct routes, fewer changes and well-equipped vehicles with toilets and light refreshments. Be sure to ask in advance regarding facilities or accessibility for passengers with disabilities. National Express coaches offer discounts on fares to holders of its Senior Discount Coach Card – for further information contact:

National Express Ltd
Head Office
Ensign Court
4 Vicarage Road
Edgbaston
Birmingham B15 3ES
Tel: 0121–625 1122

Rail Travel

People over 60 are entitled to a Senior Railcard, which offers one third off the price of leisure travel for a year from the date of purchase. Railcards may be bought for £16 from British Rail stations or selected travel agents. To apply you need some form of proof of age such as a passport, NHS Medical card, birth certificate or current Senior Railcard.

A Senior Railcard entitles people to ⅓[1] off the price of:

- Savers and Supersavers
- SuperAdvance Returns
- Network AwayBreaks
- Cheap Day Singles and Returns
- Standard Single and Open Returns
- First-Class Single and Open Returns
- First-Class and Standard Day Singles
- First-Class and Standard Day Returns
- All-zone One-Day Travelcards subject to minimum fare
- Rail Rovers

Discounts are also available to holders on some ferry services.

A Senior Railcard does *not* give a discount on:

- Travel in Silver Standard Accommodation
- Special excursions and Charters (i.e. those not listed in public timetables)
- Railair Coach Links
- Channel trains between London (Victoria) and Channel ports, or between London (Waterloo) and Southampton Docks
- Eurostar and other international services
- Any non-BR services other than those already mentioned.

Leisure First

Leisure First offers off-peak First-class travel at half the usual First-class fare. It is available on selected InterCity services throughout the week, with the exception of those running at peak business times.

To qualify for Leisure First people must spend a Saturday night away and reserve seats no later than 4 p.m. the day before they travel. Further details and conditions are available in the Bargain Fares leaflet, available from BR.

Rail Europe Senior Card

Rail Europe Senior Card is available for £7.50 to BR Senior Railcard holders and offers savings on rail and sea travel to 19 European countries. Discounts are based on full single or return fares and are for international travel only (not journeys within a country).

---

[1] Please check for full details at local stations, as there may be certain ticket, route, train and time restrictions applicable.

The Rail Europe Senior Card and details of fares to individual destinations are available at main British Rail stations, British Rail International appointed travel agents, or from:

The International Rail Centre
Victoria Station
London SW1V 1JY
Tel: 0171–834 2345

Tripscope

Tripscope provides a national travel and transport information service for people with mobility problems. It provides assistance with any aspect of travel, for those planning specific journeys both in the UK and overseas whether by private motor or public transport.

From their offices in London and Bristol the experience and friendly staff can discuss personal travel needs, thereby helping to reduce pre-travel anxiety and in-journey stress. Above all, with the assistance of their comprehensive database they can provide accurate and up-to-date information so that journeys may be arranged and undertaken with confidence.

They will also offer assistance and information about related matters such as accessible lavatories and wheelchair hire, and will deal with enquiries by telephone, letter or tape.

The service is free both to individual people with disabilities or the elderly and the professionals and organisations working with them. Tripscope is not a travel agency and cannot make bookings. For further information contact:

The Information Officer
The Courtyard
Evelyn Road
London W4 5JL
Tel: 0181–994 9294
Minicom: 0181–994 9294
  or
Pamwell House
160 Pennywell Road
Bristol BS5 OTX
Tel: 0119 941 4094

Voluntary and Community Transport Schemes

Further information on local mobility and voluntary and community transport services may be obtained from Tripscope (*see above*) or the Department of Transport Mobility Unit (*see page 190*).

Dial-a-Ride and Taxicard

DaRT – Dial-a-Ride and Taxicard Users – represents over 15,000 Londoners with disabilities who are unable to use public transport. DaRT carries out and publishes research on the two specialist transport services for people with disabilities, Dial-a-Ride and Taxicard, and works to persuade central and local Government to recognise the need for increased funding for both services. DaRT also promotes fully accessible mainstream public transport – buses, tubes and trains.

Members of Dial-a-Ride and Taxicard can join DaRT for an annual voluntary membership fee and receive regular information which keeps them up to date on all transport issues affecting people with disabilities. DaRT is funded by the London Borough Grants Committee. For free leaflets on the service, and others such as 'Accessible Buses', 'How to Get Disabled People Moving in London' and 'Transport in European Capitals', contact:

DaRT
St Margaret's
25 Leighton Road
London NW5 2QD
Tel: 0171–482 2325

Dial-a-Ride
Dial-a-Ride is a door-to-door transport service for people who are unable to use public transport. It is available to people of any age and any disability. Dial-a-Ride mini-buses are specially designed. All of them can carry wheelchair users, and Dial-a-Ride drivers will help passengers on and off the bus and see them safely to their doors.

Passengers pay their own fare – about the same as an ordinary bus – and may travel alone or accompanied to go shopping, to visit friends, etc. Dial-a-Ride cannot take people to hospital appointments, as this service should be provided by the non-emergency ambulance service.

The Dial-a-Ride service runs seven days a week throughout the year and operates throughout the Greater London area. Anyone wishing to join the service should contact DaRT for the local Dial-a-Ride address.

Taxicard
The Taxicard Scheme allows people with disabilities who are unable to use mainstream public transport to use licensed London cabs at a reduced rate. Taxicard holders can book a cab for any purpose at any time and can travel anywhere in the Greater London area.

Taxicard is operated and funded in most London boroughs; membership is usually free. In most boroughs there are restrictions to the number of trips a Taxicard holder can make.

In most boroughs Taxicard users can make a journey costing up to £10.80 on the taximeter for a flat fee of £1.50. Any amount over the £10.80 limit must be paid in full. To join the London-wide scheme contact:

LATU (The London Accessible Transport Unit)
Britannia House
1–11 Glenthorpe Road
London W6 0LF
Tel: 0181–748 7272
The British Red Cross Society (*address page 180*) provides volunteers and escorts to enable housebound people and people with disabilities to make journeys.

Hertz Rent-a-Car
Head Office
1272 London Road
London SW16 4DQ
Tel: 0181–679 1799

Hertz Rent-a-Car is purported to be the only car hire firm which is prepared to rent cars to individuals over 74 years of age.

The Chalfont Line
4 Medway Parade
Perivale
Middlesex UB6 8HA
Tel: 0181–997 3799
The Chalfont Line provides transport (and holidays) for the elderly and people with disabilities.

AIR TRAVEL

Most airlines are extremely helpful to anyone with a disability or those who cannot manage the enormous distances that they may have to cover between the terminal and the aircraft. If airlines are informed well in advance that a passenger may need assistance, they may be able to arrange transport from check-in to the aircraft and priority seating. They should also be informed if a passenger will be taking a wheelchair, walking frame or other aid.

British Airways' Travel Club offers discounts on accommodation and car hire for its over-55 members. For further information contact:

British Airways
PO Box 10
Heathrow Airport
Hounslow
Middlesex TW6 2JA
Tel: 0181–759 5511

LOW-SPEED VEHICLES

A number of different low-speed, battery-powered vehicles are on the market which do not require a driving licence. Many have optional hoods, shopping baskets and other accessories and may be driven on the pavement as they only travel at a few miles per hour. For further information contact the nearest Disabled Living Centre (*address page 179*) or RADAR (*address page 60*).

Anyone considering buying one of these vehicles should check the cost of maintenance, as replacement tyres, batteries and labour charges may be high. Brochures and 'test drives' should be free of charge.

Other suppliers include:

The Bedford Mobility Centre
FREEPOST 348
Watford
Herts WD2 8FP
Tel: 01234 266666
This company sells scooters and four-wheelers.

Ortho Kinetics UK Ltd
FREEPOST
Wedensfield
Wolverhampton WC13 3XA
Tel: 01902 866166
This company sells scooters.

Electric Mobility Euro Ltd
Sea King Road
Lynx Trading Estate
Yeovil
Somerset BA20 2YS
Tel: 01935 22156
Company selling scooters and three- and four-wheelers.

Further Reading
Directory of Aids for Disabled and Elderly People, Ann Darnbrough and Derek Kinrade (Woodhead-Faulkner, 1986), £14.95
Out and About: A Travel and Transport Guide, Richard Armitage and John Taylor (Age Concern, 1990), £6.95
Arranging Outings for Older People: A group organiser's guide, Nancy Tuft (Age Concern 1990), £4.95

chapter eleven

HOBBIES AND INTERESTS

Exploring Further Education, Volunteering, and Other New Pursuits

FOR MANY PEOPLE, retirement offers opportunities to follow up new or favourite hobbies, interests and activities for which there may not have been time previously. There is an exciting choice of activities, courses, sports and games on offer that can make retirement a new beginning.

In Chapter 2 I discussed the importance of keeping fit and of healthy exercise; in that chapter many forms of exercise and relaxation were examined. Local authorities arrange many sporting or leisure activities. It is worth checking at your local library to investigate the huge range of adult education courses which are offered – such as languages, painting, cooking or photography – and for details on facilities or classes at the nearest leisure centre. They should also have information on any local interest groups, sports clubs and other classes, societies or groups.

NEW BEGINNINGS

The Dark Horse Venture
Kelton
Woodlands Road
Liverpool L17 0AN
Tel: 0151–729 0092 or 0181–460 3016
'The Dark Horse Venture – discovering the dark horse in you!'
The Dark Horse Venture is open to all over-55s and encourages them to take up new activities and discover hidden talents. To qualify, all you have to do is select an activity which you have never tried before and pursue it on a regular basis for a minimum of 12 months. During this time you will receive guidance and advice from a chosen person with professional training or proven experience in that activity. Dark Horse Venture Certificates are awarded on satisfactory completion of the chosen activity.

There is no limit to the number of single-subject certificates that people can embark on and accomplish. Those who have been awarded one certificate from each of three categories can apply for the Gold Seal Certificate. For a general information pack and registration form, contact The Dark Horse Venture at the address given above.

Age Resource
Astral House
1268 London Road
London SW16 4ER
Tel: 0181–679 2201

Age Resource was established by Age Concern England to ensure that knowledge, skills and experience gained during the first 50 or 60 years of life should be developed, diversified, utilised and enjoyed. It promotes a wide range of opportunities for involvement by older people, and develops and expands contacts and co-operation with other organisations. In addition it makes awards to celebrate the achievements of older people in group activities.

Townswomen's Guilds
75 Harborne Road
Edgbaston
Birmingham
Tel: 0121–456 3435

Townswomen's Guilds are for all women regardless of politics, race, age, religion or circumstances. Each Guild is autonomous, meeting as convenient. There are 91,000 members in 2,000 Guilds, grouped into 115 Federations. Activities range from patchwork to parachuting!

Members enjoy a wide range of sport and creative leisure. Activities range from table tennis and bowls to cookery, gardening and drama.

Sixty Plus – The Open Age Project
1 Thorpe Close
London W10 5XL
Tel: 0181–969 9105

Sixty Plus set up The Open Age Project to develop new opportunities for older people to stay active, encouraging them to take part in education, arts, outings and visits, languages, culture and sports.

Third Age Trust
1 Stockwell Green
London SW9 9JF
Tel: 0171–737 2541

Forms over-55s groups to study a subject or to participate in leisure activities.

The Scottish Retirement Council
204 Bath Street
Glasgow G2 4HL
Tel: 0141–332 9427

The Scottish Retirement Council promotes education for retired people and runs a number of craft and hobby centres.

REACH
Bear Wharf
27 Bankside
London SE1 9DP
Tel: 0171–928 0452

A national, not-for-profit organisation; REACH finds part-time expenses-only jobs for retired or redundant businesspeople or other professional men and women who want to use their skills to help charitable organisations, depending on their experience and availability. Regional 'matchers', themselves retired professional people, send anyone interested a selection of jobs to consider.

The New Horizons Trust
Paramount House
290–292 Brighton Road
South Croydon
Surrey CR2 6AG
Tel: 0181–666 0201
The New Horizons Trust is a charity which offers cash grants to groups setting up projects that benefit the community. There must be at least ten people in the group and at least half must be aged 60 or over. The project is a new one which makes use of the knowledge and expertise of group members, aiming to use their skills to fill in gaps in social services and to improve local amenities. Grants of up to £5,000 are available and projects should involve as many retired people as possible.

VOLUNTEERING

A vast number of organisations survive thanks to the work of volunteers. Help is always gratefully received, will sometimes pay moderate expenses, will enable volunteers to choose the amount of hours they work and may require some training. Here are just a few – more are listed on *pages 61–2*:

Age Concern England
(*address page 101*)

Help the Aged
(*address page 101*)

The Samaritans (National Headquarters)
10 The Grove
Slough S4 1QP
Tel: 01753 532713
Samaritans is a voluntary organisation offering confidential emotional support 24 hours a day every day of the year, to those in distress, despair or feeling tempted to suicide. Their service is free and confidential and anyone can phone, visit or write to any of the 200 branches throughout the UK and Republic of Ireland.

The Samaritans seeks volunteers from those about to retire or the recently retired to help maintain this service; preparation or training is given – contact your local branch for details or look in the telephone book under 'S'.

The Winged Fellowship
Angel House
20–32 Pentonville Road
London N1 9XD
Tel: 0171–833 2594
The Winged Fellowship is a charity which provides holidays and respite care for people with physical disabilities at five UK holiday centres. Fully trained staff at the centres are helped by over 6,000 volunteers a year who assist in providing companionship and care to the guests. 'Mature' volunteers are particularly welcome and The Winged Fellowship pays board, lodging and travel within the UK, so all it costs is time!

RSVP and Community Service Volunteers
237 Pentonville Road
London N1 9NG
Tel: 0171–278 6601
The RSVP programme within CSV encourages the over-50s or retired people to participate in voluntary activity for the benefit of themselves

and the local community (*see also Chapter 3, page 61*). They have 260 different types of project.

Homestart
2 Salisbury Road
Leicester LE1 7QR
Tel: 0116 233 9955
Homestart is a registered charity whose volunteers befriend parents with children under five who are feeling isolated and stressed. Like the RSVP, Homestart welcomes volunteers with experience (in this case of parenting/being around young children). Volunteers usually visit one or two families a week for two to three hours. Branches nationwide.

Saneline
199–205 Old Marylebone Road
London NW1 5QP
Tel: 0171–724 6570 (admin only)
Saneline always needs more mature volunteers to help on the phoneline. Please write for more information (*see also Chapter 3, page 52*).

British Trust for Conservation Volunteers
36 St Mary's Street
Wallingford
Oxon OX10 0EU
Tel: 01491 839766

Voluntary Service Overseas
317 Putney Bridge Road
London SW15 2PG
Tel: 0181–780 2266
VSO encourages all ages to work on agricultural, business, social, technical, health or teaching projects overseas.

National Association of Leagues of Hospital Friends
Second Floor
Fairfax House
Colchester
Essex CO1 1RJ
Tel: 01206 761227
Volunteers are required to help on fundraising, helping in the shop, canteen, or wards of hospitals befriending or reading to people.

National Association of Volunteer Bureaux
St Peter's Court
College Road
Saltley
Birmingham B8 3TE
Tel: 0121–327 0265
NAVB supports and represents a network of 250 volunteer bureaux throughout England, Wales and Northern Ireland. Volunteer bureaux are the local experts on volunteering and they enable people to get involved in voluntary action. Bureaux interview and advise volunteers, collect information on local volunteering opportunities, match volunteers with opportunities and offer support and training.

FURTHER EDUCATION

Council for the Accreditation of Correspondence Colleges
27 Marylebone Road
London NW1 5JS
Tel: 0171–935 5391
The Council for the Accreditation of Correspondence Colleges is a registered charity which accredits organisations offering home-study courses. It aims to promote education and training and to raise standards of tuition in distance education. Some 200 courses at 41 colleges are currently listed in an information leaflet which is available free of charge.

Education Resources for Older People

The City Lit
Bolt Court
Fleet Street
London EC4A 3DY
Tel: 0171–583 4748
EdROP aims to develop and monitor learning opportunities in the adult education service for men and women over retirement age in London.

The Scottish Community Education Services
40 Torthicken Street
Edinburgh EH3 8JJ
Tel: 0131–229 9166
For information about further education in Scotland.

The Welsh Joint Education Committee
245 Western Avenue
Cardiff CF5 2YX
Tel: 01222 561231

The Wales Access Unit
Main Block, Ty Oldfield
Llantrisant Road
Llandaff
Cardiff CF5 2YT
Tel: 01225 575932
For further information about education opportunities in Wales.

The Open College
FREEPOST
Warrington WA2 7BR
Tel: 01925 232899
The Open College offers courses by correspondence, linked with either business or academic pursuits.

Skill: National Bureau for Students with Disabilities
336 Brixton Road
London SW9 7AA
Tel: 0171–274 0565
Advice or information available on request.

University of the Third Age (National Office)
1 Stockwell Green
London SW9 9JF
Tel: 0171–737 2541
The University of the Third Age works to increase self-help educational or learning opportunities for retired people. It enables members to share many educational, creative and leisure activities which are organised mainly in small groups that meet regularly, often in each other's homes. A small start-up grant, advice and speakers are available.

The National Extension College
18 Brooklands Avenue
Cambridge CB2 2HN
Tel: 01223 316644

The National Extension College is an education charity providing long-distance learning courses for adult learners, and resource materials for use in a wide range of educational and training areas. The National Extension College offers a variety of courses to older people. One of its aims is to enable people to have a second chance at education through distance learning (through to GCSE and A level) – courses include basic English, maths, computing, business, languages, engineering, birdwatching, writing, animal management – around 80 different subjects.

The Royal London Society for the Blind
105 Salusbury Road
London NW6 6RH
0171–624 8844

Charity which provides education training and employment for blind people.

The National Adult School Organisation
MASU Centre
Gaywood Croft
Cregoe Street
Birmingham B15 2ED
Tel: 0121–622 3400

The National Adult School Organisation aims to promote friendly discussion groups throughout the country. Groups meet in community centres, church rooms, public halls and members' homes. A handbook containing 40 topics for discussion is produced each year for use by the groups. Study weekends, a summer school and study tours abroad are organised to complement handbook topics.

Workers' Educational Association
17 Victoria Park Square
London E2 9EB
Tel: 0181–983 1515

The WEA is a voluntary, democratic and nationwide organisation providing a wide range of courses for adults. It receives financial assistance from central and local Government. Friendly, enjoyable classes are held in a variety of locations; costs to students are kept to a minimum.

National Institute of Continuing Education
19b de Montfort Street
Leicester LE1 7GE
Tel: 0116 255 1451

Courses for older adults throughout England and Wales as well as residential short courses. A book called *Time to Learn* is published twice a year, price £4.25.

Retirement Education Centre
Bedford College
6 Rothsay Gardens
Bedford MK40 3QB
Tel: 01234 360304

The Open University
Walton Hall
Milton Keynes MK7 6AA
Tel: 01908 274066

The Open University offers literally hundreds of correspondence courses in numerous subjects: arts, science, technology, maths, etc. The cost varies depending on whether students are pursuing the 'study pack' or a full degree course.

GARDENING

Please also see In the Garden (*Chapter 8, pages 175–6*)

The Royal Horticultural Society
80 Vincent Square
London SW1P 2PE
Tel: 0171–834 4333
The Royal Horticultural Society offers many benefits to RHS members. The £23 (plus £7 enrolment fee) membership fee provides free entry to gardens all over Britain, *The Garden* magazine monthly, special entry to the Chelsea Flower Show and other gardening fairs and free advice on gardening projects and problems. They also hold an educational programme which qualifies participants for awards and diplomas, and arrange lectures and holidays.

The National Society of Allotment and Leisure Gardeners Ltd
Odell House
Hunters Road
Corby
Northants NN17 1JE
Tel: 01536 266576
The National Society of Allotment and Leisure Gardeners helps people to enjoy the recreation of gardening and encourages the formation of local associations. It promotes education and publicity and protects allotments for future generations.

Horticultural Therapy

Horticultural Therapy
Trunkwell Park
Beech Hill
Reading RG7 2AT
Tel: 01734 884844
Horticultural Therapy demonstrates that age or disability need be no barrier to successful and rewarding gardening. It promotes gardening in all its forms as a therapeutic activity and advises on techniques, equipment and tools as appropriate. It runs study programmes and diploma courses. Numerous books and leaflets are available – contact them for a list.

DIY and Gardening

People over 60 are entitled to a 10 per cent discount on all DIY and gardening goods at the 260 *B & Q Supercentre* stores on Wednesdays. For the address of your local store, look in the Yellow Pages under DIY or ring Readicall on 0181–460 4166. Application forms are available in the stores and will require some form of identification that can confirm the applicant's age.

Further Reading
Gardening in Retirement, Isobel Pays (Age Concern England, *address page 101*), £1.95

SPORTS

A number of local authorities run special 50+ sports activities. For further information contact the Recreation Department of your Town Hall.

The Sports Council
16 Upper Woburn Place
London WC1H 0HA
Tel: 0171–388 1277
The Sports Council encourages over-50s to participate in sport and physical recreation and will give advice about where courses, facilities and advice may be found. Phone for further details and publications.

The Scottish Sports Council
1 Caledonia House
South Gyle
Edinburgh EH12 9DQ
Tel: 0131–317 7200
The Scottish Sports Council encourages participation in sport among all age groups through promoting the benefits of active physical recreation and by encouraging sports facilities and organisations to increase opportunities and access for special groups.

The Sports Council for Northern Ireland
House of Sport
Upper Malone Road
Belfast BT9 5LA
Tel: 01232 381222

The Sports Council for Wales
The National Sports Centre for Wales
Sophie Gardens
Cardiff CF1 9SW
Tel: 01222 397571

The Amateur Swimming Association
Harold Fern House
Derby Square
Loughborough LE11 0AL
Tel: 01509 230431
This Association encourages people of all ages to take up swimming, and has a national award scheme.

The National Association of Swimming Clubs for the Handicapped (NASCH)
The Willows
Mayles Lane
Wickham
Hants PO17 5ND
Tel: 01329 833689
Aims to encourage, develop and promote swimming among handicapped people.

The Scottish Association for the Disabled
c/o Fife Sports Institute
Viewfield Road
Glenrothes KY6 2RA
Tel: 01592 771700
Aims to promote sporting activities for people with disabilities.

The Veterans' Lawn Tennis Association
26 Marryat Square
Wyfold Road
London SW6 6UA
Tel: 0171–386 0484
The VLTA organises competitions, championships and events throughout the UK and internationally. It also maintains special clubs and keeps a list of affiliated clubs.

The Ramblers Association
1–5 Wandsworth Road
London SW8 2XX
Tel: 0171–582 6878
The Ramblers Association is a voluntary organisation which promotes rambling, protects rights of way, campaigns for access to open country and defends the beauty of the countryside. It has over 360 local groups who organise programmes of walks all year round. Membership (reduced rate for retired people: £8) includes an Annual Yearbook and Accommodation Guide and free copies of its quarterly journal *Rambling Today*. Factsheets (with sae) cost 25p each and include:
'Walking Facts and Figures'
'Maps and Navigation'
'Walking in Britain'
'Walking Holidays in Britain'

The Senior and Veteran Windsurfers Association (SEAVETS)
34 Nash Grove Lane
Wokingham
Berks RG11 4HD
Tel: 01734 734634
Aims to encourage the not-so-young to take up the sport of windsurfing and participate in national events.

The British Amputee Sports Association
Harvey Road
Stoke Mandeville
Bucks HP21 9PP
Tel: 01296 84848

The Yoga for Health Foundation
Ickwell Bury
Biggleswade
Beds SG18 9EF
Tel: 01767 627271

The British Wheel of Yoga
1 Hamilton Place
Boston Road
Sleaford
Lincs NG34 7ES
Tel: 01529 306851

The British Deaf Sports Council
7a Bridge Street
Otley LS21 1BQ
Tel: 01943 850214

British Ski Club for the Disabled
Springmount
Berwick St John
Shaftesbury
Dorset SP7 0QH
Tel: 01747 828515

British Veterans' Athletic Federation
67–71 Goswell Road
London EC1V 7EN
Tel: 0171–261 8685
Your local library has information about BVAF courses and activities that are held at the nearest leisure centre.

British Veterans Athletic Sports Foundation
360 Harvey Road
Stoke Mandeville
Bucks HP21 9PP
Tel: 01296 84848

Central Council of Physical Recreation
Francis House
Francis Street
London SW1P 1DE
Tel: 0171–828 3163
As the UK's national association of sport and recreation, the CCPR aims to promote and develop measures to improve sporting opportunities, particularly for the disadvantaged and those with disabilities.

TALKING BOOKS

The National Listening Library
12 Lant Street
London SE1 1QH
Tel: 0171–407 9417
The National Listening Library provides a postal service of unabridged talking books and lends anyone with a disability a special machine to play these long-playing tapes. The annual subscription is £25; this covers all postage on cassettes in both directions. Members are provided with a catalogue which contains some 3,000 titles. Membership application forms can be obtained from the NLL, together with a descriptive leaflet. The form requires certification that a member has a disability which makes it difficult for him or her to read a book in the normal way. The visually impaired obtain their talking books from the Royal National Institute for the Blind.

British Wireless for the Blind Fund
Gabriel House
34 New Road
Chatham
Kent ME4 4QR
Tel: 01634 832501
Radio-lending agency providing free, permanent loan to the registered blind.

Wireless for the Bedridden Society
159a High Street
Hornchurch
Essex RM11 3YB
Tel: 01708 621101
This organisation can supply a wireless to the 'aged poor' by application either to social workers or Age Concern.

ARC Section
National TV Licence Records Office
Bristol BS98 1TL
Tel: 0117 923 0130
The Accommodation for Residential Care (ARC) section of the TV licence authority offers TV licences at a reduced fee to people in strictly defined accommodations. These include people with physical disabilities in their own rooms in residential and nursing homes and certain sheltered housing schemes. Details of conditions of eligibility for reductions are available in a leaflet.

Cassette Library of Recorded Books (Calibre)
Aylesbury
Bucks HP22 5XQ
Tel: 01296 432339
Calibre is a lending library of recorded books for the blind and those with disabilities. Its purpose is to provide a free, easy library for anyone who is unable to read printed books. Membership forms are available on application and the service is free, but donations are most gratefully received.

Free Tape Recorded Library for the Blind
105 Salusbury Road
London NW6 6RH
Tel: 0171–624 8844
Please telephone for an application form – the service is free but donations are gratefully received.

The Talking Newspaper Association
90 High Street
Heathfield
East Sussex TN21 8DB
Tel: 01435 866102
The Talking Newspaper Association is a registered charity which records over 140 newspapers and magazines on audio cassette for the visually impaired. The annual subscription fee is £12.50 for as many titles as required from the publications list. There is also a network of community groups.

The Housebound Readers Service
Brompton Library
210 Old Brompton Road
London SW5 0BS
Tel: 0171–244 6469
Library service supplying books for people who are housebound.

THE ARTS

Shape London
The London Borough Grant Service
356 Holloway Road
London N7 6PA
Tel: 0171–700 0100
Shape is a federation of independent regional arts organisations which work to increase access to the arts for many groups of people who are often excluded from mainstrean arts provision. It works for the rights of people with disabilities and other under-represented groups to complete access, opportunity and equality at every level of the arts in London. The Shape network extends through England, Scotland and Wales – phone for nearest organisation.

ITHACA
Unit 1
St John Fisher
Sandy Lane West
Blackbird Leys
Oxford OX4 5LD
Tel: 01865 714652
ITHACA (part of the Shape network) aims to make the arts available to people who do not normally have access to them in Oxfordshire and Berkshire.

Artability
St James Centre
Quarry Road
Tunbridge Wells TN1 2EY
Tel: 01892 515478

Part of the Shape network, this voluntary organisation was formed to increase opportunities for people with disabilities to participate actively in creative arts in Kent, Surrey and Sussex.

Age Exchange Theatre Trust
11 Blackheath Village
London SE13 9LA
Tel: 0181–318 9105
The Age Exchange Theatre Trust is a reminiscence centre and museum which arranges social activities and theatre productions, education, publishing and health training for the growing national interest in reminiscence and oral history. Pensioners act in the shows and the theatre tours the UK and Europe.

Exploring Living Memory co-ordinates reminiscence groups in the Greater London area, offers advice and runs workshops.

The Arts Connection
Cumberland Centre
Reginald Road
Portsmouth
Hants PO4 9HN
Tel: 01705 828392

This is a charity which promotes access to the arts for the elderly and people with disabilities in the Isle of Wight, West Sussex and Hampshire.

Conquest (The Society for Art for the Physically Handicapped)
3 Beverley Close
Ewell
Epsom
Surrey
Tel: 0181–393 6102
Conquest encourages adults with physical disabilities to pursue creative art activities in the home, in company and in the community by encouraging them to lead full and more active lives and, wherever possible, assisting them to overcome their disability through participation in creative art activity. No experience necessary. Art groups are set up, exhibitions organised, workshops, slide and video shows held. Training days are held frequently and there is a guide for group leaders. Video £10 (£2 to hire) including p & p. Book £3 including p & p.

GENERAL INTERESTS

The National Trust
36 Queen Anne's Gate
London SW1H 9AS
Tel: 0171–222 9251
The National Trust preserves historic buildings, gardens, parks, countryside, coastline and historic sites (entry is free to members). It publishes a free booklet 'Facilities for Disabled and Visually Handicapped Visitors'; the annual subscription allows free entry into National Trust properties.

Camping for the Disabled
20 Burton Close
Dawley
Telford
Tel: 01743 761889
Camping for the Disabled offers advice to people with disabilities and their families on camping and caravanning, and organises group camps at adopted sites.

British Jigsaw Puzzle Library
8 Heath Terrace
Leamington Spa
Warwicks CV32 5LY
Tel: 01926 311874
The Leamington Spa British Jigsaw Puzzle Library is a postal lending library for jigsaws. Membership is £65 per annum (just over £5 per month) and the library can supply from its 3,000 jigsaws – write or phone for an application form.

The Older Feminists Network
54 Gordon Road
London N3 1EP
Tel: 0181–346 1900
The aim of the Older Feminists Network is to counter the negative stereotypes of older women in society, to challenge the ageism and sexism which older women suffer and to provide contacts, mutual support and the exchange of ideas and information by mobilising the skills and experience of older women in campaigning for change. The network arranges meetings, social events and a newsletter.

The British Pensioner and Trade Union Action Association
Norman Dodds House
315 Bexley Road
Erith
Kent DA8 3EZ
Tel: 01322 335464
The Association aims to bring about improvements in the provisions made for older people by the State and in industry, commerce and daily life.

Wales Pensioners
Transport House
1 Cathedral Road
Cardiff CF1 9SD
Tel: 01222 225141
Wales Pensioners provides information and support for all pensioners throughout Wales.

NEWSPAPERS AND MAGAZINES

Active Life
Christ Church
Cosway Street
London NW1 5NJ
Tel: 0171–262 2622
Active Life, the lively magazine for the years ahead, is a bi-monthly publication full of news and features on law, money, travel, interests, well-being and practical matters. Single issues cost £1.75 plus p & p; a subscription is £9.99 per year.

Choice
2 St John's Place
St John's Square
London EC1M 4DE
Tel: 0171–490 7070
A lifestyle magazine for active over-50s.

Civil Service Pensioner
7 The Beeches
Shaw Hill
Melksham
Wilts SN12 8EW
Tel: 01225 702416
Quarterly magazine for members of the CSP Alliance.

Mature Tymes
Sycamore House
PO Box 25
South Glamorgan CF7 7XU
Tel: 01446 775522
Monthly magazine for the over-50s.

Pensioners' Voice
Melling House
14 St Peter Street
Blackburn
Lancs BB2 2HD
Tel: 01254 52606
Newspaper of the organisation which campaigns for a better deal for older people. Subscription £6 or available through pensioners' clubs.

Prime of Life
15 Trafalgar Street
Plymouth
Devon PL4 9PE
Tel: 01752 250984
Monthly tabloid newspaper for over-50s in the West Country and south coast.

Saga
Saga Publishing Ltd
The Saga Building
Middelburg Square
Folkestone
Kent CT20 1AZ
Tel: 01303 857523
A magazine for the over-50s, published ten times a year.

Yours
Apex House
Oundle Road
Peterborough PE2 9NP
Tel: 01733 555123
A monthly magazine for retired people.

Other Useful Organisations and Addresses

Achievements Ltd
79–82 Northgate
Canterbury
Kent CT1 1HE
Tel: 01227 462618
How to trace family ancestry.

British Antique Dealers Association
20 Rutland Gate
London SW7 1BD
Tel: 0171–581 5259
The BADA Cultural and Educational Trust was founded as an educational sponsor. Friends of the BADA may participate in a programme of cultural events, receive free entry into a number of antique fairs and exhibitions, receive free advice on the purchase, insurance, care and sale of antiques, and receive a number of other benefits.

British Chess Federation
9a Grand Parade
St Leonard's-on-Sea
East Sussex TN38 0DD
Tel: 01424 442500
Write with sae for details of nearest chess club and calendar of events.

Embroiderers' Guild
Apartment 41
Hampton Court Palace
East Molesey
Surrey KT8 9AU
Tel: 0181–943 1229
Educational charity promoting classes, exhibitions, groups and bookshop.

Ehrman Kits Ltd
Lancer Square
London W8 4EP
Tel: 0181–573 4866
Tapestry by mail (catalogue £2).

Holmfirth Wools
Egypt Road
Thornton
Bradford BD13 3RG
Tel: 01274 835365
Mail-order knitting wools.

Memories on Video
24 York Gardens
Winterbourne
Bristol BS17 1QT
Tel: 0117 977 2857
This company will transfer old cine films on to videos.

Memory Makers
1 South Street
Exmouth
Devon EX8 2SX
Tel: 01395 264000
Restores old photographs.

The Oral History Society
c/o The British Library National Sound Archive
29 Exhibition Road
London SW7 2AS
Tel: 0171–412 7415
The Oral History Society encourages and supports the recording and archiving of older people's reminiscences and life stories. Two conferences are held each year to bring oral history practitioners, young and old, together. Two journals are published each year. The society provides practical advice through its regional network of local representatives all over Britain and there is also an international membership. Books include:
  Oral History: Talking about the Past (1992), £3.

The Writers Bureau
FREEPOST BY1743
Manchester M1 1JB
Tel: 0800 262 382
Learning to write.

Further Reading
Age Concern (*address page 101*) produces Factsheets 30 'Leisure Education' and 31 'Older Workers'
An Active Retirement, Nancy Tuft (Age Concern Books, 1993), £7.95
Looking Good, Feeling Good, Nancy Tuft (Age Concern Books, 1991), £7.95
Directory for Older People: A Handbook of Information and Opportunities for the Over-55s, Ann Danborough and Derek Kinrade (compilers), (Harvester Wheatsheaf, 1992), £17.95
Piatkus Books (tel. 0171–631 0710 for further details) publish several books of interest to older readers, including:

Growing Old Disgracefully – New Ideas for Getting the Most Out of Life (£6.99)
Jobs for the Over 50's (£8.99)
Look Younger, Feel Better, Dr James Scala and Barbara Jacques (£9.99)

chapter twelve

DEATH AND BEREAVEMENT

Arranging and Paying for the Funeral in Advance, What Friends and Relatives Need to Know after a Death, Coping with Grief and Loss and Administering the Estate

DEATH IS A SUBJECT that many of us wish to avoid, for a number of reasons. However, the death of a partner, parent, child or other close relative or friend is a particularly stressful experience which can be eased if, in various practical ways, preparations have been made in advance.

In this chapter I look at different ways in which planning can help people to come to terms and cope more easily with the thought of death. I also consider the effect that a bereavement can have on people, and some ways of dealing with grief, and also the practical arrangements that have to be followed after a death.

PLANNING FOR DEATH

Although death is considered a taboo subject in many families, a great burden can be removed from the family if older people are able to face up to the inevitability of their own passing and make their wishes known. No better illustration of this can be shown than with the writing of a Will, as described in Chapter 7.

In addition to the preparation of a Will, there are a number of practical aspects which can be considered. If you have a partner or dependents they should understand, where practical, the tasks that you normally perform. These may encompass such things that are taken for granted such as the paying of bills, arranging insurance, changing the fuse, cooking a simple but healthy meal or even relighting the boiler. Being unable to cope with day-to-day tasks when a partner dies will leave the survivor with a sense of frustration and possibly anger.

It is also beneficial to discuss with your partner or other members of the family your wishes about the way the funeral is to be arranged, the type of service that may be conducted (perhaps even the order of service) and your wishes about what should happen to you after death *vis-à-vis* burial, cremation, etc. Often survivors will be in a state of shock immediately following a death and, because there is a great deal to do in a short space of time, may not prepare or arrange everything with their normal consideration. For instance, they might arrange a more lavish funeral than they can afford, or buy certain types or quantities of flowers or specify an order of service which, however small an issue it may seem at the time, they may subsequently regret.

A great many of these problems can be anticipated in advance. However, it is a difficult subject to broach, even though it is one that will have been considered on more than one occasion by anyone who might ultimately be responsible for the arrangements. Openness in this, as in other emotional matters, will invariably produce a reassuring response as opposed to the uncertainty of silence. Choose your moment to discuss it carefully and with sensitivity. Perhaps you could begin by talking about your Will, and where it is kept. This can lead to a general discussion about your affairs and any specific wishes that you may have that your successors should be aware of. As can be seen later in this chapter, it is also useful that your children or likely successor knows the name of your doctor and solicitor.

Further Reading
'Who Wants to Think about Dying?' – leaflet (£1.20 plus 25p p & p) from CRUSE – Bereavement Care (*address pages 228–9*)

Imminence of Death

If you know that your partner, a friend or relation with whom you are very close, or one of your parents is dying, it is often difficult to carry on a normal relationship, particularly if that person is living at home with you. However, everyone should make a conscious effort to act calmly and as normally as possible. In such circumstances it is as well to be prepared for the question 'Am I going to die?' or to have to break the news that he or she might not have much longer to live. In either case it will depend upon your relationship with and knowledge of that person to determine what you should say.

For some people the knowledge that death is imminent is very difficult to come to terms with and might disturb the peace of their last days or weeks. For others it has the opposite effect and allows them time to prepare themselves mentally and spiritually.

There are a number of organisations which can give advice:

The Natural Death Centre
20 Heber Road
London NW2 6AA
Tel: 0181–208 2853
The Natural Death Centre is an organisation launched in 1991 which has as its overall aim to help to improve the quality of dying. The Centre:
- provides information and support for families looking after a dying person at home
- gives families information to enable them to arrange funerals with or without using undertakers
- publishes information on the best and most helpful undertakers, crematoria and funeral suppliers
- hosts workshops for the general public on 'exploring our own death', as well as meetings and dinner discussions to break the taboo of discussing death and

dying. These are all held around the country
- provides bereavement and individual counselling
- assists in the preparation of *A Living Will* (which indicates how much high-tech medical intervention the signatory would want if suffering from a terminal disease)
- issues a Declaration of Rights for the person dying at home.

The Natural Death Centre will send a complete information pack in return for four first-class stamps, and asks for donations if possible from people wanting specialised advice. They will also send details on *The Living Will* in return for two first-class stamps.

The Befriending Network
11 St Bernards Road
Oxford OX2 6EH
Tel: 01865 512 405

The Befriending Network aims to introduce trained volunteers to people living at home with a life-threatening illness. The volunteer will help the person who is ill in whatever way is appropriate in the circumstances, including just being there while the usual carer has a break. They would not provide nursing care, but will have acquired some practical and listening skills through their training. Visits will normally be for two to three hours, once a week.

Further Reading
The Natural Death Handbook, produced by The Natural Death Centre and available from the Centre (£10.95 including p & p)
This book covers the subjects of improving the quality of living and dying, and includes, among other topics, details of how to care for someone dying at home, how to prepare for dying and a consumers' guide to the best undertakers, crematoria and similar organisations.
Who Dies? An Investigation of Conscious Living and Conscious Dying, Stephene Levine (Gateway Books, The Hollies, Wellow, Bath BA2 8QJ), £7.95
Deathing, An Intelligent Alternative for the Final Moments of Life, Anya Foos-Graber (Airlift, 26 Eden Grove, London N7), £13.50
Both books are recommended by The Natural Death Centre as the best reading on spiritual preparations for dying.
The Living Will – Consent to Treatment at the End of Life (Age Concern and Edward Arnold), £5.99
A working party report available from Age Concern (*address page 228*), this analyses the potential role and effects of advance directives, and in particular the 'Living Will'.
Coming Home, A Guide to Dying at Home with Dignity, Deborah Duda (Airlift, 26 Eden Grove, London N7), £13.50
Recommended by The Natural Death Centre as the best book on dying at home.

Desire for Death
It is natural to hope that when our time comes, each one of us shall die peacefully, with dignity and without prolonged suffering. There will be many, however, who endure a long-drawn-out and deeply distressing period of pain

and suffering. As medical technology advances, the practice of sustaining life in a body that is irreversibly incapacitated is no longer a miracle but a routine procedure.

There is a strong case, based upon common sense and compassion, for granting the wish of incurable patients for a merciful release from prolonged and useless suffering. Despite this there are a number of action groups who are actively lobbying against any form of legalisation of voluntary euthanasia. These mainly come from religious groups and medical associations for people with disabilities. Their underlying fear is that the right to die might become a duty to die; once the principle was established, they fear, some groups of people might become categorised as 'expendable'.

The Voluntary Euthanasia Society
13 Prince of Wales Terrace
London W8 5PG
Tel: 0171–937 7770
The principal objective of the Society is to make it legal for a competent adult person who is suffering severe distress from an incurable illness to receive medical help to die at his or her own considered and persistent request. The Society produces an information pack (£3) and a free leaflet called 'The Last Right: The Need for Voluntary Euthanasia', in addition to a number of publications concerning patients' rights and legal choices at the end of life.

Further Reading, Viewing and Listening
All the publications listed below are available from the Voluntary Euthanasia Society.
Advance Directives (Living Wills) (£3)
The Last Right (audio cassette by Dirk Bogarde; £3)
Euthanasia – The Good Death, Ludovic Kennedy (£3.60)
Your Ultimate Choice (collected articles; £5)
Voluntary Euthanasia: the facts (video presented by Tom Conti; £10)

Paying for the Funeral in Advance
It is possible not only to plan one's funeral arrangements in advance but also to ensure that there will be adequate money to pay the costs. With the cost of an average funeral exceeding £1,000, and with price increases which have been greater in the past 20 years than the rate of inflation and are predicted to continue in the same manner in the future, such schemes have attractions. In principal someone will pay today's prices for a funeral which may take place in a month or in a decade or more. In the United States, one in seven people has paid for his or her funeral in advance, but in this country less than 175,000 prepayment schemes have been sold.

Price, however, is not generally the main motivation for someone taking out a plan. After a death the bereaved family is unlikely to be in a state to wish to enter into commercial negotiations with a funeral director (*see below*) or concern themselves about whether there is money available for the funeral. The prepaid plan is therefore able to offer peace of mind. In the US it is considered almost 'socially irresponsible' to have neglected one's funeral arrangements, thereby leaving the burden on one's survivors at the time of their grief.

Several companies have schemes which may offer a number of plans at varying levels of expense (from as little as £100) which guarantee the actual type of funeral selected to be paid for in advance at the prices prevailing at the date of entering the plan. The costs covered may include only the bare essentials of the funeral or may meet all the ancillary costs such as cremation fees, a contribution to a minister of religion, and other similar items. You should always check to see what exactly is covered. For instance, is the actual burial covered, as well as the minister's and doctor's fees?

These types of plan can be an attractive proposition, because not only can they fully cover the costs of the funeral, they can also be used to arrange the exact service you require. The selected funeral directors will sign a legally binding contract which guarantees that the selected funeral arrangements will be carried out exactly as and when required, at no further cost.

The main companies operating these schemes will put the money paid in advance into a trust fund which is held independently by one of the large banks. This provides security over the money. Anyone looking at such schemes should always ensure that the company does put the money into an independent trust fund; therefore if anything happens to the company, the money remains safe. There is generally no age limit for applicants to these schemes.

Many companies also offer similar sounding schemes, which are actually traditional life assurance schemes. Under these, various types of policy and payment can be put together, either by a single lump sum payment, by regular payments for a fixed period or until death, or by a combination of these two options. In general the non-profit plans (i.e. plans that return a fixed amount of money, rather than ones which increase each year or guarantee to cover the cost of a certain event, such as a funeral) sold by leading insurance companies are not good value; the majority of the plans are started when people are in their early sixties, and actuaries calculate that someone in this age group would need to contribute to a typical plan for 13.5 years to have paid in what they are due to receive. As two out of three will be alive after this time, and two out of five after a further six years, the scheme may not be cost effective. It is possible to have paid into the scheme more than the scheme returns, and also to find that the amount ultimately paid out is insufficient to meet the funeral costs, which have continued to increase in the mean time.

If the plans do allow for an element of inflation-linking of the amount assured under the scheme, it is much less likely that rising prices in the cost of funerals will mean that there is insufficient money to meet the full costs of the funeral. These types of scheme also have an advantage over funeral prepayment schemes in that they can be used for any purpose if considered necessary.

Co-operative Funeral Services
29 Dantzic Street
Manchester
M4 4BA
Tel: 0161–832 8152 or Freephone 0800 181 818 (24-hour answering service)

The Co-operative Funeral Service is the UK's largest Funeral Director, with branches nationwide. They are also a major provider of funeral pre-payment plans, for which enquiries should be made at their local branch or by telephoning Chester (01244) 341135 for details.

Chosen Heritage
Farringdon House
Wood Street
East Grinstead
West Sussex RH19 1EW
Tel: 01342 312266 or Freephone 0800 525 555

Chosen Heritage, which is recommended by Age Concern, offers a choice of guaranteed funeral plans whereby people can arrange and pay for the service of their choice at today's prices. A plan gives peace of mind and spares relatives the anxiety and expense of organising the funeral at the time of bereavement. All payments go into an independent trust fund, with Barclays Bank acting as custodian trustees.

Golden Charter
Crowndale House
1 Ferdinand Place
Camden
London NW1 8EE
Tel: 0800 833 800

Provides guaranteed funeral plans.

Perfect Assurance Funeral Trust
618 Warwick Road
Solihull
West Midlands B91 1AA
Tel: 0121–709 0019

Perfect Assurance is a prepayment plan.

Dignity Ltd
FREEPOST BM2415
Sutton Coldfield
West Midlands B72 1BR
Tel: 0800 269 318

The Funeral Expenses Plan
Royal Life Insurance
Bretton Way
Peterborough PE3 8BQ

Abbey Life Assurance
Direct Mailing Dept
Abbey Life Centre
80 Holdenhurst Road
Bournemouth BH8 8AL
Tel: 0800 262 422

The Independent Order of Odd Fellows
Manchester Unity Friendly Society
40 Fountain Street
Manchester M2 2AB
Tel: 0161–832 9361

The Society offers policies to people up to age 85 on their next birthday.

Age Concern (*address page 228*) Factsheet No 27, 'Arranging a Funeral', describes a number of alternative schemes.

Donation of Body and Organs

Many people, feeling that to do so will help others, wish to donate part or all of their body to the medical profession after death. If you wish to be a donor it is important not only that you complete a donor card (*see below*) but that you also notify your immediate family of your wishes.

You must be specific about whether you wish to donate certain organs or your whole body. The reason is that, if the circumstances are suitable for a possible donation at the time of death, your immediate family will be approached about the donation. If you have at any time expressed to your family an objection to the removal or use of any of your organs, and your objection was not changed subsequently, that objection may not be overridden.

However, despite the constant need for organs the circumstances under which an organ may be removed for use are very limited – usually if a person dies in an intensive care unit in hospital, where the heart may be kept beating even after brain death. There are certain exceptions; the British Organ Donor Society (BODY) is a voluntary organisation which can offer advice to both donors and their families. They provide a factsheet, 'Organ Donation and Transportation', which gives further details.

The British Organ Donor Society (BODY)
Balsham
Cambridge CB1 6DL
Tel: 01223 893636 or Freephone 0800 444 136

It is possible to donate the whole body, and if you are interested in this your family must take immediate action upon your death to contact the nearest medical school or, if in London:

The London Anatomy Office
Rockefeller Building
University Street
London WC1E 6JJ
Tel: 0171–387 7850

Acceptance by the medical school or Anatomy Office is not automatic and will depend upon a number of factors including the cause of death, the need for a post-mortem and the condition of the body at the time of death.

If a whole body donation is accepted, the body may be kept for up to two years, thus effectively preventing funeral arrangements. Once it is released a private ceremony may be arranged or the arrangements may be left to the medical school, who will organise at their own expense a combined service for several donors at once.

If you wish to donate organs or your entire body, you must complete a *donor card*. These cards are available from a number of public places such as most libraries, post offices and doctor's surgeries. Otherwise, they can be obtained from the following:

Department of Health
Leaflets Department
PO Box 21
Stanmore
Middlesex HA7 1AY
Tel: 0171–210 5983

All driving licenses which are now being issued also have a donor section incorporated into the license. It is entirely voluntary as to whether this is completed.

There is always a need for organ donors, whereas there are generally more whole-body donors than are required for training purposes. BODY recommends that a multi-organ donor card should be used, and if it is wished it is possible to insert on this 'Whole Body Donor'. There is no age limit for donors of organs for transplant.

What to Do After a Death

When someone dies there are a great many decisions to be taken and arrangements to be made in generally a short space of time. Bereavement is not an easy experience for anyone to cope with and usually results in great personal distress to the people responsible for making the decisions and arrangements.

Basic guidance is given below, together with details of books and leaflets which may be obtained for further detailed advice. Many, such as the Social Security leaflet 'What to Do After Death – A Guide to What You Must Do and the Help You Can Get', provide simple and straightforward explanations of the procedures that are recommended to be followed. In practice much reliance will be placed upon family and friends to provide advice, as well as on the professionals involved such as doctors, priests and funeral directors.

The Doctor's Certificate

Death at Home
If someone dies at home you must call the family doctor. If the doctor is able to verify the cause of death he or she will issue a certificate giving the cause of death. If there is to be a cremation, another certificate must be issued and signed by two doctors who are professionally independent of each other. Your own doctor will help you to find the other signatory.

Death in Hospital
The hospital authorities will issue the 'cause of death' certificate to the local Registration Office.

Unexpected Death

If the death is unexpected or unusual, your doctor has a duty to tell the police; they will report it to the coroner who may call for a post-mortem. If there is any doubt about the cause of death, a coroner's inquest may be set up. Also a coroner may be involved under other circumstances, such as when a death occurs within 24 hours of admission to hospital, or while a person is being operated on in hospital, or if the deceased person was getting a War Pension. In these cases the coroner will then notify the Registrar and issue an order for burial or a cremation certificate, as appropriate.

Registering a Death

The 'cause of death' certificate must be registered within five days (eight in Scotland) unless the death has been referred to a coroner. If the coroner held a post-mortem which established that the death was by natural causes, a Form 100, which is issued by the coroner, must also be provided to the Registrar.

The certificate must be taken to the Registrar of Births and Deaths for the area in which the death has occurred. An address for the Registrar will be known by the local doctor, post office, police or local authority or library, or will be in the telephone directory (under Registration of Births, Deaths and Marriages). The certificate should be taken by a member of the family, or by someone with sufficient knowledge to provide the Registrar with the following information:

- the full name of the deceased
- date and place of birth
- (if the deceased was a married woman), her maiden name and the full name of her husband.
- (in Scotland) the full names of both parents of the deceased, and the profession of the father of the deceased.

The Registrar will want to see either the deceased person's National Health Service number or Medical Card, which has to be handed in. He or she will then issue two certified copies of the entry in the Death Register (the Death Certificate), as well as a Certificate for Burial or Cremation (known as the Green Form, which will be required by the funeral director or undertaker) and a Certificate of Registration of Death (Form BD8 [rev]) which is for Social Security purposes only.

Further copies of the Death Certificate can be obtained for a small fee. It is advisable to obtain some as they may be needed for probate purposes or to release money before probate from insurance policies, bank deposits or pension funds.

FUNERAL ARRANGEMENTS

Although there is no obligation to hold any ceremony after a death, there can be immense psychological value in so doing. It is a time when family and friends can openly express and share their sadness and is considered an important and necessary part of the process of continuing life after bereavement.

The final funeral arrangements should not be made until you are certain that the death does not have to be reported to a coroner, since this may affect the date when the funeral can be held. If you are uncertain about the wishes of your deceased spouse or relative in connection with the funeral, it is advisable to check his or her Will to see if there are any directions therein.

Although it is not strictly necessary (*see* Alternative Funeral Arrangements, *below*), the majority of funerals in the UK are arranged by a funeral director. As the arrangements will be discussed at a time of personal distress, it is advisable to obtain written estimates from at least two funeral directors. Even discussing the possibilities available with more than one person helps clarify what is available and at what cost.

There are a large number of funeral directors in the UK, most of whom provide a 24-hour service. The majority are members of the National Association of Funeral Directors (NAFD), a trade association of 2,200 funeral directors which is governed by a code of practice approved by the Office of Fair Trading.

The most significant features of the code are that the funeral directors must provide a price list upon request together with full information on the services that they can provide; they must also provide a basic simple funeral if required and a firm estimate. The basic funeral will include the supply of a coffin or casket (respectively tapered or rectangular), a conductor, bearers and a hearse. A basic funeral will not cover the cost of things which funeral directors are generally responsible for, such as church or cremation fees, flowers, additional following cars at the funeral, embalming or notices in the newspapers.

It is necessary to remember that if there is to be a burial in an existing family grave or vault, the funeral director will need the grave ownership document, called a grave grant, which gives permission to use the grave as a vault. You should know where this is and transfer the ownership to another member of the family after the funeral.

For further information contact:

Co-operative Funeral Services
See page 218

Oaktree Funeral Services Ltd
Plantsbrook House
94 The Parade
Sutton Coldfield
West Midlands B72 1PH
Tel: 0121–354 1557

National Association of Funeral Directors
618 Warwick Road
Solihull
West Midlands B91 1AA
Tel: 0121–711 1343

The Society of Allied and Independent Funeral Directors
Crowndale House
1 Ferdinand Place
Camden
London NW1 8EE
Tel: 0171–267 6777

The Society represents the interests of independent family-owned Funeral

Directors. Many are also members of NAFD.

The Cremation Society of Great Britain
Brecon House
16 Albion Place
Maidstone
Kent ME14 5DZ
Tel: 01622 688292
The Society publishes a quarterly journal, *Pharos International*, and annually a *Directory of Crematoria* (£16.50 complete with binder or £12.25 for insert only) which includes statistics, details of crematoria costs and siting and planning of crematoria. It also provides, free of charge, information on all aspects of cremation to all members of the public, organisations, local authorities and any other interested parties. It issues several publications on the subject of cremation.

National Association of Bereavement Services
20 Norton Folgate
London E1 6DB
Tel: 0171–247 0617

Alternative Funeral Arrangements

Burial on Land

For those not wishing to use a Funeral Director, there are a number of organisations who will advise on the alternatives, such as the Natural Death Centre (*address page 214*) and the Independent Funeral Advisory Service (address below). Although few people are willing to go to the necessary lengths required, it can be a very rewarding and intensely personal experience.

At present, according to the Natural Death Centre, fewer than 1 per cent of people take care of their own funerals. But as the green generation ages, this percentage is certain to rise. Statistics indicate that about 437,000 wooden coffins are burned each year, polluting the atmosphere with dioxin, acids and dioxides. At least burial, even with a wooden coffin, locks the carbon underground and does not add to the greenhouse effect. It can also help protect land from being used by humans for development, thus saving it for wildlife. The Natural Death Centre receives a dozen letters each day from older persons wanting to know if they can be buried in their own back garden. There are few legal controls at present over the fate of your body; all that is required is a death certificate from the doctor and a burial certificate from the Registrar. Care should be taken that the burial takes place in ground that has no restrictive covenant preventing burials (refer to the property deeds) and where it will not cause a nuisance, such as pollution, nor affect the local water supply (check with the National Rivers Authority – tel: 0171–820 0101). Costs can be relatively cheap, with a complete funeral being organised for as little as £100.

A common problem that a number of people have identified is the possibility of buying coffins without reverting to a funeral director. It is, however, possible to make them very inexpensively from veneered chipboard panels. The Natural Death Centre makes reference to the following sources for coffins and body bags:

James Gibson Funeral Directors
342 St Helens Road
Bolton
Lancs BL3 3RP
Tel: 01204 655869
Makes coffins for as little as £90 including handles and delivery

Green Undertakings
c/o 79a Gloucester Road
Bristol BS7 8AS
Tel: 0117 924 6248
They are able to offer an oak veneer standard coffin for £95 with handles and lining. They also have cheaper cardboard coffins.

Lears of London
Bryson House
Horace Road
Kingston upon Thames
Surrey KT1 2SL
Tel: 0181-546 2633
They are willing to sell to the general public such things as body bags (including non-toxic bags), cremation urns and coffin linings.

Carlisle and Brighton Cemeteries (*for address see below*) supply to the general public a regular chipboard coffin for about £90, cardboard coffins for about £55 or a body bag for £14, together with accessories such as coffin lining material and lowering webbing for burials.

Further information (and flat-pack cardboard coffins) can also be obtained from the Natural Death Centre (tel: 0181-208 2853).

There is now a growing movement for farmers, local authorities and wildlife charities to establish Woodland or Nature Reserve Charities, often with a commemorative tree for each body there. Several local authorities have set aside sites as burial grounds (*see below*), and several non-local authority burial grounds have also been approved. They wish to be able to represent a 'life from death' memorial. The Natural Death Centre has formed an Association of Nature Reserve Burial Grounds. The purpose of the Association is not only to keep a central record of the location of sites as permission is obtained for them from the local authorities, but also to put forward a Code of Practice for its members to adhere to so that potential clients approaching a burial ground can be assured that it will reach certain specified standards. It will also help members through the planning stage and help promote the concept of natural burial.

AB Wildlife Trust Fund
7 Knox Road
Harrogate
North Yorks
HG1 3EF
AB Wildlife Trust Fund is a charity dedicated to bringing more choice in funeral arrangements and giving added protection to wildlife sites.

Carlisle Cemetery
Tel: 01228 25022

Harrogate Stonefall Cemetery
Tel: 01423 883523

Woodvale Cemeteries
The Woodvale Lodge
Lewes Road
Brighton
BN2 3QB
Tel: 01273 604020

Stapenhill Cemetery
38 Stapenhill Road
Burton on Trent
DE15 0QE
Tel: 01283 508572

Independent Funerals Advisory Service
Belmont
Brendon Road
Watchet
Somerset TA23 0AX
Tel: 01984 632285
The Independent Funerals Advisory Service has been established to provide information, advice and material services for those people who would prefer to make funeral arrangements wholly or partly independently of funeral directors. This nationally available service is particularly useful to people wishing to plan ahead of a death, so as to be sure the funeral is arranged as they would like it for themselves, their family members and friends.

They also publish a number of informative leaflets, including:
'Laying Out Coffins'
'Burials in Private Ground'

Further Reading

Green Burial: The DIY Guide to Law and Practice, John Bradfield (£9.85 including p & p from The Natural Death Centre)
Funerals: And How to Improve Them, Dr Tony Walter (Hodder & Stoughton, Mill Road, Dunton Green, Sevenoaks, Kent TN13 2YA), £8.99
Both these books are on the subject of DIY funerals, and are recommended by The Natural Death Centre.
Age Concern's Factsheet No 27, 'Arranging a Funeral' (*address page 228*). This factsheet is concerned with help for those who have to arrange a funeral, or who wish to make plans for their own.

Burial At Sea

There are many people who have a close affinity to the sea and wish to be buried there. There are three sites off the British coast which are approved for burial – the Isle of Wight at the Needles, Newhaven, and Plymouth. Licenses must be obtained from the local district inspector for the Ministry of Agriculture, Fisheries and Food. The Mare Marine Protection Division can provide further information, and may be contacted on 0171–238 5872.

There are a number of regulations and guidelines in force; these tend to discourage people from arranging sea burials, and only about 20 are arranged each year. You need to inform the Registrar when registering the death that you plan a sea burial, and you can then obtain a 'Coroners Out of England Form' (Form 104) – and the local coroner's address to which this should be sent. The type of coffin that can be used, in order to prevent pollution, and to ensure that the body is not washed ashore or caught in the nets of trawlers, is quite specific, although it may vary slightly from district to district. The coffin can only be made from certain specific materials which will not endure in a marine environment (no persistent synthetic materials), it has to be weighed down with 3 cwt of concrete or iron and must have holes of at least three quarter-inch diameter in the side to allow the water to enter and air to escape. The body should also be weighted, should not be embalmed and should have a plastic tag around the ankle with a permanent inscription stating the deceased's name and date of burial. Unlike burial in a cemetery or in a nature reserve, burial at sea can be expensive, with costs likely to exceed £3,000. This is not only for the special preparation of the coffin, but also for the hire of a boat with specific navigation equipment and a knowledgeable captain. Details of local boats may be obtained from the local district inspectors, and the Natural Death Centre can provide names of local funeral directors who can assist.

Non-Religious Funerals

There are many people who do not feel comfortable with religion or have made a clear decision to live their lives without it. Often for these people a religious service would be hypocritical or would lack sincerity, and would bring little consolation to the bereaved.

There is no obligation for anyone to hold a funeral ceremony. Undertakers may be asked to remove the body for funeral without any ceremony. However, there is a distinct psychological benefit in holding a ceremony of some kind; it is an occasion on which those who are deeply aggrieved may share their feelings. The sharing of feelings can be of great relief to the bereaved, and is an occasion when the finality of death has to be faced. This is considered an important part of mourning, an element in the necessary process of eventually re-establishing and continuing life after bereavement.

It is possible to hold non-religious funerals. These are a dignified alternative to a religious funeral and can be tailor-made to suit the wishes of the deceased and the mourners. The service is conducted by an officiant. The order of service may include music and readings, with the express intention of remembering and perhaps celebrating the life of the deceased.

The officiants, who are trained, come from a variety of backgrounds; they are men and women who are able to empathise, often from personal experience, with those experiencing grief and loss.

British Humanist Association
14 Lambs Conduit Passage
London WC1R 4RH
Tel: 0171–430 0908 or 01608 652063 for the National Co-ordinator for funeral ceremonies.
The theory of humanism is based on the assumption that this life and this world are all we know, and that the most important factor in all our thoughts and actions is our common humanity. The British Humanist Association is the national voice of humanism. It is not anti-religious as such, but seeks out an alternative moral view of current personal and social issues. It plays an important part in arranging non-religious funerals.

National Secular Society Ltd
702 Holloway Road
London N19 3NL
Tel: 0171–272 1266
The National Secular Society is the leading organisation in the free-thought movement, supporting 'non-believers' in the face of religious privilege. It has a large number of officiants able to conduct non-religious funerals. For further information, please send sae.

South Place Ethical Society
Conway Hall
Red Lion Square
London WC1R 4RL
Tel: 0171–242 8032
The Ethical Society is an organisation whose chief objectives are the study and dissemination of ethical principles and the cultivation of a rational and humane way of life.

Further Reading
Funerals without God – A Practical Guide to Non-religious Funerals (British Humanist Association), £3.50 including p & p
Coping with Death, Leslie Scrase (British Humanist Association), £4 including p & p

Paying for the Funeral

You should ensure that you are able to pay for the funeral before finalising the plans for it. The bank account of the deceased will be frozen, unless it is a joint account. Building societies and life assurance companies will generally pay out a limited sum on the production of the Death Certificate before probate has been proved. They are not bound to do so.

If payment has been arranged before death, no problem will arise. However, if no arrangements have been made it is advisable to check that the deceased did not belong to an occupational pension scheme that would pay a lump sum to help with funeral costs. In addition, lump sum payments may be available from the deceased's trade union, professional body or other association.

If you are having problems with paying for the funeral the Social Fund may assist towards the cost of a simple funeral. Further details are provided in Chapter 6. Certain criteria are laid down to determine whether you are eligible for assistance. These are whether you are responsible for arranging the funeral, and whether you or your partner are receiving any of these Social Security benefits:
- Income Support
- Family Credit
- Housing Benefit
- Council Tax Benefit.

A claim should be made to your Social Security office within three months of the death. Any payment received from the Social Fund will have to be paid back from any estate of the person who has died.

In addition to the Social Fund, assistance may be sought from the local council or health authority.

BEREAVEMENT

We all expect to experience a death in the family at some stage in our lives. Although it is often inevitable, very few people wish to consider the emotional implications in advance. Even if mentally prepared for a death, it is always a time of sadness; if the death is unexpected it will naturally come as a complete shock and cause severe distress.

Grief is a natural emotion which will invariably follow a bereavement. Often it is mingled with feelings of guilt, anger, frustration, loneliness and despair. Many people find the range of emotions confusing and difficult to cope with, particularly if the bereaved is a partner, relative or friend whose support has been relied on for many years.

Although time is the greatest healer of grief, there are a number of stages to helping overcome it. As the severity of the grief and the ability to cope with it will vary from person to person, there is no instant formula that can be produced to heal the spirit.

To begin with, it is important that those who are grieving learn to accept what has happened. They must also try and continue life as normally as possible, taking care of their health and not foregoing regular meals. Often if someone has been cooking for two or more people for many years there is a tendency to ignore meals when alone. It is important to meet other people and speak or correspond with other family members or friends. It is also necessary to begin to gradually reshape your life.

Every attempt must be made to ensure that there is as little to worry about as possible. Once all the legal and administrative formalities are over, the bereaved will need the support of those close to him or her. Although there is no universally correct way to act, an openness with the emotions and willingness to talk should be encouraged. Grief cannot be resisted; therefore it is better that the bereaved come to terms with their feelings and accept that it is right and natural to mourn – to be unhappy and express that unhappiness.

There are a number of organisations that are able to help people suffering from grief after bereavement.

Age Concern England
Astral House
1268 London Road
London SW16 4ER
Tel: 0181–679 8000
Age Concern has a number of local groups which provide services for elderly people. Some offer bereavement counselling.

CRUSE – Bereavement Care
CRUSE House
126 Sheen Road
Richmond
Surrey TW9 1UR
Tel: 0181–940 4818
Cruse Bereavement Line: 0181–332 7227. This number provides a direct link to a counsellor.

Cruse offers a comprehensive service of counselling by trained and selected people, advice on practical matters and opportunities for social support. This service is available to all bereaved people either through one of its 195 branches or National membership. There is a wide range of supportive, informative and advisory literature and a monthly newsletter for bereaved people. In addition Cruse arranges training courses for those who work either in a professional or lay capacity with the bereaved.

Self-referral is the usual way most people contact Cruse; however where the bereaved person has given consent they will accept referrals from family, friends or the various caring professions.

National Association of Widows/Widows Advisory Trust
54–57 Allison Street
Digbeth
Birmingham B5 5TH
Tel: 0121–643 8348
The Association, by way of branches throughout the UK, runs a service providing friendly support, information and advice to all widows to help them to overcome the many problems they face in society today.

National Association of Bereavement Services
68 Charlton Street
London NW1 1JR
Tel: 0171–247 1080
The Association acts as a referral agency for people who are seeking a local or specialist bereavement service.

The Compassionate Friends
53 North Street
Bristol BS3 1EN
Tel: 0117 953 9639 (24-hour answering service)
The Compassionate Friends is a nationwide self-help group of bereaved parents and grandparents offering friendship and support to others whose child (of any age, including adult) has died from any cause. Friendship, understanding and personal and group support is offered through meetings (one-to-one or in a group). A quarterly newsletter, large postal library and range of leaflets are available upon request. It is a befriending rather than counselling organisation, with links around the world.

Gay Bereavement Project
Vaughan M. Williams Centre
Colindale Hospital
London NW9 5HG
Tel: 0181–200 0511
Helpline: 0181–455 8894
The Project is designed to help gay men and lesbians in the event of a partner's death. It intends to raise public awareness that the death of a lover is as traumatic as that of a spouse.

Samaritans
(National Headquarters)
10 The Grove
Slough S4 1QP
Tel: 01753 532713
The Samaritans is a telephone helpline for people feeling in despair or suicidal. It offers confidential support 24 hours a day, 365 days a year. There are over 170 branches in England, Scotland and Wales. For your nearest branch, look in the local telephone directory.

Other Sources of Help

Your local minister or other religious leader will be experienced in counselling the bereaved and will always be helpful, even if the person seeking help is not a regular churchgoer.

There is also a practical organisation which can assist in preventing a specific type of worry after a death. Housewatch offer a service that will provide live-in security if a house is empty after a family bereavement. They will perform such basic tasks as looking after animals, forwarding mail, dealing with suppliers of essential services and tradesmen and ensuring that the property is maintained in good order and repair. They will also assist with house clearance during the period of probate, if required.

Housewatch Ltd
Little London
Berden
Bishop's Stortford
Herts CM23 1BE
Tel: 01279 777412

Further Reading
'Bereavement' – A free leaflet covering the emotional and practical aspects of dealing with bereavement (Help the Aged; *address page 182*)
DSS Guide D 49, 'What to Do after a Death'
After the Death of Someone Very Close, Caroline Morcom (CRUSE), 80p plus 30p p & p
Written by a CRUSE counsellor, the reader is guided through some of the feelings experienced during the grief of bereavement.
Beyond Grief: A Guide for Recovering from the Death of a Loved One, Carol Staudacher (Souvenir Press; available from Bookpoint Ltd, 39 Milton Trading Estate, Abingdon, Oxfordshire OX14 4TD), £7.95
A detailed book on the problems facing those dealing with the death of a loved one or for those helping others who are grieving.
Secret Flowers: Mourning and the Adaptation of Loss, Mary Jones (The Women's Press, 34 Great Sutton Street, London EC1V 0DX), £2.95
A compassionate book that is written out of the personal experience of the author; it treats the experience of grief and loss after a death as being a positive spiritual experience.
Through Grief: The Bereavement Journey, Elizabeth Collick (Darton, Longman and Todd in association with CRUSE), £3.95 plus 65p p & p.
Also available on cassette from CRUSE for £5.50 plus 60p p & p. The cassette is complementary to the book and contains a series of direct personal talks to bereaved persons on a range of topics such as grief, anger, guilt, loneliness and depression. It is intended to bring the emotions of bereavement into the open, thus helping the listeners to a point of reassurance and self-awareness.

Financial Help for Those Who Are Left

Depending upon the individual circumstances, it may be possible to claim extra Social Security Benefits or Pensions when a member of the family dies.

These include:

Widow's Payment
This is a tax-free lump sum paid to a widow if her husband has paid enough NI contributions and either she is under 60 or her deceased husband was not getting Retirement Pension when he died.

Widowed Mothers Allowance
This can be claimed if a widow has at least one child for whom she can claim Child Benefit.

Widow's Pension
This is paid to a widow with no dependent children who is over the age of 45, but not yet able to claim Retirement Pension.

Retirement Pension
If a widow and her deceased husband were receiving Retirement Pension when he died, the widow may be able to use his NI contributions to obtain extra pension.

War Widow's or Dependant's Pension
Widows and orphans, near relatives or widowers may be able to claim War Pensions if the deceased died as a result of service in HM Armed Forces.

Guardian's Allowance
If someone is entitled to Child Benefit for a child taken into the family as the result of a death, the family can also claim Guardian's Allowance.

Further details of these and other benefits, with details of how to claim, can be found in the following DSS booklets:
D 49, 'What to Do After a Death'
NP 45, 'A Guide to Widow's Benefits'
NI 51, 'National Insurance for Widows'

Administering the Estate

If There Is a Will
If a Will was prepared, the original must be found. Generally it will be kept with the solicitor who assisted in the preparation of the Will, or with the deceased's bank. Once found its validity must be ascertained. Consideration must be given to whether the testator had sufficient mental capacity when the Will was drawn up and whether the appropriate formalities were complied with.

If there is a Will, it is the responsibility of the executors named in it, acting as the deceased's personal representatives, to obtain the Probate Court's authority to carry out its terms. They will then be responsible for administering the estate. The executor will not be recognised by the organisations with whom he or she must deal and from whom he or she must obtain legal control of the deceased's assets unless he or she has a document issued by the Court which is known as the Probate or Letters of Administration.

If assets are held in joint names, these may normally be transferred to the survivor merely by producing a copy of the Death Certificate. Otherwise only limited amounts of money will be released to an executor on production of a death certificate by banks and insurance and pension companies. It is then necessary to have the Will 'proved' and to produce a 'grant of probate' before any money can be released. An exception to this is if the total amount of money left by the deceased is £5,000 or less; it is then a case of asking the bank or other institutions holding the money what the formalities are; this normally involves only completing a simple form.

If There Is No Will

If no Will has been made, the deceased is said to have died 'intestate' and a personal representative, usually a close relative, must administer the estate. The representative must normally need to apply to a probate registry for a 'Grant of Letters of Administration'. Whereas an executor has full legal authority to administer the estate by virtue of the Will and needs probate only by way of confirmation, a personal representative in intestacy has no authority unless and until letters of administration are granted.

The distribution of the estate of someone who dies intestate can be complex, especially if it is large and there is a widow or widower and children. It is recommended that professional advice is sought.

Probate and the Duties of the Executor

The main tasks of the executor are:
- to find out what the deceased has left. This involves writing to all the organisations where the deceased had money, and obtaining valuations where necessary.
- to ascertain how much inheritance tax will have to be paid, when is it likely to be paid and calculate how the funds will be raised to pay it.
- to complete forms required by Probate Registry (*see below*), including an Inheritance Tax Return for the Inland Revenue.
- to appoint a time to visit the Probate Registry to swear the forms.
- to visit Probate Registry in person to swear papers.
- to pay Inheritance Tax. The demand is normally received two to three weeks after probate is sworn. The first £150,000 of an estate is treated as exempt, with tax at 40 per cent on anything above this threshold. The rates and the threshold change periodically. Inheritance Tax on freehold property and on a business can be paid by instalments, but on all other assets it must be paid

before receiving Grant of Probate. This can create a problem with the timing of releasing funds from the estate, and it may be necessary to obtain a temporary overdraft facility.
- to receive Grant of Probate or Letter of Administration. This is normally received four to five weeks after probate is sworn.
- to use the Grant of Probate to get hold of assets within the estate (*see below*).
- to sell property if necessary.
- to pay outstanding debts.
- to hand over legacies and bequests.
- to deal with whatever money/assets are left (the residue).

The forms required by the Probate Registry and available from them are:
PA 1, *Probate Application Form*
CAP 44, *Return of Assets and Debts*
CAP 30, *Schedule of Stocks and Shares*
CAP 37, *Schedule of Property*
PA 45, *Matrimonial Home Questionnaire*
In addition the executor will receive a guide to making a personal application for probate (PA 2), a list of probate offices (PA 3), a table of fees (PA 4) and an envelope in which to return the forms.

When the Grant of Probate or Grant of Letters of Administration is received, it should be sent to all the organisations where the deceased held money as listed in form CAP 44. With certain types of assets, such as shares, there are special forms to be filled out and procedures to follow, so it is as well to seek help from a professional such as an accountant or a bank's financial advisor.

All major towns in England and Wales have district probate registries which should be able to help with any queries; they are not able to give legal advice. Otherwise go to the local Citizens Advice Bureau or contact:

The Personal Application Department
Principal Registry of the Family Division
Probate Office
Somerset House
Strand
London WC2R 1LP
Tel: 0171–936 6938

In Scotland you should contact any Sheriff Court or:

The Sheriff Clerk (Commissary Office)
16 North Bank Street
Edinburgh EH1 2NS

Other Points to Remember

There may be other practical arrangements to make or refunds due on certain items in the estate.

For example, if the deceased had a car the estate may be due a part refund of insurance premiums. However, this should be kept in place while the car is on the road, until it is sold or the ownership and insurance transferred.

The deceased's credit card bills will need to be paid and then the cards cut up and returned to the issuers.

Gas, electricity and telephone companies should be contacted regarding the supply and payment, and the post office told where to redirect mail.

Season tickets and club memberships could be due to refund the estate – check with each issuer.

If the deceased lived in a council house or received Housing Benefit, you should advise the local authority.

Legal Costs

Often families who are unaccustomed to dealing with solicitors come into contact with them for the first time when they are required to administer an estate. It is quite possible that one solicitor might charge two or even three times more than another for doing approximately the same work by having different levels of charges. The Law Society does not lay down a recommended scale of charges, although it does have basic guidelines within which solicitors set their own fees.

Most solicitors charge a basic fee. Many mark this up for assisting in the administration of an estate, and also levy a charge based on the value of the estate of the deceased. The best solution is to shop around. If, however, you feel you have reason to complain, you should first ensure that you have gone as far as you reasonably can to get the firm to resolve your problem themselves. If this fails, refer to Chapter 7 (*page 156*) of this book.

Further Reading

How to Sort Out Someone's Will: A Straightforward Guide to Dealing with Probate (Consumers' Association, Way, Hertford SG14 1LH), £7.95
This book contains a pack listing the main probate registries and local offices, a progress checklist and a checklist of the essential steps to take.

Wills and Probate (Consumers' Association), £9.95
One of the most comprehensive guides on the subject and written for the layperson. The book is regularly updated.

What to Do When Someone Dies (Consumers' Association), £9.95
A regularly updated guide to the practical arrangements following a death. Recommended by the Natural Death Centre as the 'best book on red tape surrounding death'.

Age Concern's Factsheet No 14, 'Probate: Dealing with Someone's Estate' (*address page 228*). Scottish law differs, therefore Age Concern Scotland (*address page 101*) issues different factsheets on the subject.

'When Someone Dies' (leaflet from Money Management Council, PO Box 77, Hertford, Herts SG14 2HW), free

Taxation When Someone Dies

The executor of the estate will normally be responsible for completing an income tax return covering the period from the beginning of the financial year (6 April) up to the date of death. As in a normal tax return, all income and capital gains must be declared. It is a useful exercise to compare the previous return submitted to the Inspector of Taxes to ensure that everything is included. If a copy is not available the Inspector will provide one.

A full year's personal allowances are granted in the year of death. Therefore it is quite common to receive a tax rebate. If tax is due, it must be paid from the estate of the deceased. If the tax return reveals a source of income of which the Inspector was not previously aware, the Inspector is entitled to claim arrears of tax for the previous six years. The executor should therefore satisfy him- or herself that all taxes have been paid before the estate is distributed.

During the period between the death and the distribution of the estate (the administration period), any income that may arise is entered on a tax return by the executor. Income tax is paid at the basic rate. When the income is distributed to the beneficiaries, they are credited with this tax. If they pay higher rate tax they may be liable to pay more, but if they pay no tax they will be eligible for a refund.

Capital gains tax (CGT) is charged only when an asset is sold, exchanged, given away or disposed of in any other way. When someone dies there are no CGT liabilities on gains up to the date of death on assets held, but there may be on any assets that were sold prior to death or on assets that need to be sold by the executor in order to raise money to pay Inheritance Tax liabilities. The executor, or any beneficiary, is deemed to have 'acquired' assets for future CGT purposes at their value as at the date of death.

Inheritance Tax (IHT) is charged on an estate only if the total value of everything (less certain deductions) that the deceased owned at the time of death is over a certain threshold (currently £150,000). There are also certain exemptions, the most important being the one for assets left to a surviving spouse. Large gifts made during the deceased's lifetime may be taxable. For further information, *see Chapter 7 (page 156)* or you can get details of relief, exemptions and the rate of tax and the current 'threshold' from the Capital Tax Offices. Their addresses are:

Capital Tax Office – England and Wales
Minford House
Rockley Road
London W14 0DF

Capital Tax Office – Scotland
Mulberry House
16 Picardy Place
Edinburgh EH1 3NF

Capital Tax Office – Northern Ireland
Law Courts Building
Chichester Street
Belfast BT1 3NU

If you have any more specific enquiries about taxation after death, any Tax Office or Tax Enquiry Centre will be pleased to help you. Their address will be in the local phone book under 'Inland Revenue'.

Further Reading
IR 45, 'What Happens When Someone Dies'
This free leaflet produced by the Inland Revenue gives a brief description of Income Tax, Capital Gains Tax and Inheritance Tax.

INDEX

AB Wildlife Trust Fund 224
Abbey Life Assurance 218
Abbeyfield Society 70
abroad, travelling 87–93
   insurance 88–9
   medical treatment 89–90
   pension arrangements 88, 104
abuse, of elderly 53–4
ACCA (Chartered Association of Certified Accountants) 150
ACCAS 49
ACCAS Northern Ireland 50
ACCAS Scotland 50
ACCAS Wales 49
accidents, in the home 183, 186–7
accommodation 64–86
accountants 150, 163, 165
Achievements Ltd 210
Action for Dysphasic Adults 42
Action on Smoking and Health (ASH) 22
Active Life 209
acupuncture 43
Additional Earnings Related Pension 103
Adjustamatic Beds 174
administration of estate 231–6
advisory services (stockbrokers) 153
Age Alliance 145, 146
Age Concern England 15, 46, 85, 101, 199, 228

Age Concern Insurance Services 88–9, 143
Age Concern Northern Ireland 15, 46–7, 85, 101
Age Concern Scotland 15, 46, 85, 101
Age Concern Wales 15, 46, 85, 101
Age Exchange Theatre Trust 208
Age Resource 198
Age-Link 55
Aid Call plc 185
air travel 195
Airtours Golden Years Holidays 88
Al-Anon 25
alcohol 24–5
Alcohol Concern 25
Alcohol Counselling and Prevention Services 25
Alcohol Problem Advisory Service 25
Alcoholics Anonymous 25
Allchurches Life Assurance Ltd 146
Almshouse Association 83–4
alternative medicine 43–5
Alzheimer's disease 37–8, 50
Alzheimer's Disease Society (England) 37–8
Alzheimer's Disease Society (Northern Ireland) 38
Alzheimer's Disease Society (Wales) 38
Alzheimer's Scotland 38

Amateur Swimming Association 204
Anchor Housing Association 70
Animal Aunts 90
Animal Welfare Trust 62
annuities 135–6
Annuity Bureau Ltd 136
Annuity Direct 136
ANS Contract Healthcare 84
appeals (Social Fund payments) 124–5
Aquasun Senior Sun 92
ARC Section 206
Arena Travel 91
Arkle Lodge Nursing Home 82
Army (war pensions) 105
Artability 207
Arthritic Association 39
Arthritis Care 39, 95
Arthritis and Rheumatism Council 39
arts activities 207–8
Arts Connection 208
Ashbourne Homes plc 81
Asset Financial Planning 141
Association of British Credit Unions Ltd 126
Association of British Insurers 89, 138
Association of British Travel Agents (ABTA) 87
Association of Charity Officers 57, 127
Association for Continence Advice 34
Association of Crossroads Care Attendant Schemes (England) 49
Association of Independent Care Advisors 80
Association of Investment Trust Companies 139
Association of Jewish Friendship Clubs for Over-60s 55
Association of Nature Reserve Burial Grounds 224

Association of Private Client Investment Managers (Apcims) 153
Association of Unit Trusts and Investment Trusts 138
attack victims 54
Attendance Allowance 114
Attorney, powers of 156–9

B & Q discount 187, 203
BA Publications 100
back pain 40
BACUP (cancer patients) 40
Bakers Coaches 92
Banham Burglary Prevention 186
Banking Ombudsman 150
banks 132, 155
bathroom equipment 174–5
Bedford Mobility Centre 196
beds 173–4
Befriending Network 215
Belgrave International Trust and Taxation Consultants 166
benefits 88, 99–127
Benefits Enquiry Line 100
bereavement 91, 228–30
BESt Investment 135
Beth Johnson Housing Association Ltd 72
BIIBA (British Insurance and Investment Brokers Association) 150
blind 28, 84, 95, 178, 189, 202, 206–7
body bags, sources 223–4
Bonds 133–4
bones 31–2
books:
  for the housebound 207
  talking 206–7
Boots Company plc 181
BREAK 94
Breakthrough Deaf-Hearing Integration 30, 176
Brendoncare Foundation 81

British Acupuncture Association and Register 43
British Airways 195
British Amputee Sports Association 205
British Antique Dealers Association 210
British Association for Counselling 52
British Bankers Association 138
British Chess Federation 210
British Chiropractic Association 44
British College of Naturopathy and Osteopathy 44
British Colostomy Association Group 35
British Deaf Association 30, 95
British Deaf Sports Council 205
British Diabetic Association 41, 95
British Federation of Care Home Proprietors 78
British Footwear Manufacturer's Association 32
British Geriatrics Society 21
British Heart Foundation 37
British Homoeopathic Association 44
British Humanist Association 226
British Jigsaw Puzzle Library 209
British Limbless Ex-Servicemen's Association 59, 81
British Nursing Association 52
British Nutrition Foundation 23
British Organ Donor Society (BODY) 219
British Pensioner and Trade Union Action Association (BPTUAA) 54, 209
British Red Cross Society 52, 60, 95, 180, 189
British Resorts Association 93
British School of Osteopathy 44
British Ski Club for the Disabled 205
British Spas Federation 92
British Tinnitus Association 30

British Trust for Conservation Volunteers 200
British Veterans' Athletic Federation 205
British Veterans Athletic Sports Foundation 206
British Wheel of Yoga 205
British Wireless for the Blind Fund 206
Budgeting Loans 123
building societies 132, 155
Building Societies Association 138
Building Societies Ombudsman 150
Building Society Shop 133
burglar alarms 186
burglaries 183–4
burial, at sea 225–6
bus fares 117
bus travel 191

Caledonian Nursing Homes Ltd 83
Camping for the Disabled 209
Cancer Help Centre 41
Cancer Relief Macmillan Fund 40–1
Cancerlink 41
Canine Concern Scotland Trust 63
capital, from own home 68, 144–7
capital gains tax 235–6
Capital Release 68
Capital Tax Office:
    England and Wales 235
    Northern Ireland 236
    Scotland 235
care, at home 68
Care Alternatives 52
Care in the Community 67, 75
Care and Repair Cymru Ltd 66
Care and Repair Ltd (England) 65–6, 118
Care and Repair Scotland 66
Carefree Holidays Ltd 91
Carequest 80
carers:
    and elderly abuse 53
    help for 48–51, 113–16

Carers National Association 49
caring organisations 46–63
Carlisle Cemetery 224
Carlyle Life Assurance Company Ltd 146
Cash Plan 146
Cassette Library of Recorded Books (Calibre) 207
Castle Rock Housing Association Ltd 71
cataracts 27
CC Products 180
Central Council of Physical Recreation 206
Centre for Accessible Environments (The Centre) 66
Centre for Policy on Ageing 16, 54
CGA Direct 143
chairs 173–4
Chalfont Line (Holidays) 94, 195
charities 57–9, 126–7
Charity Search 58, 127
Chartered Society of Physiotherapy 40
Chase de Vere 132
Chester-Care 181
Chinese medicine 43
chiropody 32
chiropractic 44
Choice 209
Chosen Heritage 218
Church of Ireland Housing Association (Northern Ireland) Ltd 73
Cinnamon Trust 63, 84
Citizen's Advice Bureau 48
 see also NACAB; National Association of Citizen's Advice Bureaux; Scottish Association of Citizen's Advice Bureaux
City Lit 201
Civil Service Pensioner 210
Cleshar Community Care 51
Clover 181
CNA Scotland 49

CNA Wales 49
Co-op Holiday Care 92
Co-operative Funeral Services 218, 222
coach travel 191
coffins, sources 223–4
Cold Weather Payments 109, 121–2
Coldline 56
ComCare Messenger 183
Commercial Union Assurance Company Ltd 142
community alarms 183
community care 67, 120–1
Community Care Act 1993 121
Community Care Grants 121, 123
Community Home Care 71
Community Hospitals Group plc 83
Community Service Volunteers 61, 199–200
community transport schemes 193–5
Compassionate Friends 229
compensation (investments) 153–5
Complan 24
Concern for Comfort 174
Conquest (Society for Art for the Physically Handicapped) 208
Constant Attendance Allowance 114
Contact 55
Continence Foundation 34
Coronary Prevention Group 37
Cosyfeet 33, 178
Council for the Accreditation of Correspondence Colleges 201
Council Tax Benefit 108, 115
Counsel and Care (for the Elderly) 47, 85–6, 110, 127
Country House Retirement Homes Ltd 83
Country Houses Association 71
Countrywide Holidays 91
Court Cavendish Group Ltd 83
Court of Protection 158–9
Credit Unions 125–6
Cremation Society of Great Britain 223

INDEX

Crestacare Ltd 83
Crime Concern 184
crime victims 54, 185
Criminal Injuries Compensation Board 185
Crisis Loans 124
CRUSE: Bereavement Care 91, 228–9

Dark Horse Venture 36, 197–8
DaRT 193–4
David Aaron Partnership 135
day centres 117
deaf see hearing
deaf-blind 31, 96
death:
  desire for 215–16
  imminent 214–15
  planning for 213–27
  registration 221
  what to do after 220–1
Death Certificate 220–1
debt 163–4
Declaration of Rights (death at home) 215
dementia 37–8, 42
  see also Alzheimer's disease
Dementia Services Development Centre 38
dental care 20, 31
Depression Alliance 42
Derwent Housing Association Ltd 73
diabetes 41–2, 95
DIAL 102
Dial-a-Ride 194
DIEL (telecommunications) 177
diet 23–4
Direct Line Insurance 143
disabilities, people with:
  benefits 110–13
  help for 59–60, 65
  holidays 93–6
Disability Alliance Educational and Research Association 113

Disability Information Trust 179, 191
Disability Living Allowance 112–14
Disability Rights Handbook (Disability Alliance) 113
Disability Scotland Information Service 179
Disability Wales 179
Disabled Housing Trust 82
Disabled Living Centres Council 179, 189
Disabled Living Foundation 33, 59, 179
Disabled Living Services 94
Disabled Traveller 95
Disablement Information and Advice Line (DIAL) 102
discretionary payments (Social Fund) 122–3
Distressed Gentlefolks Aid Association 56, 127
divorced people, and pensions 104
Doctor's Certificate (of death) 220–1
Dolphin Special Needs Bathrooms 175
donation (of body or organs), after death 219–20
donor cards 219–20
door, answering 186
doorbell, and hearing difficulties 29, 176
Dressense 181
drinking, helpful gadgets 172
driving see motoring
DSS Benefits Agency 105
DSS Freeline 100
DVLC 189–90
dysphasia 42

Eagle Star Life Assurance Company Ltd 140
eating, helpful gadgets 172
eczema 42
education, further 26, 201–3

241

Education Resources for Older People 201
EEZEE-Rise 174
Ehrman Kits Ltd 211
elderly abuse 53–4
Elderly Accommodation Counsel 69
Elders Voice 56
Electric Mobility Euro Ltd 196
electrical appliances 188
Electricity Regulation, Office of (OFFER) 27
Embroiderer's Guild 211
emergencies, help in 183
Enduring Power of Attorney 157–8
Energy Action Grants Agency 27, 118
Energy Efficiency Office 118
English Churches Housing Group 74
English Courtyard Association 71
English Tourist Board 96
Enterprise 92
Equitable Life 144
Equity and Law Life Assurance Society plc 144
estates, administration 231–6
Europ Assistance Ltd 89
euthanasia 215–16
Everstyl Reclining Armchairs 174
ex-service personnel 58–9
execution-only services (stockbrokers) 153
executors 161–2, 232–5
exercise 35–7
Exeter Friendly Society 142
Extend Exercise Training Ltd 37
Extrasure Holdings 89
Eye Care Information Service (EIS) 28
eyes 27–9

fabric supports 20
Family Policy Studies Centre 16
fees, for residential/nursing homes 75–6, 139–41
feet 32–3

FIMBRA (Financial Intermediaries, Managers and Brokers Regulatory Association) 149
finance 98–155
financial advice, sources of 125–7, 147–53
financial advisers 148, 151–2
fire precautions 187–8
fixed income investments 132–4
Fold Housing Association 74
footwear 32–3, 178
Forces Help Society and Lord Roberts Workshops 58, 82, 107
Foundation for Age Research/Research into Ageing 17
Free Tape Recorded Library for the Blind 207
Friends of the Elderly and Gentlefolks Help 74, 81
Friends Provident Life Office 144
Funeral Expenses Plan 218
Funeral Payments 121, 122
funerals:
  advance payment 216–18
  arrangements 221–7
  non-religious 226–7
  paying for 121, 122, 227
  planning 213–14
  without a Funeral Director 223–7
future requirements, financial planning for 129

garden gadgets 175–6
gardening 175–6, 203
gas appliances 187–8
Gas Supply, Office of 27
Gay Bereavement Project 229
General Accident 144
giddiness 33
Gilts 133–4
Gimson Stairlifts 173
glasses 20
glaucoma 27–8
Godwins Ltd 17

Golden Charter 218
Golden Rail Holidays 91
Golden Years 92
Government Stock (Gilts) 133–4
Grace 80
Graduated Pension 103
grants:
   Community Care Grants 121, 122–3
   Local Authority 65
   for renovations/adaptations 65–6
Great British Cities 93
Greater London Association for Disabled People (GLAD) 60, 94
Green Undertakings 224
Greenacre Group plc 82
Grey Agency Newsletter 10
guaranteed acceptance policies 135
Guaranteed Equity Funds 135
Guaranteed Income Bonds 135
Guardian's Allowance 231
Guernsey Tourist Board 96
Guinness Trust 74

Hadleigh Retirement Homes 75
Haemophilia Society 42
Hanover Housing Association 73
Hargreaves Lansdown Asset Management Ltd 132
Harrogate Stonefall Cemetery 224
health 19–45
   annual check 19
   insurance 141–2
Health Benefits Division 119
Health, Department of, Leaflets Department 220
Health Education Authority Customer Services 49
Health Education Authority (England) 21
Health Education Authority for Wales 21
Health Education Board for Scotland 21

Health Promotion Agency for Northern Ireland 21
Health Publications Unit 90, 119
hearing 29–31, 176–8
hearing aids 29, 176–7
Hearing Concern: The British Association of the Hard of Hearing 30
heating appliances 188
Help the Aged 22, 47, 72, 80, 85, 101–2, 182, 199
herbalism 44
Hertz Rent-a-Car 195
H. F. Holidays 93
hobbies 26, 197–212
Hodgkin's Disease Association 41
Holiday Care Service 89, 93
Holiday Services for Disabled Holidaymakers and their Families 95
holidays 87–97, 117, 183–4
Holmfirth Wools 211
Home and Capital Trust Ltd 146
Home and Comfort 180
Home Energy Efficiency Scheme (HEES) 118
home helps 117
Home Income Plan 146
home, own:
   care services 51–3, 68
   helpful gadgets 117, 171–81
   insurance 142–3
   security 90, 183–4, 230
   as source of capital 68, 144–7
   staying put 65–8
Home Responsibilities Protection 114
home reversion schemes 145–6
Homecraft Supplies Ltd 181
Homelife DGAA 66
Homesitters Ltd 63, 90
Homestart 200
homoeopathy 44
Horticultural Therapy 203
Hospice Information Service 84–5

hospital friends 57, 200
hospitals:
  inpatients, and pensions 104
  travel costs 20
Host Consultancy 16
Housebound Readers Service 207
household insurance 142–3
Housewatch Ltd 89, 90, 230
housing 64–86
housing associations 68–71
Housing Benefit 99, 108, 116
Housing Organisations Mobility and Exchange Services (HOMES) 69–70
Humanist Housing Association 71

IBRC (Insurance Brokers' Registration Council) 150
ICAEW (Institute of Chartered Accountants in England and Wales) 150, 163, 165
IFA Promotion Ltd 148
Ileostomy Association of Great Britain and Northern Ireland 35
Immediate Funding Plans (long-term care insurance) 139
IMRO (Investment Management Regulatory Organisation) 149, 154
income and growth bonds 134
Income Support 99, 108–9
Income Tax 166–8, 235
incontinence 34–5
Incorporated Society of Registered Naturopaths 45
Independent Financial Advisers 151–2
Independent Funerals Advisory Service 225
Independent Health Care Association 80
Independent Living 1993 Fund 128
Independent Order of Odd Fellows 218

Independent Review Service (Social Fund) 125
inflation, and investments 129
Infratech 181
Inheritance Tax 168–70, 235–6
injury benefits 110–13
Institute of Chartered Accountants 150, 163, 165
Institute of Chartered Accountants in Scotland 150
Institute of Complementary Medicine 43
insurance 88–9, 134–7, 138–44
interests 197–212
International Glaucoma Association 28
International Rail Centre 193
intestacy 232–3
Invalid Care Allowance 48, 113–14
Invalidity Allowance 110
Invalidity Benefit 103, 110
Invalidity Payment 110
Investment Ombudsman 150
investment schemes (insurance) 134–7
investment trusts 131
investments 128–38
investors, protection 153–4
Investors Compensation Fund 155
Irish Tourist Board 96
ITHACA 207

Jaguar Alarms 186
James Butcher Housing Association 74
James Gibson Funeral Directors 224
Jephson Homes Housing Association Ltd 74
Jewish Care 84, 127
John Groom's Association for the Disabled 80

Keep Able 181
Kirk Care Housing Association 72

INDEX

kitchens:
 fire precautions 188
 gadgets 171–2
Kleinwort Benson 140

LATU (London Accessible Transport Unit) 195
laundry services 117
LAUTRO (Life Assurance and Unit Trust Regulatory Organisation) 149
Law Society 156, 159
Law Society of England and Wales 150
Law Society of Scotland 150
Leaflets Unit 100
Lears of London 224
legal costs, of estate administration 234
legal matters 156–65
Legal Services Ombudsman 160
Leisure First (rail travel) 192
Leisurely Days 92
Leonard Cheshire Foundation 80
Lewisham Pensioners Link 55
life insurance 135, 144
lifters 175
lifts 172–3
lighting 28
listeners (someone to talk to) 52–3
Living Will 215
Loan Plan (will-writing technique) 170
loans 123–4
Lodge Care plc 83
London Anatomy Office 219
loneliness 56
long-stay holidays 88
long-term care insurance 139–41
low-speed vehicles 195–6

McCarthy and Stone 70
Macmillan nurses 41
Major and Mrs Holt's Battlefield Tours 91

Mangar Booster Multi-Purpose Lifter 175
Mangar International 172
Mare Marine Protection Division 225
marriage guidance 53
Masta's Travellers Health Line 87–8
Mature Tymes 210
MAVIS (Mobility Advice and Vehicle Information Service) 190
meals on wheels 51, 117
Medau Society 36
Medical Department (Wellcome Foundation) 37
medical treatment, abroad 89–90
medicines 187
 safety 33–4
Memories on Video 211
Memory Makers 211
mental alertness 26
mental health 42, 52, 95, 200
Merseyside Improved Homes 74
Methodist Homes for the Aged 55, 72, 80
MIND 42, 95
minorities, homes for 84
mobility 189–96
Mobility Advice and Vehicle Information Service (MAVIS) 190
Mobility Allowance 190
Mobility Information Service 191
Mobility Unit 190
Money Management Council 137, 164
Money Management Fee-based Advice Register 148
money problems 125–7
 see also financial advice
mortgage annuity schemes 146
Morton-Wilson Limited 140
Motor Neurone Disease Association 43
motoring 189–91

insurance 142–3
Multiple Sclerosis Society 42, 95

NACAB 51, 101
NACAB N. Wales 101
NACAB Northern Ireland 101
NACAB S. Wales 101
NADFAS Tours Ltd 93
National Adult School Organisation 202
National Association of Bereavement Services 223
National Association of Citizens Advice Bureaux (NACAB) 51, 101
National Association of Deafened People 30–1
National Association of Estate Agents 70
National Association of Funeral Directors 222
National Association of Leagues of Hospital Friends 57, 200
National Association of Swimming Clubs for the Handicapped (NASCH) 204
National Association of Victim Support Schemes 185
National Association of Volunteer Bureaux 62, 200
National Association of Widows 53, 229
National Association of Women's Clubs 55
National Back Pain Association 40
National Benevolent Institution 128
National Canine Defence League 62
National Care Homes Association 78
National Council for Voluntary Organisations 62
National Deaf-Blind League 31, 96
National Debtline 164
National Eczema Society 42
National Express Ltd 191

National Extension College 50, 202
National Federation of Credit Unions 126
National Federation of Housing Associations 72
National Federation of Spiritual Healers 45
National Institute of Continuing Education 202
National Institute of Medical Herbalists 44
National Insurance 102–3
National Listening Library 206
National Osteoporosis Society 32
National Savings (Department) 133, 138
National Secular Society Ltd 227
National Society of Allotment and Leisure Gardeners Ltd 203
National Trust 91, 94, 208
Nationwide Housing Trust 73
Natural Death Centre 214–15
naturopathy 44
Neighbourhood Energy Action 27, 119
Network Homesearch 79
New Horizons Trust 199
NHS 20, 119
NHS Spectacle Voucher 27
nominee services (stockbrokers) 153
North British Housing Association 70
North Housing 73
Northern Caring Homes Ltd 83
Northern Counties Homes 73
Northern Ireland Co-ownership 73
Northern Ireland Federation of Housing Associations 72
Northern Ireland Housing Executive 66
Northern Ireland Information Service for Disabled People 179
Northern Ireland Tourist Board 96
nursing care, at home 68
Nursing Home Fees Agency 141

nursing homes 75–86, 109, 141

Occupational Pensions Advisory Society (OPAS) 105
Office of Fair Trading 165
Office of Population, Censuses and Surveys 16
Officers Association (RBL) 107
Older Feminists Network 209
Ombudsmen 150, 160
Open College 201
Open University 202
Oral History Society 211
Orange Badge Scheme 190
Orbit Housing Association 71
organ donation 219–20
Ortho Kinetics UK Ltd 196
osteopathy 43–4
osteoporosis 31–2

Parker Bath Developments 175
Parker Hilton Ltd 181
Parkinson's Disease Society of the United Kingdom 42–3, 95
partially sighted 28, 178
Partially Sighted Society 28
Payments by Right 121
Pensioners' Voice 210
pensions 88, 102–7, 231
People's Dispensary for Sick Animals 63
Perfect Assurance Funeral Trust 218
Personal Equity Plans 132
Personal Investment Authority (PIA) 146, 149,151
Personnel and Logistics (Legal Services) 170
pets, caring for 62–3
PHAB Scotland 60
PHAB Wales 60
Physically Handicapped and Able Bodied (PHAB) (England) 60
physiotherapy 40
PIA (Personal Investment Authority) 146, 149, 151

placement agencies 79–80
policy, public 54
Policy Studies Institute 17
Population Concern 17
Portuguese Painting Holidays 93
possessions, marking 184
post-mortems 221
Power of Attorney 156–9
Pre-funding Schemes (long-term care insurance) 139
Pre-Retirement Association of Great Britain and Northern Ireland 17
Pre-retirement Association Holiday Courses 91
Premier Unit Trust Brokers 131
Presbyterian Housing Association Northern Ireland Ltd 73
prescriptions, NHS 20, 118–19
pressure sores 174
Prime of Life 210
Princess Royal Trust for Carers 49
Private Health Partnership 141
Private Patients Plan 142
probate 232–3
Probate Office 233

Quality Care Homes Ltd 83
questionnaire 11
QUIT 22–3

Racal Chubb Products 185
RADAR 49, 60, 65
RAF Association 58
Raglan Housing Association 72
Rail Europe Senior Card 192
rail travel 117, 192–3
Ramblers Association 205
REACH 198
Recognized Professional Bodies (RPBs) 150, 151
Red Cross see British Red Cross
Reduction in Yield (investment products) 152
Register of Traditional Chinese Medicine 43

Registered Nursing Home
  Association 78
Registry of Financial Planning 148
Relate/National Marriage Guidance
  53
Relatives Association 78
Relaxation for Living 36
REMAP GB 180
residential homes 75–86, 109, 117
Response Electronics plc 185
Retired and Senior Volunteer
  Programme (RSVP) 61
retirement: counselling and courses
  17
Retirement Counselling Service 17
Retirement Education Centre 202
Retirement Insurance Advisory
  Service 143
Retirement Lease Housing
  Association 71, 74
Retirement Pension 102–4, 231
returns, and investments 129–30
reviews (Social Fund payments)
  124–5
Richmond Fellowship for Mental
  Welfare 42
risk, and investments 129
roll up loans 147
Royal Air Force (war pensions) 105
Royal Air Forces Association
  (housing) 74
Royal Association for Disability and
  Rehabilitation (RADAR) 60, 65
Royal British Legion 59, 81, 107
Royal British Legion Housing
  Association Ltd 75
Royal Horticultural Society 203
Royal London Society for the Blind
  202
Royal National Institute for the
  Blind 28, 84, 95, 178, 187
Royal National Institute for Deaf
  People 29, 176
Royal Navy and Marines (war
  pensions) 106

Royal Society for the Prevention of
  Accidents (ROSPA) 183, 186
RSVP (CSV) 199–200
RUKBA – Royal United Kingdom
  Beneficent Association 56, 66

safety 182–8
Saga 210
Saga Holidays 90
Saga Private Healthcare Plan 142
Saga Services Ltd 143
St George's Nursing Home 82
Samaritans 53, 199, 229
Sandown Private Nursing Homes 83
Saneline 52, 200
savings see investments
Scandinavian Seaways 92
Scottish Action on Dementia 42
Scottish Amicable European 140
Scottish Association of Citizen's
  Advice Bureaux 101
Scottish Association for the Disabled
  204
Scottish Community Education
  Services 201
Scottish Equitable Life Assurances
  144
Scottish Federation of Housing
  Associations 72
Scottish Retirement Council 198
Scottish Sports Council 204
Scottish Tourist Board 96
sea, burial at 225–6
Second Adult Rebate 116
Securities and Futures Authority Ltd
  (SFA) 149, 155
Securities and Investments Board
  (SIB) 148, 153–5
security, home 90, 183–4, 230
Select Retirement 75
Self Regulatory Organisations
  (SROs) 149, 153–4
Senior and Veteran Windsurfers
  Association (SEAVETS) 205
SeniorLine 26, 67, 102, 109

Sequal Trust 176
Severe Disablement Allowance 110–11
Severnside Associates 143
sexuality 25
SFA (Securities and Futures Authority Ltd) 149, 155
Shape London 207
shares (equities) 130–2
Shearings Ltd 92
Shelter: National Campaign for Homeless People 67
sheltered housing 68–75
Sheltered Housing Advisory and Conciliation Service 69
Sheltered Housing Services Ltd 71
Sheriff Clerk (Commissary Office) 233
Shiatsu Society 44
SHIP Campaign 145
shoes 32–3, 178
SIB (Securities and Investments Board) 148, 153–5
sick benefits 110–13
sight 27–9
 see also blind
sight tests 20, 27–8
Sixty Plus 56
Skill: National Bureau for Students with Disabilities 201
SMD Agency 79
smoke alarms 176, 187
smoking 22–3, 188
Social Fund 65, 121–5
Social Services Department, local services 50–1, 67, 75–6, 117–18
Social Work Department (Scotland) 67, 75–6
social worker advice 117
Society of Allied and Independent Funeral Directors 222
Society for the Assistance of Ladies in Reduced Circumstances 127
Society of Chiropodists 32
Society of Homoeopaths 44

Society for Horticultural Therapy 176
Society of Trust and Estate Practitioners 165
Society of Voluntary Associates 62
Soldiers' Sailors' and Airmen's Families Association 58
Sole-Mates 33
solicitors, complaints against 160
Solicitors Complaints Bureau 160
Somerset Care Ltd 52, 81
SOS Talisman 185
Sound Advantage 176
South Place Ethical Society 227
Special Collection 180
special needs, homes for 84
Speechly Bircham 170
spiritual healing 44
SPOD 25
sports 204–6
Sports Council 204
Sports Council for Northern Ireland 204
Sports Council for Wales 204
stairlifts 172–3
Stalwart Assurance Co Ltd 146
Stannah Stairlifts Ltd 173
Stapenhill Cemetery 225
State Retirement Pension 102–4, 231
Stock Exchange 138
stockbrokers 153
Stroke Association 43
strokes 43
Sue Ryder Foundation 81
suicide 53
Sun Alliance Insurance UK 143, 190
Sun Island Holidays UK 92

Takare plc 82
talking books 206–7
Talking Newspaper Association 207
Tameside Care Group Ltd 82
Tax Exempt Special Savings Accounts (TESSAs) 133
TaxAid 167–8

taxation 165–70
  deceased persons 235–6
  and investments 129
Taxicard 194
teeth 20, 31
telephones 117
  and hearing difficulties 29, 176, 177–8
television 117
  and hearing difficulties 29, 176
Theraposture Ltd 173
Third Age Trust 198
Tibble Trust 208
tinnitus 30
tools, helpful 175
Tourist Boards 96
Townswomen's Guilds 198
Towry Law Group 134, 137
trains see rail travel
travel see abroad; mobility
Travel Companions 90–1
Travelin' Talk 95
Tripscope 193
Two Care 81
Typetalk 177

unit trusts 131
United Kingdom Home Care Association 51, 78
University of the Third Age 201
Urostomy Association 35

Vegan Society 24
Vegetarian Society of the United Kingdom 24
vehicles, low-speed 195–6
Veteran's Lawn Tennis Association 205
Victim Support 54
Victim Support Schemes 185
Victim Support Scotland 54, 185
Voluntary Euthanasia Society 216
Voluntary Service Overseas 200
voluntary transport schemes 193–5
Volunteer Stroke Scheme 43

volunteers 61–2, 199–200

Wales Access Unit 201
Wales Pensioners 209
Wales Tourist Board 96
walking trolleys 175
War Disablement Pension 106–7
War Pensioner's Welfare Service 107
War Pensions Agency 106
War Pensions Helpline 106
War Pensions Schemes 105–8, 114
War Widows Association of Great Britain 59
War Widow's or Dependant's Pension 107, 231
warm, keeping 26–7
Warner Holidays 93
Weight Watchers UK Ltd 24
Welsh Federation of Housing Associations 72
Welsh Joint Education Committee 201
Western Trust and Savings Ltd 147
Westminster Healthcare plc 82
Widowed Mothers Allowance 231
widows 53, 59, 107, 229, 231
Widows Advisory Trust 229
Widow's Payment 231
Widow's Pension 231
wigs 20
Will Registry 163
William Sutton Housing Trust 73
Willis Owen t/a The Building Society Shop 133
wills 156, 160–3, 213, 231–2
Winged Fellowship 50, 94, 199
Winter Warmth Line 109
Wireless for the Bedridden Society 206
'with profit' endowment policies 137
With-Profit Bonds 134
Women's League of Health and Beauty 37
Women's Royal Voluntary Service (England) 57, 61

Worker's Educational Association 202
WPA (Western Provident Association) 142
Writers Bureau 211

WRVS Scotland 61
WRVS Wales 61

Yoga for Health Foundation 36, 205
Yours 210

Of further interest...

HEALING OUR HEARTS AND LIVES
Inspirations for Meditation and Spiritual Growth

Eileen Campbell

The true meaning of healing is to become more whole. None of us escapes pain and suffering and we all have to deal with healing our hearts and lives. Healing ourselves is a first step towards healing our relationships, our communities and our world.

In the process of healing we need to focus on what is uplifting and inspiring, for we are responsible for our thoughts, whatever our outward circumstances may be. We also need to let go of the past; forgiveness of ourselves and others is a vital aspect of the healing journey. Through the wisdom of forgiveness we will find lasting peace.

A Manual for Living
A Little Book of Living

Epictetus

Presenting the essence of perennial Stoic wisdom in aphorisms of stunning insight and simplicity, this book contains throughout contemporary and pragmatic reflections on how best to live with serenity and joy.

Epictetus was a former Roman slave and great Stoic philosopher whose talks have been admired for more than 1,500 years.

Embraced by the Light
What Happens When You Die?

Betty J. Eadie

Betty Eadie died after an operation, but was later to recover. It was during the intervening period of a few hours that she had what has been described by Raymond Moody as 'the most profound near-death experience ever'.

You will not fail to be moved by Betty's story. A devoted mother with a loving family, she embarked on a voyage of discovery, leaving her body and vising an afterworld of understanding, peace and joy. She was given a message to share with others that has filled hundreds of thousands of people with hope. *Embraced by the Light* recounts the people she met, the truths she learned and the magnificent realities of the spirit world. Her experiences changed her life forever. Reading this fascinating, dramatic and thought-provoking book may change yours too.

HEALING OUR HEARTS AND LIVES	1 85538 436 1	£7.99	☐
A MANUAL FOR LIVING	0 06 251111 4	£4.99	☐
EMBRACED BY THE LIGHT	1 85538 411 6	£9.99	☐

All these books are available from your local bookseller or can be ordered direct from the publishers.

To order direct just tick the titles you want and fill in the form below:

Name: _____
Address: _____
_____
_____ Postcode: _____

Send to: Thorsons Mail Order, Dept 3, HarperCollins*Publishers*, Westerhill Road, Bishopbriggs, Glasgow G64 2QT.
Please enclose a cheque or postal order or your authority to debit your Visa/Access account –

Credit card no: _____
Expiry date: _____
Signature: _____

– to the value of the cover price plus:
UK & BFPO: Add £1.00 for the first book and 25p for each additional book ordered.
Overseas orders including Eire: Please add £2.95 service charge. Books will be sent by surface mail but quotes for airmail despatches will be given on request.

24 HOUR TELEPHONE ORDERING SERVICE FOR ACCESS/VISA CARDHOLDERS – TEL: 0141 772 2281.